ELIHU WASHBURNE

---

*The Diary and Letters of America's Minister to France
During the Siege and Commune of Paris*

MICHAEL HILL

Foreword by David McCullough

SIMON & SCHUSTER

New York   London   Toronto   Sydney   New Delhi

Simon & Schuster
1230 Avenue of the Americas
New York, NY 10020

First Simon & Schuster hardcover edition November 2012

SIMON & SCHUSTER and colophon are registered trademarks
of Simon & Schuster, Inc.

For information about special discounts for bulk purchases,
please contact Simon & Schuster Special Sales at
1-866-506-1949 or business@simonandschuster.com.

The Simon & Schuster Speakers Bureau can bring authors
to your live event. For more information or to book an event,
contact the Simon & Schuster Speakers Bureau at
1-866-248-3049 or visit our website at www.simonspeakers.com.

Designed by Ruth Lee-Mui

Manufactured in the United States of America

1   3   5   7   9   10   8   6   4   2

Library of Congress Cataloging-in-Publication Data
Washburne, E. B. (Elihu Benjamin), 1816–1887.
Elihu Washburne: the diary and letters of America's minister to France during the
Siege and Commune of Paris / [edited] by Michael Hill; with a foreword by David
McCullough.
p.   cm.
Includes bibliographical references and index.
1. Washburne, E. B. (Elihu Benjamin), 1816–1887—Diaries.
2. Washburne, E. B. (Elihu Benjamin), 1816–1887—Correspondence.
3. Paris (France)—History—Siege, 1870–1871—Personal narratives.
4. Paris (France)—History—Commune, 1871—Personal narratives.
5. Ambassadors—United States—Diaries.   6. Ambassadors—United States—
Correspondence.   I. Hill, Michael.   II. Title.
DC314.W37 2012
327.73044092—dc23
[B]   2012013304
ISBN 978-1-4516-6528-4
ISBN 978-1-4516-6531-4 (ebook)

We have been through fire and blood . . .
during the reign of the brigands.
Elihu Washburne,
June 16, 1871

CONTENTS

ELIHU WASHBURNE

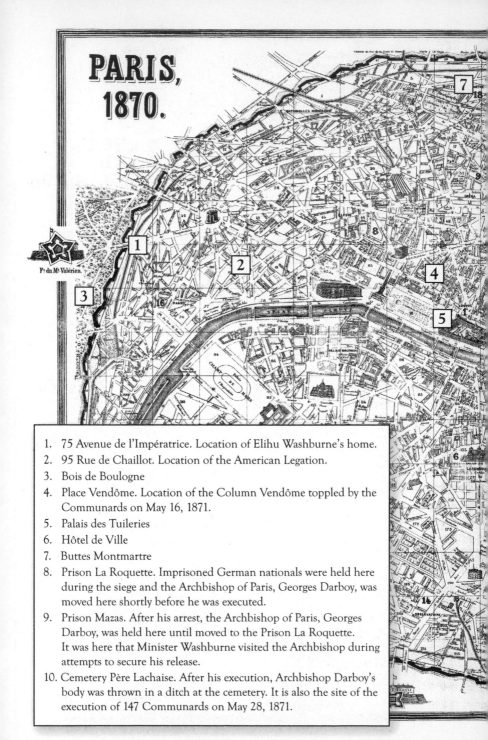

PARIS, 1870.

F.t du Mt Valérien.

1

3

16

2

8

4

5

7
18

9

6

14

1. 75 Avenue de l'Impératrice. Location of Elihu Washburne's home.
2. 95 Rue de Chaillot. Location of the American Legation.
3. Bois de Boulogne
4. Place Vendôme. Location of the Column Vendôme toppled by the Communards on May 16, 1871.
5. Palais des Tuileries
6. Hôtel de Ville
7. Buttes Montmartre
8. Prison La Roquette. Imprisoned German nationals were held here during the siege and the Archbishop of Paris, Georges Darboy, was moved here shortly before he was executed.
9. Prison Mazas. After his arrest, the Archbishop of Paris, Georges Darboy, was held here until moved to the Prison La Roquette. It was here that Minister Washburne visited the Archbishop during attempts to secure his release.
10. Cemetery Père Lachaise. After his execution, Archbishop Darboy's body was thrown in a ditch at the cemetery. It is also the site of the execution of 147 Communards on May 28, 1871.

Ft de l'Est.

Ft d'Aubervilliers.

Ft Romainville.

Ft de Noisy.

Ft de Rosny.

Ft de Nogent.

Ft d'Ivry.

Ft de Charenton.

FOREWORD

BY DAVID MCCULLOUGH

The medals and high commendations he so deserved were never bestowed on Elihu Washburne because he wanted it that way. An official letter from Secretary of State Hamilton Fish recognizing the sacrifices and trials Washburne had endured, and lauding his high sense of duty, was, he insisted, quite enough. He feared too much praise, Washburne said, wary of becoming too popular.

But in his role as American Minister to France the summer of the sudden outbreak of the Franco-Prussian War, in August 1870, and through the mounting horrors of the months that followed in Paris, he played a heroic part unlike that of any other American diplomat before or since. As Michael Hill writes, Elihu Washburne's life is a great American story. And it ought to be far better known and appreciated for all it says about such laudable old attributes as courage, kindness, and patriotism.

Raised in a family of ten children in rural Livermore, Maine, he had been "hired out" as farm help at age 14. What little education he had he acquired largely on his own. Heading west with a law degree at 24, he settled in Illinois, became a friend of Abraham Lincoln, and served eight terms in Congress, where he became an ardent voice for abolition and a strong supporter of President Lincoln, seeing him almost daily throughout the Civil War.

At the time of his appointment to Paris by President Ulysses S. Grant, however, many in Washington considered the Congressman thoroughly unsuited for the job. He was too plain, too like a farmer, and quite obviously void of the diplomatic experience necessary for almost any post of importance, let alone Paris. So it was with much surprise that word of his accomplishments under duress was first received in Washington. That he could, in fact, prove to be one of the most effective representatives of his country ever, and a hero of the hour, would have seemed preposterous.

With the German army rapidly advancing on Paris, and throngs of Americans desperately fleeing the city, along with most foreigners, Washburne chose to stay, not because of orders from Washington, but out of his own sense of duty. As long as any American remained, he felt he must, too. As it was, he would be the only minister or ambassador of a major country to stay at his post.

For the security of his wife and children, he saw that they were safely relocated to quarters in Brussels—all but one grown son, Gratiot, who bravely stayed on at his father's side.

Meanwhile, at the request of both the French and German governments, Washburne had immediately assumed the responsibility of organizing a swift, mass exodus by special trains of the thousands of poor German laborers and their families then living in Paris who were seen now as enemies and who, if not summarily executed as spies, were certain to suffer terribly. They were, as he reported to Secretary of State Fish, "without work, without money, without credit, without friends, without bread. Pinched with hunger, terrified by threats of violence, with no means of leaving the country, they have come to me to save them."

Working harder than he ever had in his life, and with the help of others, Washburne succeeded in getting some 20,000 German men, women, and children safely out of Paris and back to Germany.

No one "could have been better suited for the difficult task," wrote the first Secretary of the Legation, Wickham Hoffman.

> Had he been brought up in diplomacy he would have hesitated and read up on precedents . . . It is quite as well that the head of an embassy should be a new man. He will attach much less importance to trifles, and act more fearlessly in emergencies.

Later, after the German army had the city surrounded and under siege, Washburne saw that more than 600 destitute Germans who had been unable to escape received food and shelter within the safe confines of the American Legation. In the words of Shakespeare, the writer Washburne most liked to quote, he had great "fortitude of soul."

Through the whole of the siege lasting four and a half months, he worked fervently, sometimes eighteen hours a day. At one point he succeeded in arranging the release from the city by carriage caravan a total of 56 Americans, which left no more than 200 behind in Paris. Still, Washburne refused to leave.

With the approach of winter, food and fuel grew ever more scarce. By Christmas people were surviving on horse meat, cats, dogs, sparrows, rats, anything to keep alive. In January the German bombardment began.

When at last in March 1871, Paris was starved into surrendering, there followed, with the return of spring, a return of supplies and a stretch of comparative calm and order, as though the worst were over—until the horrific civil war known as the Commune burst upon the city, a calamity more hideous even than the siege. Paris, Washburne wrote, became "hell upon earth."

Again he kept to his post, doing everything in his power to alleviate suffering and to observe all that was happening in order to report back to Washington, but also in an effort to foresee what might happen next.

He went everywhere—by carriage, on horseback, and on foot—and very often at great risk. The night the Communards set fire to the Tuileries Palace and much of Paris, he watched in horror from a top floor at the Legation, hour after hour, the whole city spread before him. The morning after, he went at once to survey the damage, going where few would have dared set foot. If he feared for his life, he is not known to have said so.

He seemed tireless, but from his private writings we know how often he felt entirely "used up" and down at heart, barely able to keep going. At times he was ill to the point of being unable to leave the house. But then the next day, out the door he went back to work.

At only one effort did he fail. In early April of 1871, after the Archbishop of Paris, Monsignor Georges Darboy, was arrested and imprisoned by the Communards, the Nuncio of the Catholic Church appealed to Washburne to intervene, and Washburne, fearing for the Archbishop's life, moved immediately "to do everything in my power." But his efforts were to no avail. On May 24, the Archbishop was executed.

Washburne took the news very hard. He had gone three times to see the Archbishop in prison and had grown extremely fond of him. Like Washburne, he, too, had refused to leave Paris because he felt it his duty to stay with his people through their time of trial.

Others knew that Washburne, an American Protestant, had tried harder than anyone to save the Archbishop, that he was incapable of standing by in the face of difficulties, and that tens of thousands were forever indebted to him for so much he had done.

But there was a further side to his contributions and one of great benefit to history, the full extent of which has only recently come to light, and it is this that makes the publication of this book such an exceptional event.

Beginning the summer of 1870, Elihu Washburne had been keeping a diary, his own amazing eyewitness Paris chronicle set down day by day, no matter how much else weighed on his mind, no matter how exhausted or down in spirit he felt. Nor were his entries mere abbreviated notes or hurried jottings. He wrote at length, the pages filled with great descriptive detail and much feeling, and all from a vantage point like that of no one else caught up in the crisis.

In a two-volume memoir, *Recollections of a Minister to France* published in 1886, Washburne quoted frequently from the diary, but like others of his time, he would often edit or rewrite what he had said originally, or leave out large portions of the whole—his struggles with illness and depression, for example. It was only in 2009, one hundred and twenty-three years later, thanks to the efforts of Mike Hill, that the full extent of the original document was discovered in—of all places—the Library of Congress.

Washburne, it turns out, had not written his daily entries in a conventional diary book but on loose sheets of stationery, and copies of these had been made by letterpress, the nineteenth-century equivalent of carbon paper. Later these copies were bound in with similar copies of his Paris correspondence, all together chronologically, in two volumes and given to the Library of Congress. For years it was assumed they were correspondence only—until Mike Hill looked more closely.

As often said, the task of the historian is to a great degree detective work. And this is also a big part of the pleasure and pull of history. For nearly thirty years, Mike and I have worked together on research for my books, and I know no one more skilled and resourceful, or so tireless at the job, or who has such a good time at it.

Handwritten manuscripts—letters, diaries, court records— are the biggest, richest part of so-called primary sources, and Mike can decipher old handwriting, even the most atrocious of scrawls, with uncanny ease and transcribe it with the speed of lightning.

Living as he does not far from Washington, he draws heavily on the collections at the Library of Congress, where he has long been regarded by the staff as a valued colleague. Many of my most rewarding days have been working with Mike there at the Library as well as presidential libraries, universities, historical societies, and other archival collections across the country and abroad. For my latest book, *The Greater Journey,* about Americans in Paris in the nineteenth century, a story in which Washburne plays a major part, the resources of no fewer than thirty-two such institutions were consulted.

But if the Washburne diary pages at the Library of Congress were only copies, then, we naturally wondered, where were the original pages?

The answer, we soon discovered, was the Washburne family collection in Maine. So there came the summer day at Livermore, when for the first time we saw the real thing and much more—letters, rare old photographs, scrapbooks, paintings. A banquet feast of material! At one point our heads were spinning so that we had to go outside and sit under a tree to calm down.

Still, the diary surpassed everything. It is a one-of-a-kind treasure the value of which grew greater with closer study. Not only is it filled with observations and details found nowhere else, it is superbly written page after page and in a strong clear hand. Rarely did Washburne ever cross out something, or revise after second thought. He seems to have known at the moment exactly what he wanted to say.

He expressed great admiration for the French Minister of the Interior, Léon Gambetta—"full of pluck and courage"— high praise for the French officers he came in contact with, and especially high praise for the way the people of Paris were facing up to the calamity of the siege.

Again and again appear long, vivid, almost cinematic passages leaving no doubt of how sensitive he was to the appalling human tragedy being played out. At a number of points, it is as if one is there watching with him, as when the German army makes its entrance down the Champs Élysées:

> At first the troops were met with cat calls, and all sorts of insulting cries, but as they poured in thicker and faster and forming companies, as they swept down the avenue to the strains of martial music the crowd seemed to be awed into silence, and

> no other sound was heard but the tramp of the soldiers and the
> occasional word of command . . .

As the reader will find in the pages that follow, much of what he wrote is deeply moving—his account, for example, of the unexpected arrival of French government troops in Paris the morning of May 22, 1871, and the havoc of the day, the dead left strewn in the streets.

As in so much that Washburne wrote, one feels his underlying sense of obligation to get it all down there and then, while still fresh in his mind, no matter how late the hour when at last he returned to his desk.

In a time like our own, when almost no one in positions of public responsibility dares keep a diary, the fullness and candor of what he wrote, not to say the heart he put into it, are all the more remarkable and admirable.

The final days of the Commune were the most savage of all, with such rampant slaughter committed by both sides as none present had ever seen or imagined.

"The reign of the Commune for ten weeks, pursuing its career of murder, assassination, pillage, robbery, blasphemy, and terror, finally expired in blood and flame," he reported at last on May 31 to Secretary of State Fish, in one of the selection of letters also included here.

> The incredible enormities of the Commune, their massacre
> of the Archbishop of Paris and other hostages, their countless
> murders of other persons who refused to join them in their
> fiendish work, their horrid and well organized plans for incen-
> diarism intended to destroy the entire city, and which resulted
> in the destruction of so many of the great monuments of Paris
> are crimes that will never die . . .

Elihu Washburne and all those caught up in what happened are long gone now, of course. How many today have any idea even of when the Franco-Prussian War or the Siege of Paris or the reign of the Commune happened? How many in our time have any idea who Elihu Washburne was? In a number of respected histories of the Franco-Prussian War and the Commune, his name does not even appear.

But we need to know, if only because the Franco-Prussian War was Part One of a titanic struggle between France and Germany that was to be followed by the horrors of World War I and World War II. And Washburne, a truly remarkable American from whom there is much to be learned, was there, as real in life as any of us, voluntarily playing a major part in a way most of us would like to think we might, if called upon, but as few ever could.

Now for the first time, we have the full story in his own words in print, skillfully supplemented with necessary background and editorial explanations provided by Mike Hill. The book is a landmark achievement.

PROLOGUE

On Friday, March 31, 1871, a tired, sick, and frustrated Elihu Washburne, the American Minister to France, scrawled in a diary he had been keeping for months, "There never was such a 'hell upon earth' as this very Paris . . . How long, oh, how long!"

For 257 days, Washburne had lived through war, siege, and bloody revolution. Paris was in ruins, pockmarked by shell holes from massive Prussian cannons that had pounded the city night after night. During the worst days of a nearly five-month siege, disease and starvation had ravaged the city, killing between 2,500 and 4,000 Parisians each week. The winter—one of the worst on record—had made life in Paris unbearable for the 2 million people trapped by the Prussians. To survive, people had been forced to eat rats, dogs, cats, zoo animals, sparrows, horses, and mules. Fuel shortages throughout the city caused "wood riots" in the streets as Parisians fought over dwindling supplies of wood to burn.

The Franco-Prussian War, the cause of it all, had broken

out in July of 1870. It was a war that the French Emperor Napoléon III, nephew of the great Napoléon, had attempted to avoid. But he had been drawn into it by an inflamed press and a circle of adventurous advisors outraged by Prussian diplomatic slights and the threat of an emerging German empire. For weeks, the Emperor and his badly organized, ill-equipped army struggled against the mighty Prussian forces of King Wilhelm and Prince Otto von Bismarck. The Emperor himself, worn out and ill, led the French army into battle at Sedan in September, but his forces were routed and he was taken prisoner. Defeat followed defeat as Bismarck's troops marched steadily through France, halted finally at the gates of Paris by a formidable system of forts and defenses. A frustrated Bismarck—the "Iron Chancellor"—ordered his army to lay siege to the city, intent on starving and pounding it into submission.

Finally, on January 27, 1871, France was beaten. A battered Paris could hold out no longer. A fragile French government, which had seized power after the capture of Napoléon III, gave in. France was humiliated and the final terms of surrender were denounced by the public and press. Insurrection and riots ensued and the government was toppled. A new revolutionary committee—known as the "Commune"—took control of Paris. At first a spirit of high expectation greeted the new regime, its followers hopeful that France's long-festering social ills, neglected for years by the Emperor, would now be cured. Quickly, however, the ideals of the Commune were consumed by bitter and disillusioned extremists. Reminiscent of the brutal Commune de Paris formed in 1789 during the French Revolution, the Commune of 1871 was soon taken over by a collection of vicious and sadistic revolutionaries intent on destroying the government and Paris itself. After seizing power, they embarked on a reign of terror which, for nearly two months, filled the streets with blood, chaos, and carnage. During the final bloody week of May 1871 alone—the last gasp of the Commune—some 20,000 Parisians were massacred in a final savage struggle.

When the war began, the ambassadors of every major foreign power fled the capital. "The gaudy butterflies of the *salons* speedily fluttered out of sight," mocked one newspaper as diplomats rushed out of Paris. But one diplomat, American Elihu Washburne, remained, holding fast to his diplomatic post. His superiors in Washington, President Ulysses S. Grant and Secretary of State Hamilton Fish, allowed him the option to leave, but he would have none of it. "This is my place where duty calls me and here I must remain," he wrote at the time.

Along with millions of Parisians, Washburne endured months of bombardment, brutally cold weather, and dwindling food supplies. Despite all the hardships and dangers (one Commune member insisted he be hanged and the American Legation leveled to the ground), Washburne found time to chronicle these remarkable events in his diary, personal letters, and diplomatic dispatches. Whether exhausted, sick, or cold, Washburne tended to his journal and correspondence almost each day, pouring out his thoughts and impressions onto sheets of blank paper, later interwoven into leather-bound books. He knew he was at the center of history and was determined to record it all, providing a unique and riveting account of the monumental events swirling about him.

He later incorporated portions of the diary into a two-volume book, *Recollections of a Minister to France, 1869–1877*, published in 1887. But like many nineteenth-century diarists, he edited and rewrote many entries from the journal, often deleting significant personal passages and reflections and paraphrasing others. The *Recollections* also omit his personal correspondence to family, friends, and colleagues during the years he was under siege. Those letters are invaluable, as they occasionally provide a more detailed account of events or, in some instances, fill gaps in the diary. In this book I have assembled selections from Washburne's journal and letters, drawn from the original manuscript sources at the Library of Congress and Washburne family archives in Maine.

Washburne began the diary shortly after the outbreak of the war and kept it through the end of the bloody Commune. It is a vivid personal account of life in Paris during some of its darkest hours. Separated from his loved ones and isolated from the outside world, he often took time to reflect on his parents, family, and friends back home. Filled with insight about political and military events in Paris, the diary and letters also have an unmistakable charm, at times blending homespun expressions with quotations from Shakespeare, Shelley, and the Bible. Perhaps he wrote as a remedy for loneliness, but for the reader they are pure gold. We come to know and admire Washburne as he struggles to stay alive, do his duty, and not let his country down. As he would later write, "With no experience in such matters, and with no pretension of having been initiated in what are called the mysteries of diplomacy . . . I had simply to do the best I could under the circumstances."

Above all, Washburne's story is a great American story— a man rising to greatness in the midst of difficult and extraordinary times.

Elihu Washburne arrived in Paris on May 12, 1869. It was only the second time he had ever set foot in a foreign land, and the expectations for him as a diplomat were modest. Far from the town of Galena, Illinois, where he had once struggled as a small-town lawyer and politician, he was now "a denizen of the rough west . . . [in] . . . the most polished and artistic city in the universe."

He dressed plainly, wearing a blue or black broadcloth coat. His hair was "iron gray, worn long, half rolled under at the ends like a Southerner's or a man from the rural districts," wrote a reporter for the *New York Tribune*. His eyes were "large and full . . . shining like diamonds." His manner and style were part Midwest, part New England. "The model is Yankee, but the cargo is Western," one reporter noted.

Although "without fortune in dollars and cents," he would now "hobnob" with Emperor Napoléon III and the Empress Eugénie, attend lavish state dinners, and enjoy the company of royalty and foreign diplomats from around the world.

He was representing the United States of America at the imperial court of France. It had been a long road to the magnificence and splendor of Paris, a journey that had begun nearly sixty years earlier in a country village in northern New England.

Elihu Benjamin Washburne was born in Livermore, Maine, on September 23, 1816. The sixty-acre Washburn homestead (Elihu later added the *e* to his name to reflect the old English style) rested on a rise of hills some forty miles east of the White Mountains. On a clear day Mount Washington was visible in the distance. Warm winds swept over the land in summer, but the winters were cold and severe.

He was the third of eleven children, seven boys and four girls (one boy died in infancy). The family, he would recall, was always "very, very poor." His father, Israel, a man never "habituated to manual labor," ran a general store in the village, where townspeople gathered to talk politics and religion. But bad times and "misfortune" struck in 1829, and his father's business failed, the building itself hauled away by a sheriff and a team of oxen. His father tried to make a go of it as a farmer, but the "unwilling acres" made it hard to support a family of ten children. Elihu, twelve years old by now, helped his father as well as he could, once joining him in a nine-day cattle drive to the nearest market in Massachusetts.

Despite all the hardships of life on the farm, Washburne was devoted to his father. "With me memories are awakened of his virtues, all his kindnesses, all his devotion to his family," he later wrote. "When I look back upon his life and character . . . I [am] filled with admiration and gratitude. The turf shall always grow green over his honored grave and then shall be written on his monument that he was a kind father and an honest man . . ."

Washburne adored his mother, Martha Benjamin Washburn. Born in Livermore in 1792, she was the daughter of Samuel Benjamin, an American Revolutionary War officer who had fought at the battles of Bunker Hill and Yorktown. Although of little education she "was possessed of a quick and rare intelligence and excellent common sense." She could be "firm and resolute" in tough times, but also kind and "tender-hearted." She died at age sixty-nine, on May 6, 1861, only weeks after the outbreak of the Civil War. After her death Washburne wrote, "When I think of her labors, her anxieties, her watchfulness, her good and wise counsels and her attention to all our wants, my heart swells with emotion of gratitude towards her which no language can express."

Washburne spent much of his youth as a hired hand for neighbors, trying to help support the family and pay off his father's debts. "I dug up stumps, drove oxen to the plow and harrow, planted and hoed potatoes and corn, spread, raked and loaded and stowed away hay." He worked for one neighbor for $5 a month to pay off a $25 debt. "I was called up every morning at sunrise and worked until sunset through all the days of summer," he would later write. "No slave boy under the eye of a taskmaster ever worked harder."

His early years of school were no less difficult. When he was only seven years old his parents had sent him to live with his maternal grandparents in Boston. His grandfather was "stern and severe . . . [and] to him there was no nonsense in life," Washburne would recall. They enrolled him at a local school, but as a stranger he was "not regarded kindly" and was treated harshly. He would never forget a "brutal beating" he received at the hands of the schoolmaster for some minor infraction. "The sad and heavy months wore on," he would later recall, "until finally my father came to take me home."

> He had come from Livermore with a horse and chaise and we drove back, being three days on the way . . . We arrived at home about midnight of the third day and I remember the joy of my poor mother at seeing me again.

Washburne attended schools in Livermore over the next few years, but he had little time for his studies. When he was not tending to chores or farmwork, however, he would educate himself by "eagerly" reading the newspapers and devouring books of history and biography at the local library.

By the age of seventeen Elihu had decided that farm life was not for him. "Witnessing the poverty and struggles of my parents," he would recall, "I determined to shift for myself." During the next several years he tried his hand at a variety of jobs, working as a printer's devil (an apprentice who mixes ink and fetches printing type) at a nearby newspaper and spending time as a local schoolteacher. Finally, at the age of twenty he decided to pursue law.

Before entering law school, Washburne devoted himself to two years of schooling at the Kent's Hill School in Maine and then moved to Boston, where he was tutored in the law by attorney John Otis. More than just a teacher, Otis became a "true friend," helping Washburne with room and board expenses and tuition while he attended Harvard Law School.

After Elihu's admission to the bar, his younger brother Cadwallader persuaded him to move out west to Illinois. Cadwallader had become wealthy as a Midwest lawyer handling mineral and timber land grants. "A fellow who comes to a new country, penniless and an entire stranger, cannot jump into a fortune at once," Cadwallader warned about life in the Midwest. "He has many things to contend against which are not to be overcome in a moment. But if he holds out, minds his own business, does not become dissipated . . . he will generally come out right side up."

Traveling by train and steamboat, Washburne arrived in the rough lead-mining town of Galena, Illinois, in early 1840:

> I was a passenger in the little stern-wheel steamboat Pike [he would later write] . . . We arrived at the levee before daylight, and when I got up in the morning it was bright and clear . . . The mud in the streets knee-deep, the log and frame buildings all huddled together; the river full of steamboats discharging freight, busy men running to and fro, and draymen yelling.

He was a "green Yankee boy" with nothing to aid him "except hard experience and a high resolve" to succeed. In Galena, Washburne found ". . . miners, Americans, Germans, Swiss, good men and bad men and all rough men, sturdy pioneers like himself who had gone West to succeed and would have succeeded anywhere," as one biographer wrote.

He took a room in a log cabin boardinghouse for $4 a week sleeping "in the straw" with other boarders. At night he would be kept awake by the "howl" of calves from a nearby stockyard. Washburne soon set to work on establishing a law practice, renting a small office with a "table, three chairs and a Franklin stove." Galena was a "horrid rough place," but Washburne had little trouble establishing a successful practice. The people in town, he said, "are a litigious set."

Shortly after arriving in Galena, Washburne met Adele Gratiot, the young daughter of one of the town's most prominent families. Her father, Colonel Henry Gratiot, was a successful prospector and also federal Indian agent for the region. In 1827 he had helped preserve peace in the territory by successfully mediating a dispute between settlers in Galena and the Winnebago Indians.

Adele was ten years younger, attractive, charming, well educated, and "a fine conversationalist." It was said that she was a woman "of gentle manners and quiet dignity" and "charmed everyone by the grace and amiability of her manners."

Five years later, on July 31, 1845, they were married in Galena. They would have seven children, the first, Gratiot, named for Adele's family. Throughout their forty-two-year marriage, Elihu and Adele were devoted to each other and their children. An early biographer wrote that "no personal trait . . . is as outstanding as the devotion he felt and showed" for his wife. She held a charm and influence over him that few others did. Above all, she believed in him and "never had a doubt that he could do anything which he set out to do."

Settled down with a family and a flourishing law practice, Washburne turned his ambitions toward local and national politics. By 1844 he was attending national political conventions

as a Whig delegate, and only eight years later he was nominated
by his party as a candidate for the United States Congress.

He later described the exhausting and exhilarating days he
spent on the campaign trail:

> I made a canvass of some ten weeks, almost single-handed,
> and alone . . . not wanting in energy or activity. "No dangers
> daunted and no labors tired." I made one, and very often two
> speeches, each day. There were but a few miles of railroad in the
> whole district stretching from the Great Lakes to the Mississippi
> river. I travelled in buggies, in stage-coaches, on horseback and
> on foot, in farmer's wagons; any way to get along and meet my
> appointments. I visited the leading men at their homes, talked
> with their wives and caressed their children, went to church on
> the Sabbath and contributed to the support of Sunday schools.
> I attended all the parties and danced with the young ladies, and
> made them promise to have their sweethearts vote for me. I
> attended all the county fairs, and made speeches, praising very
> justly the magnificent exhibits, and the more beautiful display of
> wives and daughters. I went through the floral halls and "toted"
> the young ones in my arms, drank cider and ate cakes at the
> booths on the outside of the ground.

At times, however, his stops on the circuit proved less color-
ful and more frightful, requiring the full measure of his fortitude and charm:

> I called one afternoon to see Mr. J, a well to do farmer, an old
> line abolitionist and a man of some influence in his neighbor-
> hood, but very mean, and with a wife still more mean. She was
> a thin visaged, long nosed, cadaverous looking creature, with a
> pair of spectacles tied on her head with a tow string. She first

saluted me by saying that she did not know what business these politicians had to be running about the county keeping honest people from their work. I withdrew after her first fire in a somewhat damaged state, never expecting to see her again. But as luck would have it, I had an appointment to make a speech in the . . . school house in the neighborhood that evening. When the meeting broke up it was raining in torrents—I could not go to the neighboring village some ten miles away . . . and Mr. J was the only man I knew there. He saw my plight and could not but ask me to go home with him and I had no alternative but to go . . .

When Washburne arrived back at Mr. J's house, an annoyed and grim-faced wife met them at the door. She had no bed for him, she snapped.

I put on my blandest smile and said that I never slept in a bed—had not such an institution in my house, but that I always slept on the floor when I was at home, and I begged her to let me sleep on the floor. No, she would not agree to that, but said "I'll take the two gals with me and you and the old man shall sleep together." When I took another look at the dirty old codger I was horror struck, but there was no getting out of it and with many mutterings the old woman packed us off into a dirty old straw bed alive with bugs. I jumped into the back side . . . leaving as wide a space as possible between us. After a long talk . . . fatigue finally brought sleep. The morning came. I congratulated the old woman on her nice bed and the splendid sleep I had had—told her that everything showed she was an elegant house keeper and that I hoped her daughters would prove her equal, and if so they would make splendid wives. Soon the "gals" appeared and I congratulated them on their genteel appearance and expressed my regret that I had no boys large enough to be their sweet-beaus. And now the old woman began to relent and she flew round & got me some breakfast which I declared to be superior to any breakfast I ever ate in Boston.

From that day forward, Washburne would proudly proclaim, Mr. and Mrs. J became "the firmest and most devoted friends" he ever had in the county.

Finally, on November 2, 1852, the "great day of trial finally came." Washburne spent election day on horseback canvassing the district, seeking any last-minute support he could muster. At the end of the day he arrived home, worn to the bone and with his "green blanket coat . . . completely covered with mud." Although the outcome of the election was uncertain, he knew he had done his best and considered his "duty accomplished."

The next day Washburne learned he had been elected to Congress by a slim majority of 286 votes. He would go on to serve eight consecutive terms in the U.S. House of Representatives.

In Congress, Washburne quickly developed a reputation for independence and honesty. In 1856, only four years after first being elected, he became chairman of the Committee on Commerce. (Three other brothers, Israel, Cadwallader, and William, would also serve as members of Congress from the states of Maine, Wisconsin, and Minnesota, respectively; Elihu, Israel, and Cadwallader made history by serving in Congress at the same time between 1855 and 1860.) As chairman, Washburne took a keen interest in legislation affecting the development of the West, such as the building of the transcontinental railroad and improvements to navigation on the Mississippi River. All four brothers would eventually champion the antislavery cause in Congress.

Later, as chairman of the Committee on Appropriations, Washburne assumed a role as a "Watchdog over the Treasury," taking every opportunity he could to protect the "public purse as if it had been his own."

He was "one of the ablest and most faithful of the representatives of the people," one newspaper declared. "He steadily set his face against corruption and extravagance in every form, and incurred the bitter hostility of the hungry and plundering hordes who annually came to Washington with all manner of schemes to rob the Treasury . . ." Others found him impossible to deal with, calling him the "meanest man in the House."

Washburne also had the good political fortune to meet two figures who would shape the rest of his public life: Abraham Lincoln and Ulysses S. Grant. Washburne first met Lincoln during the winter of 1843–1844 when they were both in Springfield, Illinois, attending a session of the state Supreme Court. At first, Washburne was hardly impressed, seeing only an "awkward" lawyer wearing a "swallow-tail coat . . . thin pantaloons . . . a straw hat, and a pair of brogans with woolen socks."

But Washburne took an "active . . . interest" in Lincoln's career, supporting him for two unsuccessful bids for the Senate in 1855 and 1858 and then for the presidency in 1860. As "an old friend of twenty years," Washburne gave his "whole soul and energies" to Lincoln's presidential bid. He delivered a speech in support of Lincoln on the floor of the House on May 29, 1860, and had copies of it published and distributed throughout the nation.

After Lincoln's election, Washburne counseled him on political developments in Washington (particularly with regard to threats of Southern secession) and advised him on Cabinet appointments. In early 1861, as Lincoln headed toward Washington for the inauguration, there were rumors of plots to assassinate him along the way. In Baltimore, as his train headed to Washington in darkness, Pinkerton agents persuaded Lincoln to disguise himself in an "old overcoat and a new soft wool hat." Washburne was the only person to greet him on his arrival in the capital and immediately whisked him off by carriage to the Willard Hotel.

Washburne would see Lincoln often during the next several years as the nation plunged into civil war. "The door of the President's house was never to be closed against the man," the *Chicago Tribune* said of the relationship between Lincoln and Washburne. "He was expected to come each day, and any hour was the right one. Often when Mr. Lincoln's heart was full of anxiety and telegraph messages were not full enough, nor impartial enough to bring peace, Mr. Washburne would travel to the front, and bear his load of facts to the careworn man at Washington."

Washburne first met Ulysses S. Grant on April 16, 1861, two days after word reached Galena that Fort Sumter had fallen to the Confederates. They were both attending a town gathering in response to Lincoln's "call for volunteers" to aid the Union. Washburne knew nothing of Grant, who had resigned from the army seven years before and was now working as a clerk at his father's leather-goods store.

Grant had graduated from West Point in 1843 and served in the Mexican War under Generals Zachary Taylor and Winfield Scott from 1846 to 1848. In 1854 he resigned from the military and spent the next six years working as a farmer, bill collector, and finally as a clerk for his father. Because he was the only man in town with any military experience, Grant was asked to chair the town meeting. When he spoke—quietly but confidently—he told the gathering of his intention to answer Lincoln's call.

Washburne was impressed by what he saw and heard. Within months he helped Grant obtain the rank of colonel in command of the Twenty-First Illinois regiment. The new colonel was stationed for a time in Missouri, a post critical to maintaining control of the Mississippi River. In July, Washburne convinced President Lincoln to promote Grant to the rank of brigadier general. Grant was grateful and told Washburne, "I can assure you . . . that my whole heart is in the cause which we are fighting for, and I pledge myself that, if equal to the task before me, you shall never have cause to regret the part you have taken."

Grant was ordered to Cairo, Illinois, and put in charge of protecting the confluence of the Ohio and Mississippi rivers. Grant's units would engage the Confederates in a remarkable string of bloody battles in the western theater of war: Fort Donelson and Shiloh in 1862, and the siege of Vicksburg in 1863. As a result of the victory at Vicksburg, Lincoln appointed him to the rank of lieutenant general, in command of the entire Union army.

After the first shots were fired at Fort Sumter in April 1861, the war moved quickly to northern Virginia, just outside Washington, D.C. On July 21, 1861, Washburne traveled by carriage with thousands of other excited onlookers to Manassas Junction, Virginia, for an early showdown between Union and Confederate forces at the Battle of Bull Run. Everyone expected to see a rout of the Confederates by the Union army under the command of General Irvin McDowell. Quickly, however, everything turned to disaster. The rebel forces under Generals Joseph Johnston and P. G. T. Beauregard pushed McDowell's forces back, forcing a wild and chaotic retreat. Washburne, in the middle of the battle, recalled an "avalanche" of soldiers "pouring down the road" near him. He later wrote of the "perfect panic" he saw all around him:

> Never before had I such feelings. I had read of wars, and re-treats and routs, but I never expected, or wanted to live to see my own countrymen retreating before an enemy. On they came, baggage wagons, horses, carriages, foot soldiers, cavalry, artil-lerymen, pell-mell, helter-skelter . . . The soldiers threw away their guns and their blankets and divested themselves of every encumbrance. Officers, blush to say, were running with their men . . .

Washburne and a friend stopped their carriage. They jumped out and tried to "rally and form the men, but we might as well have attempted to stop the current of the Mississippi with a straw," Washburne wrote. At one point he grabbed a gun and tried to halt the retreat. "I stood almost alone in the road, threatening to bayonet every cowardly soldier who was run-ning away." But nothing worked.

With the battle lost, Washburne made his way back to Wash-ington. He rushed to the White House, where he met with President Lincoln and his Cabinet to discuss the debacle. "A more sober set of men I never before met," Washburne recalled in a letter to his wife.

Panic and defeat gripped the capital for days, but Washburne was determined. "We will whip the traitors yet," he told his wife back in Galena.

Over the next four years, Washburne would revisit the seat of war time and time again, often traveling to the front lines with his friend General Grant. In May of 1864, he joined the Union army in northern Virginia to witness two of the bloodiest engagements of the war: Spotsylvania and the Wilderness. "We are in the midst of terrific events," he told his wife, Adele. "It is fighting, fighting all the time and the most desperate and terrible of the war. The imagination cannot paint all the horrors that are around us. It is war, on the greatest scale the world has ever seen."

The Battle of Spotsylvania Court House raged for thirteen days and resulted in some 30,000 Union and Confederate casualties. After the second day of battle, he wrote to Adele, "Such a long and awful day I never went through before in my whole life and hope never to see another." Despite all the horrors of the struggle, Washburne was pleased with the success of General Grant. He "is the great head and soul of the army," Washburne said. "He is in capital spirits and seems to have no doubt of success."

Less than a year later, the war was over. Some 750,000 Americans had died in the struggle. After Lee surrendered, Washburne joined Grant at Appomattox Court House, Virginia. While there, he rode through the rebel camp as they turned over their arms and began to disperse into the countryside. As the rebel prisoners marched by hour after hour, Washburne described them as a "terrible looking set."

Days later, on his way back to Washington, Washburne received the "shocking news of the assassination of our Godgiven and beloved President." The news of Lincoln's death, he told his wife, "completely unmanned me." Selected as one of Lincoln's pallbearers, Washburne accompanied the martyred President's funeral train all the way home to Illinois.

After the assassination of Lincoln, Washburne initially supported the new President, Andrew Johnson. But soon, like
Grant, he grew disillusioned with him over Reconstruction
policies and pushed hard in the House for his impeachment,
calling him "a bad and faithless man."

In a speech on the floor of the House on February 22,
1868, Washburne condemned the embattled president:

> Let him be impeached for his last great crime that he has com-
> mitted against the Constitution and laws of his country. Let
> him be promptly tried, and if found guilty, let him be removed
> from the office he has disgraced. His longer retention in office
> is a perpetual and enduring menace against the peace and hap-
> piness and prosperity of the nation. His whole official career as
> President has been marked by a wicked disregard of all the obli-
> gations of public duty and by a degree of perfidy and treachery
> and turpitude unheard of in the history of the rulers of a free
> people.

During the trial in the Senate, Washburne felt confident
that the Constitution would be "vindicated" and Johnson con-
victed. But despite the impassioned pleas of Washburne and
other opponents in Congress, Johnson survived his trial by just
one vote.

Later that year Washburne backed his old Galena friend
Ulysses S. Grant for the presidency. On the day of the election
Grant received the returns at Washburne's home in Galena via a
telegraph that had been installed in his library. As the machine
ticked away, Grant appeared as "calm as a summer morning."

"The little old library looks like a Committee room of
ward politicians," he wrote to Adele. That night, after Grant's

election was assured, the local Galena "Lead Mine Band" came to Washburne's house and played music. "We felt pretty foxy," a jubilant Washburne reported to Adele.

In one of his first Cabinet appointments after the election, Grant named Washburne Secretary of State. Many were surprised by the choice, and the nomination was ridiculed by political foes, some in the press claiming he was "not fit for the place." The *New York World* called Washburne "a man of narrow mind" who had "never originated an important measure." Gideon Welles, who had served as Lincoln's Secretary of the Navy and often clashed with Congressman Washburne over appropriation measures, dismissed him as "coarse, uncultivated." But Grant was unmoved. "No other idea presented itself stronger to my mind . . . than I should continue to have your advice and assistance," he later told Washburne.

Washburne's nomination was confirmed by the Senate on March 5, 1869, the day after Grant's inauguration. He would serve only twelve days. Throughout the winter Washburne had been seriously ill and was confined to bed for nearly a month. At times his family and friends feared for his life. It was the latest in a series of illnesses that had plagued Washburne since his early days in Galena. He had been troubled by fevers, nervous strain, and "spinal irritations." At times he could barely walk. Once he had sought medical treatment in Europe—taking occasional injections of morphine for pain—but nothing seemed to work.*

---

*Washburne would later write in his *Recollections* (II, 245) that his serious health problems dated back to his days in Galena, Illinois, where his "system had become thoroughly impregnated with malaria, bringing me to fever and ague, and bilious and congestive fevers, and to such an extent that I was finally disabled in 1866, obliged to leave my seat in Congress in early

Knowing he would "not be able to discharge the duties of that office," he resigned. Grant accepted his resignation with regret but with the "assurance of continued confidence in [his] ability, zeal and friendship."

Washburne's eldest son, Gratiot, was relieved that his father had resigned and urged him to "take a good rest and recuperate your health."

By late spring 1869, Washburne's health had improved considerably. President Grant now offered him the post of Minister to France. Washburne was thrilled by the appointment and accepted, convinced that the time in Europe would be beneficial to his health. Above all, he was delighted to be out of Washington and the political grind. "The last few years of my life were years of great labor, activity and responsibility and I must confess I was pretty used up," he confided to friends back home. "My great enjoyment in being *abroad* is in being away from *home* and out of the incessant turmoil, strife, labor and excitement of political life. It is an immeasurable relief to me."

Despite some lingering concerns about his health, he was certain there was "nothing in the discharge of the duties" that would prevent him from getting along "well enough." He was sure the social duties of an ambassador would be the "most troublesome of all."

1867, and to spend seven months in Europe in search of health." No doubt the strain and demands of public life aggravated these medical problems both before and during his service as Minister to France. Although skeptical about the opinions of his doctors (once writing that the "whole medical profession is humbug"), Washburne always found some relief for his ills at the Carlsbad resort in Bohemia. "I . . . never failed to receive much benefit from the waters," he later wrote.

The new Minister departed alone for France on May 1, 1869. Adele had just given birth to a new son, Elihu Benjamin III, and it was decided that she and the rest of the family would join him later after he was fully settled in Paris. (By 1869 the Washburnes had seven children: Gratiot, age 20; Hempstead, 18; William Pitt, 15; Elihu Benjamin, Jr., 12; Susan Adele, 10; Marie Lisa, 6; and Elihu Benjamin III, 1.) Washburne's journey across the Atlantic on the steamer *Péreire* was frightful. Immediately after his arrival in Paris, he wrote home to Adele:

Dear Mother:

And did she roll, that Péreire, *and the storm howl, the wind blew and the tempest rage terrible, offensive. We left our shores right in the eye of a raging noreaster . . . We had head winds and stormy seas about the whole distance and in all my voyages [I] never suffered so much sea sickness. I was only able to be at dinner twice during the whole trip . . . I thought constantly of you and the children coming out . . .*

[All] our sea trouble came to an end on Tuesday night at eight o'clock when the lights on the coast of France greeted our anxious and welling eyes. At 10½ we cast anchor and in an hour and a half a tug came out and took us all on board and soon our feet pressed the shores of La Belle *France in the quaint old city of Brest. After a long delay we got to the hotel with our baggage at three o'clock in the morning. In the milieu my carpet bag got lost and I was in a tremendous fever, for it had all my papers. In due time it mysteriously came to light and it has not since been out of my sight.*

At seven o'clock yesterday morning we left Brest and arrived here [in Paris] at midnight last night after a very pleasant ride. The country looked beautiful and the day was pleasant and released from the thralldom of old Neptune we all felt happy. . . .

Once in Paris, Washburne wrote home almost daily. On May 17 he told the children how dearly he missed them and assured them that once they arrived in Paris they would "kick up" their heels and have a "high good old time."

After presenting his letters of credence on May 23, 1869, as the new diplomatic Minister from the United States of America, Washburne was warmly received by the court of Napoléon III. Thanks to Adele, Washburne had some understanding of the French language. Fluent in French herself, Adele had for years encouraged him to study the language and French history. However, shortly after his arrival in Paris, Washburne, as the new ambassador to the court of France, decided it best to hire a tutor. "I have my teacher come every morning and we gabble away at a great rate," he informed his wife. "I mean to persevere to the end."

Washburne soon settled into his new post at the American Legation, located at 95 Rue de Chaillot, just off the Champs-Élysées and not far from the Arch of Triumph. The offices of the American Minister were plain and "dreary" and, as Washburne's daughter Marie would later recall, were like a "middle-class apartment . . . furnished in the most bourgeois manner."

> The Minister's room was of medium size and depressing . . . There was a huge desk and a few chairs. Each room was gloomy, but the most depressing spot of all was a green carpet worn nearly black.

That fall Washburne was reunited with his family when Adele arrived in Paris with the children, except for eighteen-year-old Hempstead, who remained behind in America to attend school. After their arrival Adele was quite ill for a time, keeping Washburne occupied at home with her and the children, who were homesick for "Galena and their little playmates." Gratiot—nicknamed "Grack"—had also come along in hopes of finding a position at a business firm in Paris. "Grack" was headstrong and independent, qualities Washburne admired. "Gratiot is a good boy in every sense," he told a friend back home. "Honest, intelligent, excellent disposition and fine manners and good habits. He is ambitious of doing something for himself and I am glad to see it. I want my boys to paddle their canoes as you and I paddled ours."

They soon rented a house at 75 Avenue de l'Impératrice, located off the Champs-Élysées and near the Bois de Boulogne. Washburne told friends back home that it was an "elegant" house with "plenty of room, convenient, . . . [and] well furnished." It had stables, a garden, and a little yard in front. "It is really just the thing we want," he told his brother.

When the new Minister arrived in 1869, the grandeur and brilliance of Napoléon III's Second Empire was on display.

> The Emperor, residing at the Tuileries, was in the midst of a brilliant court [Washburne later wrote] and was surrounded with glittering splendor. Princes and Dukes, Marquises, Counts and Barons, maintained their butterfly existence, and the *grandes dames,* in their splendid toilets, promenaded in their gilded phaetons on the magnificent Avenue of the Champs-Élysées, or in the winding and shady alleys of the Forest of Boulogne . . . The cry of "Vive l'Empereur," uttered by the courtiers and parasites, was often heard in the streets, and was responded to by a giddy throng in Paris, which flattered by the counterfeit consideration of the government, dazzled by the glitter of the court, or, fattening on the wealth of royalty, abandoned itself to the

falsehood of pleasant dreams, and bowed down before the false glory of the material strength of the Empire.

But a growing resentment among the people and the increasing militarism of Prussia threatened the Emperor's regime. During his nearly eighteen-year reign, he had transformed Paris into a centerpiece of civilization and splendor, much of it achieved through the massive public and artistic works projects of the Prefect of the Seine, Baron Haussmann. Two years earlier, during the great Paris Exposition of 1867, the city had been the showcase of the world. But the grand empire had come at a price. While the wealthy benefited, life for the poor and working classes grew harder. Over half the population of Paris, the baron said, was "in poverty bordering on destitution." Washburne himself noticed that the city had "certain appearances of prosperity, happiness and content, but they were like the fruit of the Dead Sea, and to the last degree deceptive."

The people were restless, and attempts at reform did little to calm them. Protesters took to the streets, and the press continued to inflame the public against the government. Only weeks after Washburne arrived, he saw frightening signs of what was to come. "There have been great riots and disturbances during the last week," he wrote. "Indeed, many thought we were on the eve of another revolution. Vast crowds assembled every night on the Boulevards, singing the Marseillaise, raising seditious cries, destroying property, etc."

Napoléon III himself was sick, tired, and worn out. George Sand described him as like "a sleepwalker," and one foreign ambassador reported that "the Emperor seemed to have lost his compass."

Along with discontent at home, France faced a serious threat from an emerging Prussian empire to the east. In 1866, France had remained neutral while Prussia crushed Austria and created the North German Confederation. To maintain the delicate balance of power in Europe, Napoléon III had demanded territorial "compensations" from Prussia in return for his neutrality in the matter. But Prince Otto von Bismarck, the Prussian Chancellor, refused.

Over the next four years, tensions continued to rise between the two nations. By the summer of 1870, war seemed inevitable, especially after an abortive attempt by Bismarck to place his own "Hohenzollern candidate" on the Spanish throne, a move by Prussia that threatened the security of France's southern border and "produced the utmost excitement and indignation among the French people." As Washburne wrote:

> The Paris press teemed with articles more or less violent, calling on the government to prevent this outrage, even at the cost of war. The journals of all shades were unanimous in the matter, contending that it was an insult and a peril to France, and could not be tolerated.

Although Prussia eventually backed down, public outrage in France had been so inflamed that war seemed unavoidable.

Washburne had hoped that the move to Paris would improve his physical condition, but it did little good. "My . . . health is quite wretched at present," he told a colleague back home. "I have constant attacks of ague which bring pains and fevers." On July 3, 1870, despite being "somewhat uneasy" about the state of affairs between France and Prussia, Washburne decided to leave Paris and head for the curing waters of Carlsbad in Bohemia "in pursuit of health and recreation." While he was there, Adele took the rest of the family on holiday to

La Rochelle, a seaside resort on the Bay of Biscay in western France.

In Paris, however, the march to war continued. A reluctant Napoléon III, now caught between an inflamed French public and the imperialistic designs of Bismarck, had little will to resist. On July 15, Washburne's secretary, Wickham Hoffman,* cabled Washington from Paris: WAR IS CERTAIN. That same day Napoléon III's hand was finally forced and France declared war on Prussia.

"Thus by a tragic combination of ill-luck, stupidity, and ignorance France blundered into war with the greatest military power that Europe had ever seen, in a bad cause, with her army unready and without allies," wrote historian Michael Howard.

For the next twelve months the serene life Elihu Washburne had coveted in Paris would be upended. Through war, siege, bloodshed, and a reign of terror, he would, as he noted in his diary, be thrown into a "hell upon earth."

---

*Wickham Hoffman, a veteran of the American Civil War, was appointed Assistant Secretary to the U.S. Legation in Paris in 1866 under American Minister General John Adams Dix. When Washburne replaced Dix in 1869, he asked Hoffman to stay on and eventually promoted him to be First Secretary of the Legation. Washburne described Hoffman as a "good and competent man."

1

WAR AND REVOLUTION

Within hours after the outbreak of war, on July 15, 1870, word reached Washburne by telegraph in Carlsbad. It was "like a clap of thunder in a cloudless sky," he wrote. He quickly set out for Paris and along the way was caught up in the frantic mobilization for war. "The excitement was something prodigious, recalling to me the days at home of the firing upon [Fort] Sumter in 1861 . . . The troops were rushing to the depots; the trains were all blocked, and confusion everywhere reigned supreme." When at last he arrived in Paris on the night of July 18, the city was in chaos. "The streets, the Boulevards, the avenues, were filled with people in the greatest state of enthusiasms and excitation," he would recall.

The declaration of war had "inflamed the natural hatred of the Parisians toward the Germans." Many German nationals were arrested as spies and some later executed. A proclamation by the French government ordered the immediate expulsion of some 30,000 Germans who "came in shoals" to the American Legation, desperately seeking protection and assistance. Amid all the confusion, Washburne barely had time to dash off notes to his wife and brother after the grueling journey back to Paris.

Elihu Washburne, Paris—to Adele Washburne, La Rochelle, France—July 19, 1870

You will see I am back again in Paris. I telegraphed you yesterday from Belgium that I was on my way. I heard of the declaration of war on Saturday and left that night and arrived here at 10 o'clock last night after a terribly hard and continuous trip of 52 hours . . . I was sorry to have to give up my cure, but it was inevitable. This is my place where duty calls me and here I must remain. I have no time to write particulars this morning . . .

Elihu Washburne, Paris—to his brother Israel Washburn, Jr.— July 21, 1870

You see we are in troublesome times . . . I got back last night a good deal "banged up" and . . . worse off than I was when I left two weeks ago. The suddenness of the terrible events which we are now confronting appal the world. No human ken can measure the consequences . . . that will result from the fearful conflict which is impending. For one I had prayed never to see more war but here I am [in] the very midst of it and in a position of great responsibility and labor. I shall endeavor to meet, as best I can, all the requirements of my position . . . My Legation has been filled today with Prussians wanting to get home and I am in an important correspondence with the Foreign Office on that subject. Indeed I am overrun all the time. It is as bad as being Secretary of State at the advent of a new administration. The war is on the most miserable pretext but it could not be avoided . . . Both sides are ready . . . and will fight with unheard of desperation. I

take no sides, but preserve an "armed neutrality." Adele and the
children are well and . . . at La Rochelle, where they are taking
sea baths. The Lord knows when I will see them as I am now tied
to Paris.

On July 28 Napoléon III led his troops into battle with great ceremony. Washburne reported to President Grant that the Emperor had left Paris "with great panache and parade. He took more baggage than you did . . . when you [set] out on the Vicksburg campaign."

Although ill and worn out, Napoléon III accepted his fate and the inevitability of war, summoning his subjects to battle with a stirring proclamation: "Frenchmen! There are in the lives of people solemn moments, where national honor, violently excited, imposes itself as an irresistible force, dominates all interests, and takes in hand the direction of the destinies of the country. One of these decisive hours has just sounded for France."

But the Emperor's spirited call to war could not overcome a French army horribly disorganized, badly supplied, and badly led. They faced a Prussian force well prepared and ready to strike. It was led by the Prussian King himself, Wilhelm I, the first professional soldier on the throne since Frederick the Great; Field Marshal Helmuth von Moltke, chief of the Prussian General Staff; and the "Iron Chancellor," Count Otto von Bismarck, the King's Minister-President and architect of the war. Washburne had once seen Bismarck during a brief visit to Berlin in 1867. "He is the great *I am* of Prussia and his rod rules," Washburne wrote at the time, although he added, "But a rather gay boy, fond of wine and women."

It was a "magnificent" fighting force. Émile Zola warned of a "Germany ready, better commanded, better armed, sublimated by a great charge of patriotism; France frightened, delivered into disorder . . . having neither the leaders nor the men, nor the necessary arms."

On August 2, the first skirmish of war took place. French morale was briefly boosted when the army overran a small Prussian force at Saarbrücken. Back in Paris a great triumph was declared, but four days later, disaster struck. The Emperor's forces were crushed and routed by an overwhelming Prussian force at Weissenburg and Spicheren. "The two nations were in full war, and blood was flowing like water on both sides," wrote Washburne.

Muddled reports of French victories soon flooded the city, reminding Washburne of the Civil War when "rumors, exaggerations and . . . false reports . . . spread in times of such excitement."

Diary—August 6, 1870, Saturday evening

There was a tremendous time down town today, in a false report of a French victory. Somebody read a pretended dispatch that the French had taken 25,000 Prussian prisoners including the Crown Prince. Everybody in the neighborhood went perfectly crazy—flags everywhere went out of windows, people rushed wildly into the streets and went to yelling, hugging, kissing, singing, weeping, swearing and tearing. The Bourse went up wildly, opera singers were mounted on omnibuses and sang the Marsellaise and the whole crowd joined—never was such a scene witnessed on the face of the earth. Nobody pretended to doubt the news, everybody had seen the dispatch—it was official. But after the first furor had exhausted itself, somebody ventured to enquire a little and it turned out it was a hoax. The cry was raised that it was a stock jobbing affair, and the . . . cry was raised, "à la Bourse" [to the

Bourse] and away the crowd—20,000—rushed furiously to the
Bourse, broke in, seized every fellow they could get hold of and
threw him out of the window or door. And then how flat they all
felt—knew it was a canard from the beginning—the flags were all
pulled in and the crowd dispersed swearing vengeance.

Diary—August 7, 1870, Sunday morning

I went down to the Rue de Lafayette about four o'clock yesterday
P.M. I saw some few crowds in the street, but all was pretty quiet.
On my return through Place Vendôme I saw a big crowd in front
of the Ministry of Justice. I told the "cocher" [coachman] to hold
up in order to see what was going on. I immediately discovered
[Émile] Ollivier* at the window making a speech to this crowd,
but it was so noisy and turbulent that I could hear nothing and
so I continued on my way home. I was so tired that I did not go
out after dinner, but Mr. [Frank] Moore [assistant secretary
to the American Legation] went down town and came home
at midnight. He represents the effervescence as terrific. Place
Vendôme was filled with an excited crowd uttering menacing
cries for Ollivier. The current seems to be moving heavily against
him, as the author of that savage and terrible press law which
prevents the people getting any news from the army. The news of
the battle of Weissenburg was published Friday morning in the
London Times, but they did not let it out here till Friday noon,
and then only a few lines. The people were terribly incensed . . .
Last night the people were in the highest possible state of

---

*A republican politician who supported the Emperor and helped him main-
tain power through the creation of a "Liberal Empire" in 1869. He served
in the Cabinet as Minister of Justice. On July 15, 1870, as France and
Prussia headed toward conflict, Ollivier supported the war, crying out in
the French legislative assembly, "Avec un coeur léger." [With a light heart.]

excitement—Champs-Élysées, Rue de la Paix, Place Vendôme
and all the boulevards were filled with excited crowds singing,
yelling, threatening. There is no doubt but things are very serious,
but I am as quiet as a May morning. Yet I don't know what is to
become of all these poor Germans under my protection. The Gov't
is taking stringent measures against them, and I can do but little
for them. The crowd at the Legation continues.

When news arrived that the Prussians had crossed into French
territory, the people of Paris were shattered, "tormented with
fear and suspense," reported Washburne. This "grave news"
prompted the Empress Eugénie, now Regent in the Emperor's
absence, to issue a proclamation formally declaring Paris "in a
state of siege."

Diary—August 8, 1870, Monday morning

About three o'clock yesterday P.M. a man came in and told me
the news, and perhaps none more pregnant with great events. The
news of the morning that [General Charles Auguste] Frossard's
corps was in retreat was very significant, but I was unprepared to
learn that the crack corps of the French Army commanded by their
crack General, Marshal [Patrice] MacMahon, had been defeated
in a pitched battle, for the Emperor himself had telegraphed in
these words: "Le Marshal MacMahon a perdu une bataille."
[Marshal MacMahon has lost a battle.] And then on top of this
news we had the Proclamation of the Empress and the decrees
placing Paris in a state of siege and convoking legislative bodies.

You can well imagine the effect of all this upon such a people as
the Parisians. It was like the day after Bull Run at Washington
only more so . . . The rain which was falling nearly all day gave
additional gloom. I went down town about four o'clock P.M.

and everywhere found knots of people on the sidewalk reading
newspapers and discussing the situation. In the evening I was
down town, but while there were great crowds in the street there
was no disturbance. The blows received during the day had
apparently stunned the mob. There is no news this morning which
affords the French people any consolation. A big battle appears
imminent and it may decide the fate of the campaign. I must
now go over to the Legation where there will be a crowd all day.
But at noon I must go to the funeral of Provost-Paradol* and two
o'clock go to see the Empress unless she countermands the order to
see me.

Later that day, with Paris in an uproar, Washburne arrived at
the Tuileries for his appointment with the Empress. He found
her "in great distress of mind," having "passed a sleepless and
agitated night."

Diary—August 8, 1870, 11 o'clock evening

At two o'clock I went to the Tuileries to . . . [see] the Empress.
My interview was short. She received me very courteously . . .
[and] then enquired what news I had from my country and I
replied that it was all good. "Unfortunately, the continent is
not so—here it is all very bad—we have very bad news now." I
replied that reverses were incident to all military operations and
that we had experienced such reverses and such disappointments

---

*Prévost-Paradol (the correct spelling) was the Minister of France to the
United States in 1870. As the prospects of war became clear, he warned
his fellow Frenchmen, "You will not go to Germany, you will be crushed in
France. Believe me, I know the Prussians." Nearly a month later, he would
commit suicide in Washington. (Horne, *The Fall of Paris: The Siege and the
Commune, 1870–71*, 39–40.)

in our war, particularly at its commencement. "Yes," she said,
"I know at Bull Run but, alas! our people are not like yours—
the French people give up so quick and become so dissatisfied
and unreasonable, while your people have so much courage and
fortitude. But I don't despair and I keep up my courage . . . I
think we can retrieve all our disasters." I then explained to her
an observation on the beginning of the war and how our people
rallied after our defeats &c. After a little more talk and just as
I was about to leave I enquired for His Majesty and the Prince
Imperial. When I mentioned the little Prince the mother's tear
started in her eye and she answered trembling that so far he
was safe and well. With a few words more I made a gesture of
withdrawal and she said, "I thank you much," when I bid adieu.
The poor, poor woman—what terrible feelings she must have.
Haggard, pale, worn, she is not the bright and graceful person
you saw at the Tuileries last winter. She now confronts the sternest
realities of life. As I left I wondered under what circumstances I
should see her next time.

All of Paris was "paralyzed by the terrible events which have
burst upon them in such rapid and fearful succession," Washburne reported to Secretary of State Hamilton Fish. With the
Emperor on the field of battle and the Empress increasingly
helpless, people looked to the French Legislative Assembly, the
Corps Législatif, "for some action which might stem the tide
of disaster which was then rolling over Paris and France." (The
Corps Législatif "shared the legislative function of the government with the Emperor." Washburne, in his *Recollections of a
Minister to France,* Vol. I, described it as a body "composed of
men of more than ordinary ability, and many of them of much
political experience, and who had been somewhat distinguished
in one way or another. As a body, it was composed of older

men than the members of our House of Representatives at Washington, and the number of deputies were about the same as in our House."

**Elihu Washburne, Paris—to his brother Israel Washburn, Jr.—
August 9, 1870**

> *France is on the brink of destruction and you can imagine
> something of the feelings of the people of Paris. We are very much
> in the dark here as we have no news except what the government is
> disposed to give out to us . . .*

Diary—August 9, 1870, 10 P.M.

> *The Corps Législatif met at one o'clock P.M. and I went in good
> season to get a seat . . . I was utterly unprepared for the scene
> which took place. I supposed there was some patriotism, sense
> and self-respect left among the representatives of the French
> people, but I was mistaken. If there were one man present who
> loved his country I wonder that he did not shed tears of shame
> and indignation. The "Left" of the Chamber, as the republicans
> or radicals are called, seemed ready and Ollivier no sooner
> commenced to speak when the row commenced and for two hours
> bedlam was let loose. Jules Favre* spoke with the terrible eloquence
> of Mirabeau.† [Ernest] Picard‡ spoke and then on the other side*

*A republican member of the French Assembly, he was a longtime opponent of Napoléon III and resisted going to war with Prussia.
†A popular orator and politician during the French Revolution of 1789–1792. Considered a political moderate, Mirabeau favored a constitutional monarchy.
‡A republican member of the French Assembly. Like Favre, also voted against going to war.

[Adolphe Granier de] Cassagnac denounced the Left with fury,
winding up by calling them revolutionists and that if he had
his way, he would send them all to a military tribunal before
night. A tempest followed that awful threat. The Left rose in a
body and yelled defiance to old Cassagnac. Twenty men at a time
were on their feet bawling at [the] top of their voices and shaking
their fists. Jules Simon† rushed down to the area in front of the
tribune, bared his heart and told them to shoot him down after a
lot of yelling from the Left. Seeing something they did not like in
[Antoine, Duc de] Gramont,‡ they "went" for him. Estancelin§
rushed up in front of him making threatening gestures, and
then down swept in[to] the crowd the tall and striking form of
the venerable [Louis-Antoine] Garnier-Pagès,¶ who shook his
fist right under the nose of Gramont, who sat unmoved in his
seat. There went up yells, howls, vociferations, threats, oaths.
The President rang his bell and finally as the last token and the
sign that tumult and revolution controlled the body he "covered
himself" and put on his hat. The officers rushed in and separated
the hostile forces and finally quiet was somewhat restored. After
about two hours of violence the sitting was suspended. At five
o'clock the sitting was resumed and a vote of a want of confidence
in the ministry was taken and in a twinkling the ministry was*

---

*A Deputy of the French Assembly and powerful conservative journalist
during the Second Empire. A vocal opponent of Ollivier's Liberal Empire,
he pushed for war with Prussia.
†A member of the Assembly from Paris.
‡French Minister of Foreign Affairs at the outbreak of the war.
§According to Washburne, he was one of the young "advanced Republicans." (*Recollections of a Minister to France,* Vol. I, 77.)
¶Washburne described him as "an old time republican . . . nearly seventy
years of age, and had for a long time been a prominent man in France, a
republican always, but considered somewhat conservative." (*Recollections of
a Minister to France,* Vol. I, 77.)

out and tomorrow a new one will be formed. Ollivier is terribly odious. His ministry has been guarded by soldiers for two or three days. And today the Corps Législatif was surrounded by a heavy force of cavalry and infantry to keep off the crowd, who were breathing vengeance. Shocking times these and enough to make a man heart sick. Such men cannot face a country in peril, and it seems to me that France is on the very brink of destruction.

Despite the rush of events, Washburne took time to write Adele and to cable Washington about the state of affairs in Paris, particularly about anxiety among the American colony in Paris and the continuing plight of the German nationals.

Elihu Washburne, Paris—to Adele Washburne, La Rochelle— August 1870

I was so tremendously used up last night, that I took to my bunk after dinner, but only to be constantly interrupted by people coming to see me . . . The suspense here is awful and such silence is very ominous. The crowd of Germans is increasing. The Prussian government has sent me $37,000* to help the poor creatures out of the country. And oh! Such scenes as I am compelled to witness seeing these poor people—turned out of their lodging, no money, no bread, no friends—women weeping with little babies in their arms and nothing to eat . . . women sleeping in the streets with their little ones Oh God! How it makes my heart bleed, such desolation, such suffering, such cruelty . . . When I see all this suffering how

---

*To aid in the assistance of the German citizens trying to flee Paris, the Prussian government put $37,500 (over $600,000 in current U.S. dollars) at the disposal of Washburne and the American Legation. (Hoffman, *Camp, Court, and Siege,* 148.)

*ashamed I am that I have ever complained. I hope Grack will be
here this evening as I want him . . .*

Elihu Washburne, Paris—to Secretary of State Hamilton Fish—
August 15, 1870

*Since the breaking out of the war no Germans have been able to
get work, and the poorer classes have already exhausted the very
little they had in store. They are, therefore, today without work,
without money, without credit, without friends, without bread.
Pinched with hunger, terrified by threats of violence, with no
means of leaving the country, they have come to me to save them.
Women with little babes in their arms, and women far gone in
pregnancy, bathed in tears and filled with anguish, have come
to our Legation as their last hope . . . I shall do all in my power
to assuage the miseries of these people whose cruel situation must
challenge the profoundest sympathy of every generous heart.*

With Paris in an uproar, Washburne's wife and children grew
increasingly concerned about his health and safety. Meanwhile,
Gratiot—"Grack"—had joined his father in Paris.

Adele Washburne, La Rochelle, France—to Gratiot Washburne,
Paris—August 19, 1870

Dear Grack:

*I have just received your letter and a few lines from dear Father. I
hope he is well this morning. I am constantly anxious about him. I
hope you can render yourself useful to him in these awful times . . .*
   *Much love to dear Father & take good care of him—and
yourself. Persuade him to try the sweet oil cure—it works wonders*

in his case and tell him to keep chloroform and when his back
aches saturate a piece of paper and place it over the pain. I know
if he perseveres it will help him, but he must persevere . . .

Susan Adele Washburne, La Rochelle—to Elihu Washburne, Paris—
August 22, 1870

Dear Papa:

. . . I shall be glad when we go back to Paris to be with dear old
Papa again. Indeed I will. We all want to see you again so bad, so
bad . . . I hope your back does not ache now . . . We are all pretty
well now and we hope you are too. Good bye now, dear Papa,
please excuse this bad writing, I have not much time.

As the course of the war turned against the French, the danger
posed to Americans and German nationals in the city increased
each day. By late August, Washburne and the U.S. Legation
were being overwhelmed by daily requests for protection and
assistance. During a period of six weeks after the outbreak of
war, Washburne and the American Legation helped over 3,000
Americans leave Paris. An additional 1,000 Americans who
already held U.S. State Department passports also fled Paris at
this time.

Elihu Washburne, Paris—to Secretary of State Hamilton Fish,
Washington, D.C.—September 2, 1870

The greater part of the German population has left the city. This
Legation has viséd passports and given safe-conducts for very
nearly thirty-thousand persons, subjects of the North German
Confederation, expelled from France. We have given rail-road

tickets to the Prussian frontier for eight thousand of these people,
as well as small amounts of money to a much smaller number . . .
My time is now a good deal taken up in looking after Germans
who have been arrested and thrown into prison. The number is
very great . . .

On Saturday, August 27, Adele and the children returned
briefly to Paris from La Rochelle to see Washburne, but he
quickly dispatched them by train to Brussels for their safety.

A week later, with his family settled in Belgium, Washburne
took a moment to write to Adele and the children about events
in Paris.

Elihu Washburne, Paris—to Adele Washburne, Brussels—
September 2, 1870

I am depressed and sad at the scenes of misery, suffering and
anguish. Yesterday forenoon a poor woman came into the
Legation with three children, a babe in arms, one about three
and the oldest about five. When about to leave the depot the night
before her husband was seized as a . . . spy—and carried off to
prison. There she was left in the depot with not a cent of money . . .
and there she remained all night and yesterday made her way to
the Legation, bringing her children along with her. She wept as if
her heart would break and the two little children joined in—the
baby alone unconscious of the situation. I at once gave her money
to go out and get something to eat and sent off a man to look after
her husband. He was gone nearly all day and was not able to get
him out. I shall try again today to get him out. In the meantime I
sent the poor woman and her children to a good place to be taken
care of.

The crowd to go off last night was so great that I went to the

depot myself. There were at least two thousand persons to whom
we had given them cards entitling them to tickets and such a mob
and . . . pulling . . . squeezing, yelling and swearing you never
heard. It was impossible for the railroad to send them off and
about 500 were left. They broke down the railing and one of my
men was nearly squeezed to death. I did not get away from there
until midnight . . .

The next day, reports reached Paris of another French defeat
and the capture of the Emperor at Sedan. It was devastating
news. "A great misfortune has fallen upon the country," reported the Paris newspaper *Galignani's Messenger.** "After a
heroic struggle, lasting three days, sustained by the army of
Marshal de MacMahon, against 30,000 troops of the enemy,
40,000 soldiers have been made prisoner . . ."

The people of Paris were "alarmed, discouraged, mad-
dened," wrote Washburne. "The startling news had fallen like
a thunderbolt over all Paris. The Boulevards were thronged
by masses of excited men, filled with rage and indignation."
With this latest defeat, Washburne saw the French government "drifting to a crisis." In a matter of days, the government
would fall, the Empress would flee Paris in disgrace, and a provisional Republic would be proclaimed.

---

* *Galignani's Messenger* was a Paris daily newspaper published in English
by Giovanni Antonio Galignani (1757–1821). At the time of its closing in
1904, it was the oldest newspaper printed in English on the European continent. Galignani also founded the first English bookshop on the continent
in Paris in 1801. In 1856 the bookshop was moved to the Rue de Rivoli,
where it remains open today.

Diary—September 3, 1870, Saturday evening

*This has been a most eventful day for Paris and for France. The
absence of official dispatches put out by the French government
and the news furnished by the London Times of yesterday
convinced me that all was going against the French at the theater
of war.* But at three this afternoon I received a cypher dispatch
from Mr. [John Lothrop] Motley† to the effect that the London
Times of this morning said that M[a]cMahon had been totally
defeated yesterday between Carignan and Sedan—that the
Prussians had captured the French General and staff—4,000
men, 700 horses and 150 guns—that [Marshal François-Achille]
Bazaine‡ had been defeated before Metz and that the Crown
Prince's army was reported to be at Sedan . . . Reports were also
current that the Emperor had been taken prisoner and also that
he had fled to Belgium . . . There was a large crowd in front of
the Palais Bourbon and a great many people inside the fence
surrounding the Corps Législatif. But it was a sober crowd.
The truth, so long concealed by the French press, had at length
broken upon Paris in all its terrible reality and the people
seemed thoroughly stupefied. There was no demonstration
and no loud talk. The effect was sad to the last degree. What*

*One correspondent for the London *Times* reported on September 2,
1870: "'You are living in a fool's paradise,' an intelligent friend, of Prussian
proclivities, writes to me from England, 'The Prussians are marching on
Paris, and will be upon you before you know of their coming.'"
†American Minister in London, 1869–1870.
‡Bazaine was a Marshal of France. Known for his outstanding bravery, he
was a member of the French army for four decades, serving under Louis-
Philippe and Napoléon III. After the surrender of Metz, he was sentenced
to death, but the sentence was commuted to twenty years in exile. He eventually escaped and made his way to Madrid, Spain, where he died at age
seventy-seven in 1888.

may yet come from this revolutionary population no one can tell.

> *Gratiot has just come from the prison La Roquette,* and says there are some seven hundred prisoners confined there, mostly Germans—that they are so crowded that it is impossible for any of them to lie down, but that they all have to stand up. I am going to see the Minister of the Interior tomorrow to see if he will not release the Germans en masse if I will agree to send them out of the country.*

On September 4, Napoléon III's Second Empire collapsed. Washburne was pleased, as he had grown to detest the Emperor's decaying regime. At once, he cabled Secretary of State Hamilton Fish seeking permission to recognize the new provisional government. His request was granted and he immediately communicated the news to the new Minister of Foreign Affairs, Jules Favre. (Washburne described Favre as a "tall, heavy man, with rough, strong features, plainly dressed and with an immense head of hair." Washburne knew Favre to be a "great orator" and would often seek his assistance in resolving problems during the siege.) The United States was the first foreign nation to grant recognition to the new French Republic.

Diary—September 4, 1870, Sunday morning

> *At half past twelve this morning, my secretary Col. [Wickham] Hoffman came to the house and awakened me up to tell me of the news—the defeat of M[a]cMahon, the capture of the Emperor &c.*

---

*La Roquette prison—nicknamed "the Rocket"—was opened in 1830. It was the Paris prison in which condemned convicts were held until their execution.

. . . Mr. Hoffman said there was great excitement in the street at midnight.

Elihu Washburne, Paris—to Secretary of State Hamilton Fish, Washington, D.C.—September 5, 1870

Republic proclaimed . . . Paris quiet . . . The proclamation was received by every possible demonstration of enthusiasm. Lists were thrown out of the window containing the names of the members of the provisional government . . . During this time the public were occupying the Tuileries. Sixty thousand human beings had rolled toward the palace, completely leveling all obstacles; the vestibule was invaded, and in the courtyard, on the side of the Place du Carrousel, were to be seen soldiers of every arm, who, in the presence of the people, removed the cartridges from their guns, and were greeted by cries, "Long live the nation!" "Down with the Bonapartes!" "To Berlin!" &c. During all this time there was no pillage, no havoc, no destruction of property, and the crowd soon retired, leaving the palace under the protection of the National Guard* . . . Some discussion was raised about the changing of the flag, but [Léon] Gambetta† declared that the tri-color was the flag of 1792 and '93, and that under it France had been and would yet be led to victory . . .

*Alistair Horne in *The Fall of Paris: The Siege and the Commune, 1870–71* writes this of the National Guard: "The Paris National Guard was a kind of militia which, under the Second Empire, had originally been formed chiefly from the 'reliable' bourgeoisie, but in the emergency of August [1870] the Government had been pressed to expand it on more democratic lines, and it was already thoroughly permeated with Republican sympathizers." (55)
†A prominent French statesman and member of the French Assembly. He was one of the first members of the new Government of National Defense and served as Minister of the Interior.

*The day had been pleasant, and the night was beautiful beyond
description . . . I returned to my lodgings to ponder over the
events of the day to become memorable in history. In a few brief
hours of a Sabbath day I had seen a dynasty fall and a republic
proclaimed, and all without the shedding of one drop of blood.*

**Elihu Washburne—to Mr. Jules Favre, French Minister of Foreign
Affairs, Paris—September 7, 1870**

*It affords me great pleasure to advise you that I have this morning
received a telegraphic dispatch from my government instructing
me to recognize the government of the national defense as the
government of France . . .*

*Enjoying the untold and immeasurable blessings of a
republican form of government for nearly a century, the people
of the United States can but regard with profoundest interest the
efforts of the French people, to whom they are bound by the ties of
a traditional friendship, to obtain such free institutions as will
secure to them and to their posterity the inalienable rights of "life,
liberty, and the pursuit of happiness" . . .*

**Elihu Washburne, Paris—to his brother William Washburn—
September 7, 1870**

*You see all that has happened here . . . I am rejoiced beyond
expression at the down fall of this miserable dynasty and the
establishment of the Republic . . . You never saw anything so
quickly or handsomely done as this Revolution. It seems to me,
even now, like a dream.*

**Elihu Washburne, Paris—to Secretary of State Hamilton Fish,
Washington, D.C.—September 9, 1870**

> *At 2 o'clock P.M. yesterday M. Jules Favre called upon me in person
> to thank my government in the name of that of the national
> defense, as well as in his own behalf, for its prompt recognition
> of the republic and the tender of its felicitations. He again
> desired that I should transmit to the President and Cabinet at
> Washington the profound acknowledgments of the government of
> the national defense . . .*

Later that same day Washburne sent a second dispatch to
Washington.

**Elihu Washburne, Paris—to Secretary of State Hamilton Fish,
Washington, D.C.—September 9, 1870**

> *At about 4 o'clock yesterday afternoon a large crowd of French
> people came to the Legation, bearing the French and American
> flags, repeating the cries, "Vive l'Amérique!" "Vive la France!" A
> delegation, composed of very respectable gentlemen, waited upon
> me in my private room and read a short address, begging that I
> would transmit to my government the thanks of a great number
> of French citizens for the promptness and cordiality with which it
> had recognized the French republic . . .*

Washburne also sent a personal note to President Grant back
home, apprising him of the conditions in Paris and the sentiments of the French people.

Elihu Washburne, Paris—to President Ulysses S. Grant, Washington, D.C.—September 9, 1870

> *I would like to see you to tell you of all I have seen here for the last few weeks. Never was a nation more humbled, prostrated and butchered as France has been . . . Our country has never before stood out so prominently as now. Our prompt recognition of the Republic thrilled the whole country . . .*

That same day, despite the rush of events, Washburne took time to offer his sixteen-year-old son Pitt, now attending school in London, some fatherly advice.

Elihu Washburne, Paris—to Pitt Washburne, London— September 9, 1870

> *I am very sorry you have such a bad cold, but I hope it will not last long, for it is important now that you should be well and be able to study hard. I am glad to hear that you are going to practice economy. It is very important because I have not much money to spend on you. Your letter of the 8th, yesterday, is written very well . . .*
>
> *If the Prussians come here, it is quite likely that I shall leave the city with the whole diplomatic corps . . . You have seen that we have a Republic in France. It has been very quiet here since the Revolution of the 4th of this month . . . I am rejoiced at the downfall of the dynasty. I have no sympathy for the Emperor . . . The French people owe nothing to him, but on the other hand he has brought on them the most terrible misfortune . . .*
>
> *I am not without hope that we may have a peace before long and that we may all return to Paris. I am so lonely when you are all away. You must write at least three times a week a long letter.*

Be very careful how you spell. In this letter you spell scholar with
two l's and sorry with one r. A man who is going to be a great
doctor must know how to spell or he will be ridiculed.

After the proclamation of the new republic, "an atmosphere of
unrestrained carnival" reigned in Paris, but fears about Prussian spies remained. Near Washburne's home, on the Avenue
de l'Impératrice, a former schoolhouse was ransacked and
vandalized by soldiers believing it to be the home of Prussian
nationalists. Washburne was incensed. Wickham Hoffman, the
Legation Secretary, recalled that Minister Washburne was "in
arms at once," as he was not the type of man "to submit to any
outrage upon German or American property."

Diary—September 15, 1870

This morning I learned that the building occupied by Mr.
[Paul] Hedler and his mother as a school for American boys
had been broken into yesterday by some soldiers of the National
Guard and guard mobile, and partially sacked. The School was
run by Paul and Charles Hedler and their mother. Paul and
his mother are subjects of the North German confederation, but
Charles is a naturalized American. As the two former came
under the cruel order of expulsion, they had to leave France
and so they concluded to go to England. Pitt was at this school
but when they moved it to London he followed, but holding his
room in the building and leaving a good many of his things. In
view of the fact that Charles Hedler was an American and that
Pitt was an inmate of the school, I permitted them to put out
an American flag as protection. It seems that somebody in the
neighborhood yesterday started the story that there were Prussians
in the house, then soldiers broke in, in utter contempt of the flag,

seized the concierge and marched him off to the police, took all
Mr. Hedler's papers, smashed everything up in his office, and
then made for Pitt's room . . . broke into his drawers, threw his
things all about the room, and carried off all his letters. They
then went into the cellar and broke into the wine. They did
not do great damage in other parts of the house . . . As soon as
I learned what had happened this morning I went thither to
get at the exact facts. From there I went to the Foreign Office
and reported unofficially the outrage and the insult to our flag
to Jules Favre . . . Favre at once saw the gravity of the affair
and [the] most energetic measures should be instantly taken to
inquire into the matter, punish the perpetrators and to make the
fullest reparation . . .

After France's crushing defeat at Sedan and the surrender of
the Emperor, General Moltke commanded his troops, "Nach
Paris!" (To Paris!)

By early September, daily reports into Paris marked the rapid
advance of the Prussians. The French army was in full retreat,
now planning to make its defense inside the massive "girdle" of
fortifications surrounding Paris. Scores of people fled into the
city while displaced refugees from the provinces tried to make
their way safely inside Paris. Wickham Hoffman described the
chaos:

> They were thronged with the quaintest-looking old carts, farm-
> wagons, Noah's arks of every kind, loaded with the furniture
> of the poor inhabitants of the neighborhood flying to Paris for
> safety. On the other hand, the stations were thronged with the
> carriages of the better classes leaving the city. The railroads were
> so overworked that they finally refused to take any baggage that
> could not be carried by the passenger himself.

Within days, the city, including Washburne's neighborhood, became an armed camp. In his diary he noted the changing face of Paris and its uncertain future.

Diary, September 15, 1870

Every carriage of pleasure has disappeared. The streets are no longer sprinkled or cleaned, and before the recent rain the dust in the Champs-Élysées was so great you could hardly see a road before you . . . The city is but one big camp. Three hundred thousand soldiers passed in review before Gen. [Louis Jules] Trochu* on Tuesday. There are soldiers everywhere, organized and unorganized, of all arms, uniforms, shades, and colors . . . Streets and avenues are filled with tents and baggage wagons, horses, forage &c. The garden of the Tuileries is filled with artillery. There is a great movement of troops tonight; regiments are marching down the Champs-Élysées and as I write I distinctly hear them singing the eternal but ever inspiring, "Marseillaise" . . .

Diary, September 16, 1870, Friday morning

All communication with the outside world will very soon be cut off. I shall remain at my post of duty and await the logic of events . . .

*A French military leader who served as President of the Government of National Defense in 1870–1871.

2

---·---

SIEGE

On September 17, 1870, the siege of Paris began. For two days the Prussian army slowly enveloped the city, moving in like the "claws of a crab." Paris was fortified by a wall 30 feet high and a moat 10 feet wide plus an outer string of powerful forts. This chain of defenses comprised a circumference of some 40 miles. To succeed, the siege would require a 50-mile ring and virtually all of Prussia's army.

Inside the capital, trees in the Bois de Boulogne were cut down to provide barricades and fuel. Twelve thousand laborers frantically dug breastworks. Signal semaphores were set up in positions on top of the Arch of Triumph. Many of the treasures from the Louvre were taken to Brest, with the empty galleries converted into arsenals. Artillery camps were set up in the gardens of the Tuileries, and the manufacture of cartridges proceeded on an "enormous scale." Throughout the city, the "smell of saltpetre" filled the air.

Provisions were set aside to feed those now being sealed off in Paris, of whom 500,000 were soldiers. Some 250,000 sheep and 40,000 oxen were herded into the Bois de Boulogne. "As far as ever the eye can reach," one reporter wrote, "over every open space, down the long, long avenue all the way to Long-champ itself, nothing but sheep, sheep, sheep!"

By September 19 the gates of Paris were finally shut. For the next four and a half "dreary and mortal" months, Elihu Washburne would remain at his post, an eyewitness to the "patient suffering" of the people and the death, destruction, and starvation that would eventually bring Paris to its knees.

Diary—September 19, 1870

> *Has the world ever witnessed such a change in so short a time?*
> *It to me seems like a dream. For the first time we feel today that*
> *we are cut off from the outside world. All the roads are cut and*
> *no mails and no communication. And it seems odd to be in this*
> *great world and still not in it—shut out from all communication,*
> *no letters, no papers, no nothing. But after all, a certain part*
> *of Paris, doesn't seem to mind it much ... There are the same*
> *omnibuses, the same stores open, the same people moving about ...*
> *There are a great many troops in the street ...*

Near Washburne's home, on the Avenue de l'Impératrice, a neighbor and friend, Dr. Thomas Evans of Philadelphia, had established the American Ambulance, a well-equipped, well-staffed military field hospital for the wounded. The resourceful and ambitious Dr. Evans had operated a lucrative dental practice in Paris and had, among other notable patients, the Emperor and Empress. A close friend and confidant of the royal family, he had helped the Empress escape to England upon the collapse of the Second Empire.

The Ambulance corps was operated by two American

doctors, Dr. John Swinburne, a former Civil War field surgeon, and Dr. W. E. Johnston. During the war and siege, their efforts on behalf of the sick, wounded, and dying earned enormous praise from the French people. Washburne would visit the Ambulance often and, with pride, write of the assistance given the corps by Gratiot in helping to bring the dead and wounded in from the battlefield.

Diary—September 21, 1870

Evening. Third day of the siege and almost without incident. The weather still lovely, so many people on the street you might call it almost gay. The Champs-Élysées was clear . . . and as I rode down it at one o'clock it seemed really pleasant. Not so many people at the Legation as yesterday, but a good many straggling in . . . A balloon *started yesterday at 4 o'clock . . . to get outside the besieging forces and I entrusted a couple of letters to it to be sent to London.* At three o'clock this* P.M. *I visited the American ambulance [hospital] which is established on this Avenue, nearly opposite . . . Indeed, it is far superior to anything they have in the French army . . .*

*Wickham Hoffman, the secretary of the American Legation, later described in his memoir, *Camp, Court, and Siege,* the system of "mail balloons" set up by the Parisians to communicate with the outside world during the siege: "The French always had a fancy for ballooning, and were probably in advance of the rest of the world in this respect. They now applied their experience to a practical use, and soon a service of mail balloons was organized, starting from Paris twice a week . . . The officer of the Post-office who was charged with the organization of this service told me that, of ninety-seven balloons that left Paris during the siege, ninety-four arrived safely . . ." (182–183)

Diary—September 23, 1870

*8 o'clock—Friday morning. As I descend into the petit salon
[parlor] I see soldiers on every side. A company is drilling in front
of the house, another in the Avenue Bugeaud and yet another
is quartered in the adjoining house. The discharges of artillery
which were first heard at six o'clock this morning are now more
distinguished as I write, the sound coming from beyond the
Trocadero. An action is evidently going on. From all I see and
hear I think the Prussians will soon be in the city. The firing is
more rapid. I shall take a . . . ride around by the Trocadero as
I go to the Legation to see what I can see. This is one of the most
beautiful and lovely of mornings.*

    *Friday evening. There was quite a little action this morning
and the French claim an advantage, but I do not see that it
amounts to much. Yet they take courage from the result . . . At
eleven o'clock, I went to . . . meet the diplomatic corps to consult
as to what we should do. The ambassadors had all ran away last
week, but there were twenty-two members of the corps present. All
agreed that it was not the time for us to leave now and that we
would hereafter act together collectively . . .*

Diary—September 24, 1870

*I have given notice for all [Americans] who want to leave when
I go, if I shall deem it necessary to go, to send their names and
addresses to the Legation. It is evident that people do not find as
much fear as they expected in being shut up in a besieged city . . .*

Diary—September 27, 1870

Ninth day of the siege . . . Had quite a little dinner party tonight, eleven covers [place settings at the dinner table] . . . Dr. [W. E.] Johnston . . . Dr. [John] Swinburne of N.Y., Col. Hoffman and others. Quite a good dinner for a besieged city. But the talk was not very inspiring to people in my neighborhood . . .

Diary—September 28, 1870

It looks more and more like "grim visaged war"* in our own neighborhood . . . This morning on the main avenue directly opposite our house we saw them digging holes and on inquiring tonight, I find they are mining the street. Pleasant little neighborhood this. As I come home this evening I find them erecting a barricade the other side of Dr. [Thomas] Evans' house . . . I am the last man to stay in the neighborhood, but I shall soon have to be getting out of this, as I will be shut up from getting here. But what am I to do with all the furniture in the house. We have some seven thousand dollars worth . . . I must take away the most valuable things and leave the balance to take their chance.

Now cut off from the outside world, Washburne sought any means possible to maintain communication with his family in Brussels.

---

*Shakespeare, *Richard III*, Act I, scene 1.

**Elihu Washburne, Paris—to Adele Washburne, Brussels—
September 28, 1870**

> *By a German who is to be sent out of Paris by the Government I
> shall try to send you this brief line to assure you of our continual
> good health. We are just as well and happy as we can well be
> under the circumstances. The weather is charming and Paris
> seems wonderfully cheerful. But both Gratiot and myself are
> getting very anxious to hear from you and our wishes daily grow
> more ardent to be once more united under our own roof. I have
> never before so much realized the want of your society and the
> presence of the darling children. But I find enough to do every
> day to take up my time and so I am not idle. We still have a large
> American society here. I had some nine persons to dine with me
> last night and we were really quite jolly . . . The house is in good
> order and all goes well.*

Diary—September 29, 1870

> *Eleventh day of the siege. How magnificent is the weather still.
> I can scarcely recollect a more beautiful morning than this . . .
> After breakfast I walked out to see the new defense thrown across
> the Avenue de l'Impératrice . . . It will be formidable. They are
> still throwing up the defense that I spoke of yesterday and I will
> soon be blockaded . . .*

The French army attempted several sorties to break the Prussian lines, but to no avail.

Diary—September 30, 1870, evening

*Very heavy cannonading all the morning. After breakfast walked
out to the fortifications but no one there knew anything about what
was going on. Went to the Legation and worked till one o'clock and
then took a friend and went in search of the news . . . Returned
to the Legation and remained till five o'clock P.M. and then rode
down to the Palace of Industry, now a large hospital, where the
wounded have been brought. I there learned more of the details of
the fight this morning. The French made a sortie and attacked two
or three little towns with great courage and spirit, actually took
one or two and held them for a short time against immense odds.
When forced by overwhelming numbers to retire they marched back
like troops on parade. But their losses have been heavy—some five
hundred killed and fifteen hundred wounded . . . The wounded
soldiers were all in the best spirits, which was . . . a good sign. The
French are evidently inspired with fresh hopes. They believe that . . .
France will yet be saved and that the French soldiers will vindicate
the ancient prestige and glory of their country.*

*Even now, the twelfth day, the siege begins to be felt. Fresh
meat is scarce and the butcher's shops are surrounded by people in
a riotous spirit. Bread . . . is abundant and cheap . . . horses are
already starving. It is estimated that fifty thousand will be killed
for food. They are selling for almost nothing. I saw very decayed
horses sold at auction the other day for from five to eight dollars a
head . . .*

Diary—October 1, 1870

*Evening. Have ridden around the city a good deal today and
visited the fortifications at two points. They are amazingly
strong . . .*

No one could predict how long the siege would last. Some thought a month, others longer. Washburne himself would later write that a man "would have been deemed insane who would have predicted that the gates of the besieged city would not be open until the last day of February . . ." Anticipating the worst, Washburne and the remaining Americans had "laid in a stock of provisions" to help survive any lengthy investment of the city. Wickham Hoffman would later recall:

> The French live from hand to mouth, buying only what is necessary for the day, and laying in no stores. This comes, I think, from their system of living in apartments, and the want of storerooms. The Americans, as a rule, laid in a stock of provisions. The grocers of Paris had imported a large quantity of canned food for the use of the *colonie Americaine*, which was then, and still is, a power in Paris. The greater part of the *colonie* having gone, there remained a quantity of canned vegetables, fruit, deviled ham and turkey, oysters, lobsters, etc. etc., and, above all, hominy and grits. The French knew nothing of these eatables till late in the siege, when they discovered their merits. In the mean time, the Americans had bought up nearly all there was on hand.

Elihu Washburne, Paris—to Israel Washburn, Jr.—
October 2, 1870

I think it very likely that I shall remain here during the siege and Gratiot will stay with me. No one can tell how long it will last. I think a long time . . . The French have 500,000 troops here and the spirit of the troops and the people is good. The defenses are very strong. The city may possibly hold out eight weeks . . . I will not be likely to starve. I have a stock for sixty days. I have, however, to leave my house as it is so near the ramparts and it is getting to be surrounded by defenses—barricades on both sides and the street mined . . .

P.S. I may leave Paris if the two governments will let the Americans who are here (some 200 or 300) go with me. But if they will not, I shall remain and share their fate. It would be cowardice for me to leave and have them stay . . .

Elihu Washburne, Paris—to Cadwallader Washburn— October 3, 1870

I am afraid we are in for a long siege. If they keep the Americans here, I shall remain with them. Paris is now very strong and I think will have to be starved out . . . Paris is one vast camp with 500,000 men in arms, but they seem to do nothing . . .

Diary—October 4, 1870

Sixteenth day of the siege. I have had an unusually busy day today; everybody calling on me to do something. People now begin to want to get out of the city; and they are very persistent . . . The people of Paris are becoming very sober and much discouraged. It seems to be understood that the Provinces are doing nothing. If that be so, the "jig is up," and it is only a question of time as to how long Paris will hold out. It can resist shells and bombardments, but it cannot resist starvation. The long processions at the butcher shops are ominous.

Diary—October 6, 1870

For the first time for weeks we have had a dull, foggy morning. The servant comes in and says the streets are vacant and somber.

My feelings are in unison with the appearance of the streets. This being shut off from all intercourse with the world, when you are on dry land, is becoming tedious.

Evening. The day has run out without any incident of importance. Some little glimmer of news has come in from the Prussians and the Parisians are a little more cheerful. But it all amounts to nothing, in my judgment. Nothing is being done. The days go and the provisions go.

Speaking of provisions, I saw day before yesterday in the street a barrel of flour made at Waverly, Iowa, some seventy or eighty miles west of Galena.

Had to make a visit today to the Prefect of Police, Count de Keratry, now "Citizen" de Keratry. He formerly belonged to the French army, and is regarded as a man of courage and ability . . . He spoke quite hopefully about affairs, but I don't see it. Curious place this bad, old, dismal, dilapidated, gloomy, somber, dirty Prefecture of Police, the theater of so many crimes and so many punishments. If those frowning walls could speak, what tales of horror they might tell! . . .

On October 7, Washburne was startled by news that the French Minister of the Interior, Léon Gambetta, had made a daring escape from Paris by balloon. With the government cut off from the rest of France, Gambetta had been sent on a desperate mission to the outlying provinces to try to raise additional forces to engage the Prussian army and break the siege from outside. He was accompanied by a second balloon carrying two Americans, arms merchant Charles May and his associate William Reynolds. Once the balloons were outside the city and over the siege lines, the Prussians opened fire, but the balloons and their occupants escaped.

Diary—October 7, 1870

*The weather is changing at last; the morning was quite cool,
the afternoon cloudy and raining as I came into dinner this
evening. There has been a good deal of cannonading today, and, I
presume, as usual without results. There is still a little more news
from outside today which is interpreted as favorable. The balloon
went off at eleven this morning with six passengers, including
Gambetta and two Americans. A large crowd saw it move off,
amid great excitement. I hope that we shall hear that it landed
safely. A very quiet day at the Legation. Drove down town this
afternoon and went as far as the Hôtel de Ville [City Hall],
where we found all was quiet. I have never seen the Rue de Rivoli
so crowded in my life and one can barely conceive that we are in a
besieged city . . .*

On October 2, American General Ambrose Burnside, a veteran
of the American Civil War now in Europe on business, entered
the besieged city with a pass from Count Bismarck. The American general had been requested by Bismarck to approach Jules
Favre about the possibility of an armistice. Once inside the city,
Burnside stopped at the American Legation to pay his respects
to the Minister.

Diary—October 8, 1870

*I came to the Legation this evening to finish a dispatch to the State
Department . . . To my surprise, I found that General [Ambrose]
Burnside had been at the Legation, having come in with Mr.
[Paul] Forbes from the Prussian headquarters. They have now
gone down to report to General Trochu and Gratiot has gone
down to the Foreign Office to arrange for an interview tomorrow,*

with Jules Favre. I shall go with them, and they will stay at my house tonight at No. 75. They leave tomorrow to go through the Prussian lines. They bring no letters and no later London papers than we had before . . . This has been a blue, dull, rainy day, in Paris. There is a great deal of discontent brewing, and I learn there was a large demonstration of the Reds *[radical left-wing- Marxists, anarchists and revolutionaries] at the Hôtel de Ville this* P.M., *but I have not heard of results. No news from the balloon that went out yesterday and I am quite anxious as there were two Americans in it.* While I do not mean to complain, I should not tell the truth if I said it was not getting a little dull. This long absence of all news from . . . the outside world is depressing . . . and then this dull weather coming makes it worse . . .*

During Burnside's stay, Washburne introduced the General to some wealthy American friends, the Moultons, who had decided to remain in Paris through the German investment. Like many rich Americans, Charles, his son Charles, Jr., and wife, Lillie, had been favorites at the court of the Emperor and Empress. During the long months of siege, Washburne and Gratiot would dine and take company with them often.

Diary—October 9, 1870

Twenty-first day of the siege. All very comfortably lodged at No. 75 Avenue de l'Impératrice. Very good breakfast, and a very good dinner for starvation times . . . Quite a number of callers after

---

*As U.S. Minister, Washburne was understandably concerned about the fate of May and Reynolds, who had left with Gambetta the day before. On October 8 a carrier pigeon arrived in the city with a message announcing their safe escape. Gambetta had landed near Tours, some 150 miles to the south, and May and Reynolds at Roye, north of Paris.

dinner and at nine o'clock General Burnside and myself made a call at the Moultons. Nearly all French people there—Barons and Counts and Marquises and that sort of people, and now pretty much played out . . . Weather rainy and unpleasant, but made very cheerful by the glowing fire of the petit salon [parlor]. This finishes the third week of the siege and the fifth week of the New Republic.

On October 10, 1870, Count Bismarck informed Minister Washburne by letter that because he had taken upon himself the "officious protection of the Germans residing in France," Bismarck would, in return, allow Washburne to send out and receive through the Prussian siege lines weekly diplomatic dispatch bags containing letters and newspapers.

Diary—October 10, 1870

I was very busy until noon today getting the bag ready to send off by General Burnside. I determined to send Antoine [Antoine Schmit, messenger of the American Legation] with him to take the bag from Versailles to London and to bring back the bag from London and one from Brest. At noon another interview of Burnside, Forbes and myself with General Trochu and M. Jules Favre. It lasted an hour and a half and was very interesting. Our American friends left No. 75 at a quarter before three o'clock precisely to go into the Prussian lines. The arrival of these gentlemen has created a great excitement in Paris. There were some twenty people at the house to see them off. They were accompanied to the Prussian lines by . . . Col. Hoffman and were delivered over this time without any delay.

Washburne had been hopeful that Burnside would be able to find some "starting point" between the French and the

Prussians so that "negotiations with a view to peace may be entered upon." However, Burnside's attempt at mediation failed. Bismarck and General Moltke insisted that there be no "revictualment" of Paris during any declared armistice. "Not an ounce of food should enter Paris," Moltke demanded. In his meeting with Burnside, General Trochu had adamantly refused to accept such a condition, claiming that "from the most remote antiquity, there had always been revictualment allowed in case of armistice." Colonel Wickham Hoffman would write that this early attempt at reaching a peaceful settlement failed on this very "point of honor."

By mid-October the enormous strain of Washburne's responsibilities had begun to take a toll on his already frail health. He was sick, lonely, overwhelmed and, at times, depressed. And now, with conditions deteriorating rapidly, more and more Americans were anxious to flee the capital.

Elihu Washburne, Paris—to sister-in-law Lizzie Washburn—
October 12, 1870

> *A few newspapers have got in, but I have had no letter from*
> *Adele for a month. A gentleman sent me word from Versailles,*
> *however, that he saw her a week ago and that she and the other*
> *children were well. It is a great consolation to know that. She is*
> *at Brussels . . . Pitt followed his school to London. So you see how*
> *we are all scattered and broken and it is more than I bargained*
> *for. Sick, worn out . . . I wanted to get . . . some quiet and repose*
> *and have some peace and enjoyment with my family, but see what*
> *has been cast upon me. Made acting Minister for half a dozen*
> *countries, for three months I have been literally run to death.*
> *Even now during the siege I am engaged all the time and have*
> *no leisure at all. The military operations have driven me out*

*of my own house and Gratiot and I are stopping with a friend
downtown. Our house, charmingly situated on the magnificent
avenue of the Empress, is now between two barricades and the
beautiful lawn right across the street in front of us is all dug up
and filled with troops . . .*

*I have been laid up four or five days by a severe attack of
illness . . . How happy you must be in your own house surrounded
by your family, undisturbed by the horrors of war. I would consider
it the greatest happiness to be once again settled down in my own
house, surrounded by wife & children, and loose from political
life . . . I hear very little from the United States except what I get
from the newspapers. Few people take the trouble to write me . . .
We have no idea as to when the siege will end . . . I don't believe
the Prussians can take the city either by bombardment or assault.
It can only be by starvation and that will take a long time. Yet
I may be mistaken. As soon as I get all the Americans out I may
leave myself . . .*

**Elihu Washburne, Paris—to Adele Washburne, Brussels—
October 13, 1870**

*This is really terrible not hearing anything from anybody for so
long. To my mind things look very blue for the French. I do not
now see how they are going to get out of their trouble, but I suppose
some way will be found in the end. In these long and grievous days
my mind has been dwelling on you and the children so much. My
thoughts have all been on you and our dear old home. How varied
and grateful to our Great Father I will be if we can get back to
it once more and there live and enjoy ourselves undisturbed by the
events which make such shipwreck in the world. What a miserable
way of living is this—I am so uneasy and so anxious to see you and
the dear ones. Gratiot is a great comfort to me here. I hope you*

are enjoying yourselves. I know our dear friends are kind to you and do everything they can for you. Always give them my kindest regards. They have always been our dearest and most devoted friends.

Diary—October 14, 1870

Twenty-sixth day of the siege. Paris, Friday night. A short story for today. Was very strangely attacked last night at midnight by great dizziness followed by violent vomiting for two hours. Abed all day . . .

Diary—October 15, 1870

While my bed is being made up I sit down briefly to record this day's events, or rather not to record them, as I hear nothing of any importance. Many people have been to see me, but always the same "no news" . . . I have been suffering again all day. The terrible retching I had Thursday night has left, but so sore I can hardly move. And then the cold feet and the ague pains in my limbs . . .

Diary—October 16, 1870

I am able to get up and dress and go down to dinner. I have not been out of doors. I cannot hear any news . . . It is now four weeks since the siege commenced and but very little has yet been done on either side. With the exception of the two days when the French have made attacks, there has been a most profound quiet. It seems to me that this terrible calm must soon be broken by events which will stir the . . . world. In and surrounding Paris are nearly a million of men in arms, and inspired with a deadly hate of each other.

Diary—October 17, 1870

*I went to the Legation quite early this morning and have been
very busy all the day. Many people called. At noon went to the
prison St. Lazare to see the poor German women. I found seventy-
four of them imprisoned for no offense except being Germans.
They were induced under various pretexts to remain until after
the siege commenced and then they were all arrested and sent
to prison. I have made arrangements to have them all released
tomorrow and shall have them all cared for till the siege is over.
When I had it explained to them what I proposed to do, many of
them shed tears. They have been on rations of the very lowest diet.
Not a morsel of meat is now dealt out to the prisoners. Everything
seemed to be quite clean in the prison and many sisters of charity
were in attendance . . . A good deal of cannonading all day, but
no results.*

Elihu Washburne, Paris—to Secretary of State Hamilton Fish, Washington, D.C.—October 18, 1870

*Many of our countrymen, shut in by the investment of Paris,
having become very anxious to leave the city, I asked General
Burnside to procure, if possible, the permission of the Prussian
authorities to go through their Prussian lines. The general having
advised me that Count de Bismarck had authorized him to say
that he would permit all Americans to go through their lines
that I would ask for,* I yesterday made application to the French*

*In a letter to Washburne dated October 19, 1870, Count Bismarck
granted permission for the Americans to leave on the condition they
were "provided with passports delivered by you and stating they are
citizens of the United States." Bismarck warned Washburne, however,
that anyone leaving would "not be allowed to carry any parcels, letters or

*government for authority to the citizens of the United States to
leave the city and go through their military lines. Just as I was
about to close my dispatches . . . I received the letter from Mr. Jules
Favre which I have the honor to send herewith.* I must confess
that I was very much surprised and disappointed. If the decision
is adhered to in its full force, the disappointment to large numbers
of our countrymen now in Paris will be very great. I estimate
that there are between two hundred and two hundred and fifty
Americans now in Paris, and that about one hundred of them are
anxious to leave. Among this number desirous of going away are
found many cut off from their communications from home, who
are without funds, and who have no means whatever of living.
If the siege continues for a long time, and they cannot get away,
their conditions must become deplorable in the extreme. I need not
say that matters are becoming very embarrassing, but I hope we
shall get through in some satisfactory way . . .*

Diary—October 20, 1870

*Sent for the doctor at midnight . . . Gratiot went for Dr.
Swinburne of N.Y. Ten grams of raw chamomile. Yesterday the
31st day of the siege was abed all day and suffering a good deal
in my head. At half past one today I get up long enough to write
this down. Thought I would dress and go down to breakfast this*

---

communications whatsoever besides those to be delivered to our outposts,
and that any contravention in this respect will unfailingly bring down upon
them the full rigor of martial law."

*Although Jules Favre was sympathetic to Washburne's request to allow
the Americans to leave, General Trochu adamantly refused. He was concerned about the effect their leaving might have on the morale of the city
and disdainfully compared the Americans to "rats deserting [a] sinking
ship." (Hoffman, *Camp, Court, and Siege,* 204.)

morning but my head became so dizzy that I had to take to my bed again. I can hear of nothing of any interest transpiring. I am afraid that even now, when I have got Bismarck's permission to have the Americans go through their lines, that the French will refuse. Indeed, they write me in that sense . . .

Washburne was determined that Americans who wished should be able to leave Paris, General Trochu notwithstanding. As Wickham Hoffman later wrote, "The American Minister was not a man to sit down quietly under a refusal in a matter like this."

Diary—October 21, 1870

33rd day of the siege. Was able to go to the Legation today, and have been busy all day. At 5 P.M. went to see M. Jules Favre about Americans leaving Paris. The pressure to get out is getting to be very great, all nationalities are now calling on me. I believe that I am charged with the protection of half of the nations of the earth. It is understood that there has been a good deal of fighting today, but nothing has been heard at General Trochu's headquarters up to 6:30 this evening. I think that is ominous; if the French had been successful there certainly would have been some news of it.

Diary—October 22, 1870

34th day of the siege . . . This has been a raw, chilly, lonesome day and I think there have been more "blue devils" about than any day during the siege. The meat ration has been cut down (fresh meat) to one eighth of a pound to each person for two days, but even that much cannot be had . . . The Parisians are apparently standing up pretty well under these deprivations.

They are showing, however, symptoms of lawlessness—for a few days the people . . . have been going outside of the ramparts into the small villages and robbing the houses of everything in them. No effort is made to stop it, so far as I can learn. We are awaiting the official report of the fighting yesterday, but from what I gather, there were no particular results for the French. Thirty-five of their wounded were brought into the American ambulance.

I had an interview of two hours with General Trochu this P.M. on the subject of the Americans leaving Paris. It was far from satisfactory, and it was impossible to tell what the French government is driving at . . . I was at the house, 75, today. The entire avenue is now barricaded just as you enter it by the Arc de Triomphe and so we have to go round by the back streets to get to the house. It looks dismal.

Diary—October 23, 1870

35th day of the siege. A long, dull, tedious Sunday and raining the first part of the day. Was arranging to get my people out who have passes. They were to leave tomorrow at noon, yet I have just learned that they are to be detained yet another day. There is no end to the delays, vexations and annoyances of this business. Went to see M. Jules Favre this evening and talked it all over, once more, for an hour. I should have no trouble if I had him alone to deal with.

Finally, on October 24, General Trochu relented and agreed to Washburne's request for a group of fifty-six Americans to leave. Still ill and confined to his bed, Washburne asked Gratiot and Wickham Hoffman to escort the Americans through the Prussian lines.

**Elihu Washburne, Paris—to Israel Washburn, Jr.—
October 27, 1870**

> *When I am prostrated by my old fever and ague pains, away from
> Adele . . . and the children, I must confess to a little depression of
> spirits. It is, however, a wonderful comfort to have Gratiot with
> me . . .*
>
> *My countrymen to the number of fifty-six left today and I was
> sorry not to have been able to have gone into the Prussian lines with
> them. Col. Hoffman and Gratiot went out with them and saw
> them safely delivered over. They were received very courteously by
> the Prussians and were also very courteously escorted by the French.
> While so many went[,] a great number insisted upon remaining to
> go out when I go. I wanted all to go, so as I could leave without any
> trouble if I received instructions to do so. Some who made the most
> fuss and were most clamorous to leave declined going when they
> had a chance . . . We have been completely shut out from the world
> for the last fifteen days . . . [N]o letters from the United States since
> the first of September and no letter from Adele since the 17th . . .*

At the end of October, two events rocked Paris and nearly
brought down the National Government of Defense. On the
twenty-eighth, in an effort to break through the Prussian lines,
the French launched a sortie at the village of Le Bourget, just
outside Paris. It was a success at first, but two days later the
Prussians reclaimed the town. On October 31, word reached
the city that Metz, for months considered the "strongest fortress of France," had fallen to the Germans and 170,000 more
French soldiers had been taken prisoner. When word of these
defeats reached Paris, the city broke into chaos. Radical "Red"
leaders stormed the Hôtel de Ville and temporarily seized control of the government and its leaders.

Diary—October 30, 1870

42nd day of the siege. Sunday evening. Ill health since Wednesday last has compelled me to omit my "jottings down." Yesterday, however, I was able to be up and write a number of letters . . . This morning [I] find myself about the same. I hope my attack will wear off in a few days. The weather is very wretched, raining nearly all the time. Friday and yesterday some little military operations. The French captured a little town a short distance from Paris, Le Bourget, and they claim to have held it so far against the attack of the Prussians. But these French newspapers lie so. You can place no reliance on anything you read in them.

Today completes the sixth week of the siege and I must say within that time the most extraordinary change has taken place in and around Paris. Six weeks ago today, Col. Hoffman, Genl [John] Read and myself made an excursion through the city and along the ramparts. Nothing was completed and the confusion everywhere was complete. Had the Prussians known the weakness of Paris, they could have come right in. It was the same as Washington after the first Bull Run. But now all is changed—the amount of work that has been done in the defenses is almost incredible and the troops have all been put into shape and are now under quite a good discipline. I do not see for the life of me, how the city can be taken by assault. From all I can gather, I believe the Prussians intend bombardment. They say that they have got up the heavy guns and that they will soon open fire upon the devoted city. The French say they cannot send their shells into the city, but we shall see. The aspect of the Parisian population inspires everybody . . . no more riots, no more turbulences, but everything is sober and earnest.

Diary—October 31, 1870

Noon. Since writing the above, news comes of the fall of Metz.
That together with the disgraceful affair of Le Bourget of
yesterday has created a very bad feeling in Paris. The Official
Journal tries to soften the situation . . . All is bad as can well be
for France . . .

Diary—November 1, 1870

44th day of the siege. First as to the events of yesterday. Voilà!
Another revolution. I was very busy at the Legation all day. Some
gentlemen brought me news of the bad state of feeling in the city.
The arrival of M. [Adolphe] Thiers,* the surrender of Metz and
the disgraceful affair at Le Bourget created profound emotion
among all classes. The Reds, up to this time, cowed by the force
of public opinion, now saw their opportunity. It had become
necessary that I should see M. Jules Favre on an important matter
and I went to the Foreign Office at half past five, and on my
arrival, for the first time, learned of the gravity of the situation.
I was then told that Trochu had been dismissed, and that Favre
and all the members of the government of the National Defense
had resigned; that there was an immense crowd at the Hôtel de
Ville, and that all was confusion. I started immediately for the
Hôtel de Ville, in company with a friend, and arrived there at six
o'clock. When within two or three squares of the Hôtel we found
the way on foot through the dense crowd of people and soldiers,
and entered into the building. There we found mostly soldiers,
who were roaming around with their muskets reversed. In the

---

*A French politician who opposed the Franco-Prussian War and encouraged the Government of National Defense to enter into peace negotiations.

magnificent Hall of the Municipality there seemed to be a sort of public meeting going on, and we started to mount the staircase which led to it. We had scarcely reached the head of the stairs when we saw there had been a grand eruption of other soldiers into the building. They appeared to be composed mostly of the Garde Mobile and Garde Sédentaire. We immediately descended and got out of their way and went around by another staircase, and finally got into the hall by a side door.

It was dimly lit by two oil lamps. The room was literally packed with soldiers yelling, singing, disputing and speech-making. The side rooms were also filled with soldiers, who sat around the tables, copying lists of the new government, as they called it—the "Government of the Commune." They all seemed to regard the revolution as an accomplished fact, which was only to be formally ratified at noon today by a vote of the people of Paris . . . I then went to dinner thinking that the revolution had been practically accomplished and that we were to have the genuine Red Republic. I returned to the Legation at eight o'clock in the evening to get my dispatches ready to go out in the bag this morning. I sent two gentleman out to seek reliable information and to get at the exact status before closing my dispatches. They soon brought back word that the government of the National Defense had not resigned; but that the Reds headed by [Gustave] Flourens, [Auguste] Blanqui, and others had undertaken a coup d'état, had seized all the members of the government and held them all prisoners in a room in the Hôtel de Ville. Some of the people demanded that the members of the government should be sent to the prison of Vincennes; others demanded that they should be shot; but Flourens pledged his head that he would have them safely guarded where they were . . . A gentleman who was present during this time describes the scenes which took place as ludicrous. There was no harmony or concert among them, and they were

all quarrelling among themselves. They pulled the venerable
beard, and kicked the venerable body of the venerable Blanqui,
and denounced this one and that one as not good patriots. But
in all this confusion they issued orders and gave commands
like a regular government, the other government being in jail.
While this pleasant sort of amusement was going on, some of
the National Guard, faithful to the government, got into the
building and effected the release of Trochu and Jules Ferry,
who immediately took steps to release their associates . . .

At ten o'clock the "rappel" [the drumbeat to call soldiers to
arms] was beaten all over Paris—that terrible sound which in
the first revolution so often curdled the blood. I heard it under
the window at the Legation. It meant "every man to his post."
About ten o'clock the troops began to pour in from every direction
towards the Hôtel de Ville. They soon filled the Place Vendôme
and the neighboring streets, and formed in line of battle from the
Rue de Castiglione to the Hôtel de Ville, which they completely
surrounded. In the presence of this immense force, all shouting
"Vive Trochu!" and "À bas la Commune!" ["Down with the
Commune!"] The Red forces of Flourens seem to have realized
their weakness, and before midnight they had mostly disappeared
and the members of the government were released and
comparative quiet restored all over the city. I left the Legation to
go to my lodgings in the Rue de Londres* at half past twelve, and
going by the Champs-Élysées . . . I found all of the streets deserted
and the stillness of death everywhere. What a city! One moment
revolution and violence, the next the most profound calm . . .

I hope there is a prospect of an armistice and from that I hope

---

*Washburne and Gratiot had taken up temporary lodgings with a friend,
Mr. Leopold Hüffer, at his home at No. 18 Rue de Londres after "military
operations had driven" Washburne out of his house.

*for peace. The suffering in Paris and the devastation outside
and inside, surpass belief . . . [T]oday for the first time I saw
that they had cut down a great portion of those magnificent trees
in the garden of the Tuileries, which have withstood the ravages
of a century and the revolutions of a century, to build barracks
for soldiers. How I thought of the hundreds of thousands of little
children who have played beneath their shades! . . . When shall we
again see peace?*

Diary—November 2, 1870

*This has been a day of unusual quiet. The government seems
to be again established. The more I learn of the strange affair
on Monday, the more curious it appears. For a few hours the
revolutionists seem to have had everything their own way.
The members of the government of the National Defense were
outrageously abused when they were under arrest. They were most
grossly insulted and loaded pistols placed at their heads with
threats of instant death if they dared to stir . . .*

Still reeling from the attempted coup, on November 3 the government of National Defense sought a vote of confidence from the people of Paris. The government survived the plebiscite with an overwhelming 560,000 to 53,000 majority. However, with such turmoil and discontent in Paris, there was optimism that the government of National Defense might now seek an armistice with the Prussians to bring an end to the siege.

Diary—November 3, 1870, Thursday evening

*46th day of the siege. This has been election day. The government
of France has asked a vote of confidence of the people of Paris.*

*It is said to have been all one way—that is, for the government
of the National Defense. I hope it may give them some strength,
and enable them to prevent a repetition of the 31st of October. At
four o'clock rode out into the Bois de Boulogne, entering from the
Avenue de l'Impératrice. As you go on the road to the lake, all
the trees on the left-hand side, embracing more than a quarter
section, are cut down. It is the desolation of desolations . . .*

That same day Washburne wrote to Adele to reassure her that
he and Gratiot were doing well.

**Elihu Washburne, Paris—to Adele Washburne, Brussels—
November 3, 1870**

*I am so happy to find that you are all so well when you wrote
and that you feel so little anxiety about me, trusting that a little
starvation might do me good. But such starvation does not come
to me . . . Tho' provisions are becoming scarce, yet we live very
well. Therefore do continue to be easy about us . . . This horrid
war has broken up everything. I shall never be reconciled to the
derangement of our plans last summer. If I could only have had
the full cure at Carlsbad I think I would have escaped all my
attacks this fall. And then how glorious it would have been to have
breathed the sea air with you at La Rochelle . . . But never mind,
we will hope I will be different another time . . . Who can tell
what is in the future for poor France. I shall hope to see it out and
pray the end will come soon. Mr. Fish gives me no instructions to
leave Paris and so I must stay. And here is my post of duty. How
glad I did not run away with the other ministers . . .*

Diary—November 7, 1870

*50th day of the siege . . . [A]fter breakfast visited the defenses
for about two miles. They are a prodigy of strength and wonder.
Indeed, the defenses all round the city present a spectacle without
a parallel in the whole world. I could conceive of nothing so
complete. By the vote of Thursday the government received a very
strong endorsement. Friday and Saturday everybody believed in
an armistice, but yesterday morning all hopes were blasted by the
announcement in the Official Journal that it was not agreed
to. There is great disappointment and nobody can tell what will
happen. A few more Americans will leave tomorrow . . .*

Elihu Washburne, Paris—to Secretary of State Hamilton Fish, Washington, D.C.—November 7, 1870

*I think the large vote of confidence which the government received
was the result of a desire of vast numbers of people that it should
be so strengthened that it would be enabled to make terms for an
armistice. The question of such an armistice has been the great
topic of conversation for the last few days, and the sentiment in
favor of such an armistice as it was supposed could be had was
overwhelming. There was a general belief that there would be an
armistice which would finally lead to peace, and there was quite a
buoyant feeling. Yesterday morning, however, the Official Journal
announced, to the great surprise of the Paris public, that terms
for an armistice could not be agreed upon. The announcement
created a profound feeling of despondency, and everybody is
inquiring, "What next?"*

Diary—November 8, 1870

51st day of the siege . . . Paris is in a stupor. The circular from Jules Favre shows that there is no possibility of an armistice; and the French now ask, what can be done? The day has been gloomy and chilly.

Diary—November 9, 1870

52nd day of the siege . . . It has been one of the heaviest days of the siege, cloudy, dour, dismal. Everybody has been greatly depressed. Two Protestant clergymen called tonight to see me in the interest of peace. They want me to forward a letter to Bismarck, appealing to the King of Prussia from a religious point of view. A good deal of talk about a sortie. That is always to be resorted to when matters get very low down. "Well, now, we must make a big sortie of 100,000 men, cut through the Prussian lines and raise the siege." Such is the wild talk, but no sortie is ever made.

Diary—November 10, 1870

Evening. Went to the Legation in the rain this morning and there remained all day without leaving it. It has been raining, snowing and sleeting all day long, and dark and dreary. I had my lamp lighted before four o'clock. As wretched as the weather was, a good many people came to see me . . . The English have had great trouble in getting out, and are perfectly raving to think that I slipped out all the Americans so nicely, while they were left here. They are all coming to see me to ask if I cannot do something for them.

Diary—November 11, 1870

*54th day of the siege. Stopped raining last night and the day has
been comparatively pleasant . . . Everybody is clear down! The
papers begin to talk very plainly about an armistice.*

Diary—November 12, 1870

*55th day of the siege. Evening. I might as well stop my diary,
for there is absolutely nothing to record. There are no military
or even political movements. The streets are becoming more and
more vacant and the people more and more sober. But the papers
continue to lie to suit their purposes. Last night and this morning
they all said that an armistice was certain and some of them gave
the terms of it. I called at five this afternoon to see M. Jules Favre,
who told me that there was not one word of truth in all that the
papers had said—that the government had not heard anything
from the outside since M. Thiers had left, carrying with him the
rejection of the terms which were proposed by the Prussians. The
situation here is dreadful. They can't get an armistice and they
can't make peace. The Prussians can't get into Paris and the
French can't get out. Within the last few days the suffering has
greatly increased. The crowds at the offices of the various mayors
(for Paris has eighteen) are now very large, and all are without
food . . .*

It had now been nearly a month since Washburne had received
any word from Adele. On November 13—the 56th day of the
siege—Washburne poured out his frustrations in a letter to her
in Brussels.

**Elihu Washburne, Paris—to Adele Washburne, Brussels—
November 13, 1870**

> *This terrible isolation is hard to bear. Nothing from you since
> the 22nd instant and then you write so little and tell me so little
> about yourself and the children and what is going on in the world.
> You tell me nothing of how you pass your time, who you see or what
> the news is from home. Nothing, nothing, nothing . . . If you knew
> how much Grack and I want to hear from you and of you, you
> would take more time and think of us more during these long,
> dismal, uninteresting days . . .*
>
> *The days are long and the nights are longer. I never go out
> anymore of an evening because there is nobody to go and see
> except Mr. Moulton of a Sunday evening. How I miss the cheerful
> evenings with you and the children, with glowing coal fire in the
> grate. It seems as if this business would* never end. *It is eight weeks
> today that we have been shut up. In that time I could have gone to
> Galena and returned and have stayed there a month.*
>
> *This is Sunday noon as I write. Grack has gone out . . . to buy
> some drawers for the weather is getting to be cold . . . We don't
> think now that there will be any bombardment and I hope all will
> be safe at the house and I should be happy when we all get back
> there again . . .*

But to the Secretary of State, Washburne once again expressed
his determination to stay.

**Elihu Washburne, Paris—to Secretary of State Hamilton Fish,
Washington, D.C.—November 14, 1870**

> *Private and Confidential.*
> *All is gloom now in Paris and I can see no solution of things. I*

have concluded to stay till the end, for never . . . have we had more use for a representative than now. There are many Americans still in Paris and a great deal of property to protect. I have much to do for the Germans and am in constant correspondence with Bismarck . . . My remaining here, while the representatives of all the other great powers fled, has given a good impression. People of all countries, even Japan and Persia, are coming to me every day for advice and assistance . . .

Diary—November 15, 1870

58th day of the siege. After making my memorandum yesterday . . . great excitement was produced by the appearance of a soldier on horseback at the door of the building in which the Legation is. Two little dispatch bags hung over his saddle, like the grist in the bag which I used to put on the back of the horse to go to Gibb's mill to have ground by Abel Delano. And great excitement all through the Legation. One of the bags was filled with newspapers, but all of an old date . . . My dispatches from the State Department are all very satisfactory and my remaining in Paris seems to be highly approved. As I am not ordered to leave, I shall remain here, at least for the present . . . I did not go to the Legation today but ordered a fire built in my house, at No. 75 and thither I went with my budget [Washburne is using the term to mean a pouch or wallet] at ten o'clock this morning and remained till three entirely undisturbed, nobody knowing where I was. This was a happy time at 75 as there have been happy times before. It having been noised about that I had received a [dispatch] bag and late papers, the people began flocking to the Legation early in the morning. I had left some numbers there to be read by persons calling. There is really not much in the papers after all the waiting. The world seems to have moved very quietly along since we have been in jail here.

Diary—November 16, 1870

*59th day of the siege. Wednesday evening. Legation filled with
people reading English and American newspapers . . . It is
evident that the siege begins to pinch. Fresh meat is getting
almost out of the question, that is, beef, mutton, veal, pork.
Horse meat and mule meat is very generally eaten now and
they have commenced on dogs, cats and rats. Butchers shops have
been regularly opened for the last mentioned. So there are "cat
butchers" even in Paris. The gas is also giving out and today the
order appears that only one street lamp in six is hereafter to be
lighted at night. Only to think, Paris in darkness; but then, no
longer Paris except in name. No more foreigners to go out. The
government last night decided that in view of the fact that such
large numbers have applied to go, they say that they have given
them full opportunities to go, which were not availed of and that
now they cannot stop their military operations to permit them to
go out. The Prussians have also decided to let none hereafter go
through their lines except those who have already had permission.
Count Bismarck writes to me that some of those who have gone
out have violated their paroles and taken out letters.* A very few
more Americans would like to go, but now must stay. I was very
fortunate in getting the great body of them out before the gates
were finally closed.*

*Bismarck had written to Washburne on November 12, 1870, complaining
that certain persons leaving Paris under Washburne's "certificate" had violated the departure terms by secretly carrying out personal letters. Two days
later Washburne expressed his "regret" and assured Bismarck that he was
doing all in his power to prevent such instances from occurring.

Diary—November 17, 1870

60th day of the siege. Look at that, sixty days closely besieged in a city of nearly two millions of people. But after all I am favored, for I am the only man in all this vast population who is permitted to receive anything from the outside. Nothing to record today. Was not out of the Legation until half past seven this evening, except to go down to see the Barons Rothschilds, both very intelligent and agreeable men, talking English perfectly.* They are very much discouraged in regard to matters.

Diary—November 18, 1870

61st day of the siege . . . Two months *today since the siege commenced, and I am more disappointed that it has lasted so long as it now has, than I shall be if it lasts into the first of January. Should there be some successes in the provinces, like that reported at Orléans on the 9th instant, and should a successful sortie be made, these Parisian people will hold out indefinitely. They do not now seem to fear either an assault or a bombardment.*

By mid-November a dark gloom settled over Paris. *Galignani's Messenger* reported that the weather was "exceedingly wet and stormy," and the death rate in the city from disease and starvation had reached 2,064 during the week of November 19. Markets were nearly out of food and merchants were attacked

---

*Alphonse and Gustave Rothschild were sons of the Baron James de Rothschild who, at one time, was the greatest banker in the world. Both brothers served in the French army and helped guard the walls of Paris during the siege. After the armistice was signed between France and Prussia in January 1871, the family bank would play a major role in helping France pay off the reparations due Germany under the final treaty.

by starving Parisians. Despite the bleak state of affairs in Paris, Washburne took time to reflect on his beloved father back in Livermore:

Diary—November 18, 1870

This is the eighty-sixth birthday of my father. All hail to the glorious, great-hearted, great-headed, noble old man, in truth, the "noblest Roman of them all." How intelligent, how kind, how genial, how hospitable, how true, but yet when in the course of nature a kind Providence shall call him hence, I would have the hand of filial affection only trace this simple inscription upon his monument: "He was a kind father and an honest man." It cannot be long before the last of the earlier settlers of Livermore will have passed away. And what a class of men they were, distinguished for intelligence, nobility, honor, thrift, illustrating their lives by all these virtues which belong to the best type of New England character . . . And here in this far off, besieged city, in these long and dismal days, I think of them all and would pay a tribute of respect to their memories.

Diary—November 19, 1870

62nd day of the siege. I came to my lodgings tonight quite under the weather after a busy day at the Legation. The weather has been wretched and I can hear nothing taking place of any importance. It was said there was to be a fight and the ambulances were ordered out only to be ordered back again. It is seriously alleged, however, that there is to be a great battle tomorrow and I am invited to go out with the American ambulance and I may go if I feel well enough. I will eat no dinner, take two blue pills, go to bed and put hot water to my feet and see how I come out in the morning.

Diary—November 20, 1870

*63rd day of the siege. Sunday afternoon. I do not go out of my
room today . . . But one person has been to see me so far and he
had heard nothing of the proposed battle that was to be fought . . .
One of the features of a siege are the thousand rumors and reports
that are constantly flying about. The most absurd and ridiculous
canards are circulated . . . and these French people are in a
position to believe anything, even that the moon is made of green
cheese. Some of the editors are the most deliberate, inventive and
circumstantial liars of modern times . . . These people, gay, light,
frivolous as they are, would endure wonders could you convince
them that anything was to be gained. They are arriving down to
what we call in the Galena lead mines the* hard pan.

*Fresh meat cannot last much longer, including horse and
mule. The vegetables really seem to be holding out very well, but
the prices are so high that the poor can buy but very little. Butter
is selling for $4.00 a pound, turkey $16 a piece, chickens $6.00 a
piece, rabbits $4.00 each, eggs $1.50 a dozen, and so on. The price
of bread, however, fixed by the city, is about as cheap as usual.
Wine is also quite cheap. Bread and wine will soon be about all
the poorer classes will have to eat and drink. What misery, what
suffering, what desolation. Everyday new Germans come to the
Legation for assistance and thank fortune, I have funds to assist
them. One poor woman who was left with five little children
gave birth to another yesterday. I sent her a present of fifty francs
yesterday . . .*

Diary—November 22, 1870

*65th day of the siege . . . I have several dispatches from the
Secretary of State which were delayed in reaching me and they*

*are, each and all of them, in cordial approval of my official
acts in the difficult and trying circumstances in which I have
been placed . . . The streets are more and more deserted, yet the
omnibuses thunder along as usual, and apparently there are
as many cabs as ever. There does not seem to be a ripple against
the government just now. Nothing of interest today. Raining
outside—cold, cheerless, dreary, but a warm wood fire inside and
I read, read, read all the papers.*

Diary—November 23, 1870

*66th day of the siege. Rainy till noon. It had cleared off and I
went to the photographer, who complained of my being too sober.
Have been laying in some canned green corn, lima beans, oysters
etc. All these sort of things are being "gobbled." Nobody can
tell how long we are in for it and to what extremities we will
be pushed. I first put the siege at sixty days and here we are at
sixty-six and no light ahead. The French seem to be getting more
and more "uppish" every day. Gambetta sends his proclamations
pinned to a pigeon's tail, and tells of a great many things in
the provinces, and then all at once, here in Paris, "pop goes the
weasel." The new quotations for today are as follows: For cats; a
common cat, eight francs, a Thomas cat, ten francs; for rats, a
common rat, two francs, long-tailed rat, two francs and a half;
for dogs . . . two francs a pound; for a fat dog, two and a half
francs . . .*

Diary—November 24, 1870

*67th day of the siege. And Thanksgiving at that. Visions of beef
steak, broiled chicken, hot rolls and waffles for breakfast. Roast
beef rare, turkey and cranberry sauce, roast goose and apple sauce,*

*plum pudding, mince pie, pumpkin pie and Livermore cheese for
dinner. But not as bad, perhaps, as it might be. We make the best
of the cruel situation. Our thoughts go out warmly to the great
unbesieged world . . .*

*Return to the Legation at noon and always something to
do, which is a blessing. The people here who have nothing in
their hands are desperate. But don't imagine this is all. A
Thanksgiving dinner at a restaurant on the [Boulevard des]
Italiens . . . Quite a table full and jolly; but the portion of turkey
to each guest is painfully small. Toasts, little speeches, &c till half
past ten when I came back home . . .*

Diary—November 25, 1870

*The impression seems to be gaining ground among all classes that
the siege is going to continue yet a long time. For some reason there
is a more defiant and angry spirit among the Parisians and they
are breathing more and more vengeance against their enemy.
They believe the city impregnable and some talk about holding out
till spring . . .*

*This has been a regular Paris gray day, a sort of chilly, dismal,
dragging day, aggravating my ague pains and depressing my
spirits to the "lowest notch in the steelyards"—in fact threatening
the "softening of the brain." The poor Germans keep coming
more and more, starved like woodchucks out of their holes. A poor
Prussian woman, Mrs. Schultze, who gave birth to the child a
week ago, died three days since, leaving six little children. But a
good old Huguenot minister and his good old Huguenot wife, God
bless them, have found them out and will have them cared for.*

*The fifty-francs I had sent the poor woman was found in a
little box in a drawer after her death, where she had carefully laid
it away.*

Diary—November 26, 1870

*69th day of the siege. A miserable, dull, depressing day. I did not
leave the Legation until half past four P.M., a good many people
calling . . .*

Diary—November 27, 1870

*Sunday . . . I must confess that matters look more and more
serious. The gates of the city are finally closed and no person not
connected with the military can go outside. Everything indicates
that we are now to confront the iron realities of besieged life.
What a marvel of change in this great city in three or four weeks.
All that levity of the Parisian people seems to have disappeared.
No more fancy parades of the military with bouquets and green
strings stuck in the muzzles of their guns; no more manifestations
at the foot of the Statue of Strasbourg; no more gathering of
the mob and the National Guard at the place of the Hôtel de
Ville. No more singing the Marsellaise and no more arresting
of innocent people as "Prussian spies." Since the revolution of
the 31st October, the government of the National Defense reign
supreme, and history does not record a parallel to what we have
seen in this vast city since the siege began. With an improvised city
government, without police, without organization, without effort.
Paris has never before been so tranquil and never has there been so
little crime. You do not hear of a murder, robbery, theft, or even
a row, anywhere. You may go into every part of the city at any
hour of the night there, and you will have the most perfect sense of
security and safety.*

*There is now more serious talk then ever of a sortie. There has
heretofore been so much gabble on the subject and so many times
fixed for this sortie business, that I now pay but little attention to*

what is said in the papers. The report is that a great movement
will soon take place, headed by General [Auguste-Alexandre]
Ducrot who, I think is the best soldier in France. The attempt is to
be made to break the lines and form a junction with the army of
the Loire, if such an army exist. We have had no reliable news of
anything outside for three weeks.

Half past 5 P.M. I went out between two and three o'clock and
rode down the Champs-Élysées. Though the afternoon has been
cloudy and the ground is wet, yet there were great crowds of people
walking up and down. I am told of great movements of troops all
the forenoon . . .

On November 28, Washburne's son Pitt sent a letter to his father and brother in Paris telling them of news in London.

Pitt Washburne, London—to Elihu Washburne and Gratiot Washburne, Paris—November 28, 1870

All the London papers are very high in their praise of you for what
you have done for the foreigners in Paris and one even said that
you have more moral influence than anyone else in the besieged
city which I consider going very far for Englishmen. We hear
great stories about Paris, but they are so varied that it is very hard
to tell what to believe or not. I suppose that you & Grack keep
together all the time, do you not? . . .

By the end of November, plans were being made for a "great sortie" in an attempt to break the siege. The strike called for the army inside Paris, under General Ducrot, to hit the Prussian lines south of Paris, while the Army of the Loire outside Paris drove north from near Orléans. Ducrot was determined to succeed and pledged that he would return "either dead or victorious." Reports circulated throughout the city of a "great movement of troops," and notices were sent to the American ambulance to be on alert.

Diary—November 28, 1870

71st day of the siege . . . Sunday evening. Entering on the eleventh week of the siege and after so long a time of writing in this dismal and dreary life of siege & after so many false reports, there is this evening every indication that the hour of action has come finally to strike. The gates of the city were all shut yesterday and there were great movements of troops in all directions. Today that movement continues even on a larger scale . . . It is generally believed that the French will attack in several places at daylight tomorrow morning. The American ambulance will leave at six and I will accompany one of the carriages. A pitched battle is to be fought by the two greatest powers of Europe, under the walls of Paris . . . There is something in the atmosphere and the general appearance of the city that betokens that the time of supreme trial has at last arrived. The day is damp, chilly, gloomy, cloudy, but the streets are filled. The Avenue of the Champs-Élysées is crowded with the National Guard, marching up and down. Great numbers of people on both sides of the Avenue, and a very large crowd in front of the Palace of Industry. The Place de la Concorde is filled and, as we pass up the Boulevard we find the streets almost blocked. All is excitement, stir and bustle. We find no diminution of numbers as we proceed along the Boulevards. Cabs, omnibuses, carriages, National Guards, Mobiles, troops of the line, men, women, children, and etc . . . The scene is exciting. The people understand fully what is going on. There is an earnestness in their look, tone and conversation. There is hope mingled with fear, and yet more hope than seems to have been heretofore . . . All seem

*to know what is coming. Never have the people of Paris passed a
night of such anxiety as they will pass tonight, for before another
day may pass the fate of France will perhaps have been decided . . .*

When the French attack was launched, Ducrot met with some
success, but the Army of the Loire failed in its assault and was
pushed back to Orléans, dooming the entire offensive. Inside
Paris the city was in "great excitement and anxiety, crowds
being collected on the Boulevards and public thoroughfares"
awaiting news of the fate of the "great sortie."

Diary—November 29, 1870

*Tuesday evening, 72nd day of the siege. A great disappointment
to the people of Paris, who had hoped for better results. The
information is not full, but one of the officials told me tonight
very frankly that the "results want." The report is that Ducrot
was unexpectedly checked in his attempt to cross the Marne; not
enough pontoons, which reminds one of the incidents of our war. I
intended to have gone out today with the American ambulance.
We started at six o'clock to rendezvous at the Champ de Mars,
and on arriving there found orders to return . . . There has been
a little fight in the morning . . . but it amounted to nothing. We
went within eight hundred yards of the Prussian outposts, but
we saw nothing of interest and heard but little. Returned to the
Legation between two and three o'clock . . . It is now said great
things are to be done tomorrow, but the evident want of success
today does not promise much for tomorrow. But we shall see. These
are terrible hours to the Parisians . . .*

Diary—November 30, 1870

5 P.M. *73rd day of the siege. I came to the Legation at ten
o'clock this morning to find that we had been robbed last night.
I have been protecting a German who alleged that he had been
abused by the French and that it was not safe for him to be
about in the daytime. I therefore permitted him to come and
stay in the Legation. By that means he found out where Antoine
kept the money and valuables. He concealed himself that night
in the Legation and broke open the drawer, took ten or fifteen
hundred francs and a gold watch and a diamond ring left
here by an American lady. As he could not get out through
the door on the street without waking the concierge he took the
large window curtains and let himself down out of the window.
I hope we may catch the ungrateful rascal whom I have been
feeding and lodging for two months.*

*As the battle seemed to be raging furiously about the walls
of the city I took my carriage a little after noon and went . . .
again outside the barriers . . . We passed through several little
deserted towns and rode into the large village of Charenton. There
we heard of the fight at Créteil, a little beyond. We met many
ambulances loaded with the wounded, and all gave reports of the
ill success of the French . . . Returning we came through the gates
of Charenton, and it was a sad sight as we came within the walls
of the city. The street for half a mile was literally blocked up with
people waiting to hear the news with intense anxiety. The day
had been clear but cold, and these poor people had been standing
for hours in order to learn something. As we passed they looked at
us most anxiously and as we could not tell them anything good,
we passed along. There was the greatest number of women and
children of the poorer classes, all thinly clad and shivering with
cold, and with a look of the most saddening anxiety.*

That day a hard, severe frost hit Paris. The streets were cluttered with ambulance wagons making their way back into the
city, and the river Seine was filled with small steamboats carrying more dead and wounded. Once again, the people of Paris
spent the day burying their dead.

3

DESPERATION AND DESPAIR

The "great sortie" had failed, but Washburne reported to Secretary of State Fish that "all Paris is confronting its sufferings with fortitude and courage." It would take days to tend to the wounded and dying.

December brought no relief for Washburne or the people of Paris, only more cold, more gloom, and more death. The Seine was filled with "huge masses of ice" and the ground surrounding the city was "hard as marble." As the "outcry for wood" became desperate, riots broke out in the city. The freezing poor took to unlit streets at night tearing down fences and barricades, hunting for wood anywhere they could find it. The cold and damp brought on disease: pneumonia, smallpox, and cholera. During Christmas week alone, 2,810 people died and, by New Year's Eve, another 3,280 had perished.

However, the French government remained as defiant as ever, continuing more ill-fated sorties and resisting all calls for surrender. Once again, the radical political clubs began to stir and another revolution appeared imminent.

Washburne's mood darkened as the Christmas season approached, but he was more determined than ever to stay and fulfill his duty. Although separated from Adele and his young children, he took great comfort and pride in having Gratiot by his side.

Diary—December 1, 1870

74th day of the siege. Leaving the Legation at six o'clock last night I went to the American ambulance. About eighty wounded men had been brought in there and Dr. Swinburne was hard at work at his operations. This ambulance of ours is winning golden opinions from all sets of people. It is by far the most perfect of any here. They have now 120 wounded from the fight of yesterday. A lieutenant colonel died of his wounds there this morning. They behaved nobly on the field yesterday and went out the farthest of any of the carriages. Gratiot went out to assist and all compliment him very highly for his efficiency and even bravery, for he went to the rescue of some wounded in the very neighborhood where the Prussian shells were falling. One poor fellow died in his arms.

The report is there are no military operations today and that the French are entrenching in the positions they gained yesterday. As to the results yesterday I am unable to comprehend them. The French say the "day was good," but I observe that they have not yet got through the Prussian lines. There are no details and no information; no one knows anything really, as to what has taken place. A few official lines in the Journal Officiel is all that is vouchsafed to the Parisians. There is more known about the battle in Galena this day (from Prussian sources) than I know and I am tolerably wide awake for a "man of my years." This is the first day of winter and it is clear and cold and the soldiers must suffer much.

Diary—December 2, 1870

75th day of the siege. Cold, frosty morning—ice made last night half an inch thick. The battle seems to have commenced very early this morning. The cannon has been thundering all day, but as I have not been where I could hear anything I am in ignorance of the events of the day. I have just come up from the Boulevard Prince Eugène, and I saw many crowds shivering in the street and apparently much excitement. I walked up to 75 this P.M. to see how things looked there. While waiting, Old Père [the maître d'hôtel] rushed into the room, pale as a ghost, half dead with fright, and utterly unable to speak for the moment. As soon as he was able to articulate he said the Prussians had just broken over the ramparts . . . and were coming right upon us. I laughed at him, but he said it was so because a soldier had so informed him. He soon took courage and went out in the further pursuit of knowledge and returning reported that instead of the Prussians coming in the Mobiles and National Guard were going out to attack the Prussians—"over the left," I presume. The soldiers must suffer dreadfully tonight with the cold. From all I can hear, there has been a great movement today and all Paris at this moment trembles with anxiety. The great bravery displayed by Ducrot is talked of everywhere. He stands pledged before all France to break out of Paris or die in the attempt.

On Wednesday night one of the American ambulance carriages was unable to come in from the field, and as Ducrot knew that it belonged to our ambulance, he invited the two or three Americans, in charge of it, to stay over night with him. He took them to a house denuded of furniture, and invited them to supper, which consisted only of bread and wine—not a thing besides that. After supper, the General laid down on the floor with the balance of them, and thus passed the night. The men say he was cheerful and filled with hope and courage.

Diary—December 3, 1870

76th day of the siege. Last night after I left the Legation there was,
in the language of John Dumont [an old friend from Hallowell,
Maine] "great excitement on the lower street." There were a
thousand of the most outlandish and absurd reports, and nobody
could tell anything. There had certainly been heavy fighting,
all day an intense anxiety reigned in every circle. To get at the
facts, I thought I would walk down to the Foreign Office about
nine o'clock, and see M. Jules Favre. I found him in excellent
spirits and a radiant smile over his huge, benevolent, intellectual
face. He said the results of the day had been excellent and very
satisfactory so far as the fighting was concerned about Paris.
The news from the outside was also good—there was an army of
150,000 men marching on Paris and within twenty-five leagues.
Indeed, he was very hopeful. This morning all Paris is claiming
a tremendous victory yesterday. They claim to have beaten the
Prussians in a pitched battle. They say the enemy attacked with
great fury in the morning and drove them back, but that later
in the day, they fell upon the Prussians and routed them "horse,
foot, and dragoons," not only recovering all the ground they had
lost in the morning but even gaining some and sleeping on what
they won. I do not pay much attention to all these reports, but
I am told that Ducrot, who is a sober, solid, brave soldier, with
no nonsense, is greatly delighted with the results. At any rate the
effect on the Parisians has been like magic and the morale *of both*
the army and the people has been improved at least one hundred
per cent. While the attempt to get out on this line has failed, I
think the chances for getting out on some other line are greatly
improved. The soldiers now have a confidence they have not had
before and Ducrot has shown himself to be a true soldier and has
acquired the confidence of the army.

*There has been no fighting at all anywhere today. There was
a very light snow last night and this evening it rains a little.
The sufferings of the troops on both sides must have been fearful
during these last few days. The French were without blankets and
with but little to eat, half-frozen, half-starved, and raw troops at
that. Trochu boasts that they have thrashed 100,000 of the élite of
the Prussian army!! . . .*

*Today is the calm after the storm. I have just come from the
American ambulance where I saw a poor captain of the regular
army breathing his last and his last moments were being soothed
by some of our American ladies who are devoting themselves to the
sick & dying.*

*And amid all these scenes, the French will have their fun. One
of the illustrated papers exhibits the danger of eating rats by the
picture of a cat that has jumped down a man's throat after the
rat, leaving only the hind legs and tail sticking out of the mouth.*

On December 4, Washburne issued a private dispatch to the
Secretary of State reassuring him of his commitment to stay.

**Elihu Washburne, Paris—to Secretary of State Hamilton Fish,
Washington, D.C.—December 4, 1870**

*I hope you approve of my determination to remain here for the
present. As I have said before, my remaining here as the only
representative of a great power has created a very excellent
impression and our government stands first rate with the
government of the National Defense and the French people . . .*

*I need not tell you how irksome this besieged life is becoming
and how anxious I am to join my family, separated from them
since the last of August, but in public life, I have never had but
one rule and that was to do my duty, at whatever sacrifice . . .*

*Unless the French compel the raising of the siege by force, of
which I must confess I see no prospect, it is yet to continue a long
time. The national feeling of the French against the Prussians
has been so aroused and intensified that the Parisians would now
endure the most unheard of sufferings if they thought they could
only punish their great enemy. I will make no prediction, because
in war everything is uncertain, but I will say that I would not be
surprised to see Paris hold out till the first of February. And yet, it
may not hold one week . . .*

Diary—December 4, 1870

*Sunday morning, 77th day of the siege. A snapping cold it was
this morning, and it must have been still more chilling to the
French when they read the announcement that Ducrot's army had
recrossed the Marne and were all back again under the walls of
Paris. But after all that was the only thing to be done, so long as
they could not break the lines of the enemy. Have remained in my
room nearly all day hugging my fire very closely. This evening went
to Mr. Moulton's with G[ratiot] as usual now of a Sunday evening.
Nothing talked of or thought of but the battles and the siege and the
absent ones and our "bright and happy homes so far away."*

That same day, Washburne sent a dispatch to Count Bismarck
about the continuing plight of the Germans trapped in Paris.

Elihu Washburne, Paris—to Count Bismarck—December 5, 1870

*I have the honor to enclose you herewith a list of the names of all
the persons belonging to the nationalities at present at war with
France, and who are now imprisoned in Paris. They are not
charged with any crime, but have been arrested for being found*

*here after they had been ordered to leave, and for being without
any means of existence.*

*Their situation is miserable enough, but they are treated,
perhaps, as well as could be expected, when you take into
consideration the existing state of things in Paris. If they were
released they would have to be subsisted by this Legation, and
then they would have to be exposed to the hostility of the people
of the city. I await instructions in this regard. The number of
poor Germans applying for pecuniary assistance at my Legation
is increasing every day. It has now reached two hundred and
thirteen families, and, including children, there are four hundred
and ninety-six souls.*

*I now have to employ a man specially to look after them.
A great number of these people, reluctant to leave their homes
and not supposing that hostilities could last long, determined
to remain in Paris, keeping themselves mostly out of sight. They
have now, however, exhausted all their means and eaten their
last morsel. As a last resource they came to me to relieve their
absolute necessities. Without the assistance I render them, through
the generosity of your government, they would inevitably starve. I
have as yet ample means in my hands for the present emergencies,
but I do not know how many more will apply to me, and how long
I shall have to support them.*

Diary—December 5, 1870

*78th day of the siege . . . Ducrot's order of the day appears in
which he frankly acknowledges he failed in getting through the
Prussian lines, but says he will try again. But nothing can be done
so long as this extreme cold continues. It is a bright, cold, bracing
morning, and the most complete quiet everywhere. "Not a gun
was heard," etc.*

Diary—December 6, 1870

79th day of the siege. Bad news for the French. I was down to see Col. Claremont at the English Legation this afternoon and he told me he had just received the news from the Government that the Army of the Loire had been beaten after a three-day fight and that Orléans had been retaken . . . The day today has been cold and grey. A great movement of troops in another part of the city. Another sortie is threatened which only means more butchery. The more we hear of the battles of last week, the more bloody they seem to have been. The French have lost most frightfully and particularly in officers. They have shown a courage bordering on desperation.

Diary—December 7, 1870

80th day of the siege. No bag today and we are all disappointed. Bismarck is keeping it longer than usual, for some reason. I sent my bag out yesterday, and a great deal of matter for him and I hope by tomorrow he will send in my bag from London. The day has been a sober and a sad one for the Parisians, but they bear up well under the news of the defeat of the Army of the Loire and the retaking of Orléans. It seems to have made them more determined than ever . . . Never in the history of the world was there a more reckless and devoted courage shown than that displayed by the French officers in the battles of last week. They were always in the thickest of the fight. One regiment alone lost twenty-three officers. Went down town this afternoon. The weather having softened, there was a great many people in the streets, and the Champs-Élysées were filled with the National Guard drilling. The French seem to be making good their threat to resist "à outrance." [To the utmost, to the bitter end.]

That same day a letter arrived in Paris for Gratiot from his mother in Brussels.

**Adele Washburne, Brussels—to Gratiot Washburne, Paris—
December 7, 1870**

My dear son:

Your last letter was received a few days ago and I must confess I have had very little heart for anything. The continuance of this horrid war; the separation from your dear Father and all my sons and true old friends . . . but I must keep up joy [for] the dear children's sake. God bless them. They are the greatest blessing I have. They are so good and so happy and so well, except a little sore throat and cold once in a while. I should not say one word while thousands around me are suffering not only separation from friends but want and sickness . . . I would give anything to be home in dear old Galena with you all around but God only knows if we will ever enjoy that happiness again . . .

Diary—December 8, 1870

Thursday, 4 P.M. . . . . "Hills peep o'er hills and Alps on Alps arise."* And so one day follows another and never an end. Last week was the excitement of the battles, but now, particularly since the disaster at Orléans, all is gloom and sadness. A more doleful day than this has not yet been invented. It snowed a little last night and today it is thawing a little and the dead, leaden sky still threatens the "softening of the brain." It is so dark that Antoine lighted my lamp at half past three. No bag yet and what can Bismarck mean

*From Alexander Pope's "An Essay on Criticism."

in retaining it so long. I am slow to make predictions in such
circumstances, for no one can tell what will happen in war, but
to my mind, peace is farther off than ever. The French people are
becoming more and more enraged every day and "à outrance"
really seems to have some significance. Notwithstanding the
stunning news of Orléans, the dead and wounded of the battles
of last week, the sufferings of the people of Paris, not one man
cries peace or armistice in all France. The sentiment today is (it
may change tomorrow) let the fight go on—take Paris at the last
extremity, hold it by military power. We never will treat with you—
we will organize our government in the departments—we will levy
en masse and raise another army of a million of men—the whole
population shall fight you everywhere and with all weapons. We
have forty millions of people, a people of a proud and martial spirit
and every one of whom is instigated by a feeling of deadly revenge.
The whole resources of the country of every nature and description
shall be devoted to purging our soil of Prussian foes—it may take
one year, two years, three years, but the Prussians shall be chased
from France. This is not my talk, but French talk and it may come
true to a certain extent. And if so, we will hang by the fiddle and
the bow in Paris . . . What a scatteration of all the Americans now
living here in their apartments! Who can measure the future of
Paris and of France judging from the situation today!

On the 81st day of the siege, Washburne was in a particularly
gloomy mood when he sent off a letter to Adele in Brussels.

Elihu Washburne, Paris—to Adele Washburne, Brussels—
December 8, 1870

It looks to me darker and darker every day for France and with
the spirit now aroused peace seems impossible. The French seem

determined not to make peace in any terms which the Prussians
will grant, and although Paris will eventually be taken, the fight
will go on. The government will establish itself somewhere in the
Provinces and organize other armies. When Paris is taken and the
government goes away then the Legation must follow . . . Oh this
horrid war . . . I have had enough of all this terrible business and
I begin to hate Paris . . . It is not living[,] it is simply a wretched,
fearful, almost unendurable existence. All these precious weeks
and months are slipping away and I am separated from you and
from the dear children at their most interesting ages. Perhaps I
am unusually blue today. The weather is enough to kill me itself
and then the universal gloom in the city—the cold, the snow, the
funerals in every street, the famine, the wounded, the sick and all
increasing. "Horrors on horror's head accumulate."*

That same day Secretary of State Hamilton Fish sent Washburne a personal letter expressing to him gratitude for all he had done.

Secretary of State Hamilton Fish, Washington, D.C.—to Elihu
Washburne, Paris—December 8, 1870

There is universal approbation for your course from Americans.
Nothing has been omitted that ought to have been done and what
has been done, has been done well. I think you have earned the
title, "Protector General" . . .

---

*From Shakespeare's *Othello,* Act III, scene 3. The actual line is, "On horror's head, horrors accumulate."

Diary—December 9, 1870

*"Hail mighty day." The good maître d'hôtel, François, has brought
me for lunch two fresh eggs boiled . . . the crop from the hens in the
garden. Only think, a fresh egg the 82nd day of the siege and in
the dead of winter. Who says that Paris will be starved out? I have
no news from "outdoors" today, as no one has called, and there is
nothing in the morning papers of any interest. The report of the
battles of last week appeared yesterday and the loss of the French is
in killed 1,008 and wounded 5,022—in all 6,030, no mean loss.
The wonder now is how great the Prussian loss was . . .*

Sunday, December 11, was the 84th day of the siege. Conditions were worsening in Paris, winter weather had settled in,
and Washburne was, again, worn down and ill.

Diary—December 11, 1870

*Sunday evening. My cold worse than ever and I am unable to go
out. I read my newspapers and write letters. People come in and
say the day is horrible outside. For the first time there is talk about
the supply of bread getting short and that the rationing must soon
commence. When the people are put on a short allowance of bread,
having nothing else, it must be the beginning of the end.*

Diary—December 12, 1870

*We are now entered on the 13th week of the siege. The Journal
Officiel this morning says that there is bread enough and that
there will be no rationing. That means Paris is to hold out for a
long time yet. Père [maître d'hôtel] tells me that the baker's shops
are crammed with bread this morning. The news of the disasters*

outside begin to creep in, in one way or another, but it [does not] abate one jot or tittle of the courage of these people. They imagine something to offset it. It is hard to deal with such a spirit as the French people now exhibit, but it may all change in a day . . .

Elihu Washburne, Paris—to Secretary of State Hamilton Fish, Washington, D.C.—December 12, 1870

The government of the National Defense and the people of Paris seem to have abandoned all idea of an armistice, or of a peace, and to have made up their minds to resist to the last extremity, and until every resource is exhausted . . . A good many people think that the provisions will give out suddenly, to be followed by an irresistible clamor for a surrender. We shall see. You may infer from what I have written that I do not expect to see the siege raised by a successful sortie. Everything seems almost as bad as can be for the people of Paris as well as France . . . The mortality last week was frightful, over two thousand. A great many old people and a great many children perish from the want of suitable food and from the cold.

Diary—December 13, 1870

"Short and simple are the annals of the poor"* and very short and very simple are the annals of this, the 86th day of the siege . . . Took [an] additional cold by going out yesterday and did not get up till noon today and have since been "mulling" over the newspapers from home. I have been unable to leave my room today, and have been re-reading the newspapers from home . . .

*From Thomas Gray's "Elegy Written in a Country Churchyard." The actual line is "The short and simple annals of the poor."

Diary—December 14, 1870

*[O]ne of the most wretched, gloomy, long drawn out days of the
whole siege. The natural gloom is augmented by the sinister report
circulating in the city in regard to reverses in the provinces. But
the government is . . . following in the footsteps of the [Second]
Empire in keeping back bad news. I have not been out of my
room, and my cold is now reinforced by the ague pains. The papers
discuss the provision question. One argues there are provisions
enough for* three months *yet. But I think it is nearly all guess
work . . . I sigh for the doughnuts and hot rolls at Proctor's, the
sausages and roast potatoes at Stetson's, the Johnny cake and
fresh pork at Crooker's, and the beef steaks and apple sauce at
Gammon's.*

Diary—December 15, 1870

*Thursday, 6 P.M., 88th day of the siege. The old Latin poet
who exclaimed "jam claudite rivos"* had undoubtedly been
reading the diary of a poor devil, shut up going on thirteen
weeks in a besieged city. No wonder that he wanted the river
shut up. The sortie that was to have come off today seems to
have been "postponed on account of the weather," or for some
other reason. No fighting now for two weeks although a vast
amount of suffering. But a great deal of burying of the dead.
A great number of the wounded have died, particularly from
the ambulance of the Grand Hôtel . . .*

Went to the Legation this P.M. at two o'clock. The ante room

---

*Washburne appears to be referring to "Claudite jam rivos," from Vir-
gil's "Eclogue III," which translates "close the streams" or "shut up your
streams."

filled with poor German women asking aid. I am now giving succor to more than six hundred women and children. Bismarck writes me thanking me for what I am doing and asks me to continue. At 4:30 this P.M. called to see my colleague, Count Moltke, the Danish Minister. He says that the Parisians have had bad news, and says that in the late battle the Army of the Loire lost 23,000 men and 96 guns. It was dark when I started home . . . ill-lighted dark and dirty, it was Paris no more. Moltke agrees with me that there is no peace in sight and that we may have to "pack up our duds" as soon as Bismarck comes in, and follow the government of the National Defense. But he says further, and truly, that nobody can tell what the French people will do—they are so fickle and unstable.

Diary—December 16, 1870

Friday evening, 89th day of the siege. If anything could dishearten and discourage the French people one would have supposed that it would be the news that came this morning . . . of the disaster at Orléans, at Amiens, at Rouen. But the Parisians seem to take it rather as a matter of course and only wonder that it is not worse. No sign of giving in, but apparently a more fixed determination to hold out and make war "à outrance." These people seem to have dismissed every idea of peace from their minds and only look now at an indefinite prolongation of the contest. I saw M. Jules Favre this P.M. and much to my surprise found him in good spirits and full of courage. He said there was nothing to discourage the government in the news received and that they were never so determined to hold out as now, and that there was no such thing as a peace. It is hazardous to make predictions in regard to anything in which a people as fickle and unstable as the French are concerned, but it really seems from my standpoint

here, that peace is out of the question for a very long time. The
occupation of Paris by the Prussians is now reduced down to a
question of weeks and then my "occupation" here is gone, not to
be resumed for a long time. The removal of the outside seat of
government from Tours to Bordeaux will take the diplomatic
corps to the latter place and I shall rejoice to leave Paris and go
thither taking the "little family" . . . So long as the Prussians
shall hold military possession of Paris, and that may be for two or
three years, there is an end of all business and all society. Nobody
will want to stay here under such circumstances and I expect all
our American friends will only return to arrange about their
apartments and then leave . . . What plans deranged, what hopes
destroyed, yet "such is life." The day has been cloudy, but no rain.
The streets were unusually full of people this afternoon as I rode
down to the Rue Laffitte and when I saw all the horses in the
cabs and omnibuses, in the private carriages, in the artillery,
in the cavalry, and in the military service generally, and all in
good order, I wondered how they could be fed. It is astonishing the
amount of stuff that got into Paris before the siege. I still think
the city can hold out till the first of February, though M. Jules
Favre rather dodged the question this P.M.

The brutally cold weather in Paris continued. Wickham Hoffman would recall entering the vacant apartment of an American
who had fled Paris, where he found the sofas and mattresses
filled with dead rats who had "gnawed and burrowed" their
way into the furniture, only to die of cold and hunger.

Diary—December 17, 1870

*Saturday evening, 90th day of the siege. "Not a drum was heard,
not a funeral note"* . . . Called to see my wise old friend, Dr.
Kern, the Swiss Minister-Resident, who finds the situation very
bad for France. Next door to him, in the Rue Blanche, No. 5, is the
butchery for dogs, cats and rats. Being in the neighborhood I looked
in where I saw the genuine article on sale. The price of dog . . .
has advanced. Many people at the Legation during the day. The
distress augments on every hand. The weather continues horrible.
Not ten minutes of sun in ten days. No bag yet. Vegetated all day
over my bright fire in grim expectation. Two pigeons presented to
me today, which I have handed over to Old Père to be fattened.*

**Elihu Washburne, Paris—to Adele Washburne, Brussels—
December 17, 1870**

*No bag & no nothing since the 25th instant. I am fearful we are
cut off. "Star by star goes out; And all is night." Grackskins & I
are pretty well, still enough to eat and are likely to have, so please
do not worry, but keep up heart and hope. It cannot be many
weeks before we will be together again.*

Léon Gambetta, who had departed Paris in a daring balloon
escape on October 7, was still sending optimistic reports into
the city about his efforts to raise additional armies from the
provinces.

*First line of the poem "The Burial of Sir John Moore after Corunna"
(1817) by Irish poet Charles Wolfe. The poem describes the funeral of
Moore, who was killed in battle against Napoléon I's forces in the Spanish
Peninsular Campaign of 1809. Among Moore's last words were "I hope the
people of England will be satisfied! I hope my country will do me justice!"

Diary—December 18, 1870

Sunday P.M., 91st day of the siege. A quiet morning for writing in my room. Have only had two callers. Gambetta telegraphed news up to the 12th, and put the best face he can on things. But I think the Army of the Loire has been very badly used up. But Gambetta is always full of pluck and courage and is consumed by enthusiasm. He is all there is of the government of France outside of Paris. He is a short, thick-set man of thirty-four only. Hair long and black, and black beard all over his face. Eyes black and restless, fiery, eloquent, rash, infectious, extravagant, courageous, determined, he has displayed the most superhuman energy since he left Paris.

6 P.M. At three P.M. went out riding. The boulevards were full of people and the Champs-Élysées still more crowded, and looking quite like Paris. Rode up to 75, but it was no more a summer morning in the leafy month of June. Then to the American ambulance, then a call and then home. It is said there is to be another sortie tomorrow. But what good? Only more bloodshed and nothing affected. It seems shocking to see all these brave men go to their death. To die for one's country is one thing, but to die without doing the country any good is quite another thing.

Although Washburne occasionally enjoyed a "good dinner," the daily food stocks of the Legation were beginning to run short. On Sunday, December 18, Washburne dined on mule meat for the first time.

Diary—December 19, 1870

92nd day of the siege. No bag yet and heard nothing since the 25th ult. [ultimo, i.e., November 25]. I think Bismarck is not going to permit me to receive anything more. I guess he is a little out of sorts in not getting into Paris. It is doubtful about my bag going out as usual tomorrow, as they talk of another sortie tomorrow. It did not come off today—always tomorrow. I tremble for the torrents of blood that are to flow. I am heart sick of all this military. Nothing but soldiers, soldiers, soldiers everywhere you move. A cloudy, dour, dreary day, but not cold. We ate mule meat yesterday for dinner for the first time. It cost two dollars per pound in gold. Gratiot continues well, my cold is better though I cough a good deal.

Diary—December 21, 1870

94th day of the siege. The fighting has been going on all day, but I do not think it has amounted to "a hill of beans" for the French. Heard a few rumors at the Legation and at four P.M. rode up to the American ambulance to see what they had there. I found the carriages had just come in from the battlefield with some dozen of wounded, many of them mortally. The fight was mainly an artillery duel. The French failed in retaking Le Bourget. The day has been cold. Dined as is usual on Wednesday, at Mr. Moulton's and I would never ask to sit down to a nicer dinner. Perhaps tomorrow night I may be able to record something definite as to the fighting around Paris.

Diary—December 22, 1870

95th day of the siege. The coldest day of the season.* As this was the day the French were to break through Mr. Hüffer† and I thought

---

*Over the next several days the temperature would continue to drop dramatically from 14 degrees F. on December 21, to 5 degrees on Christmas Eve and 4 degrees on Christmas Day. (*Galignani's Messenger,* Dec. 21, 24, 25, 1870.)

†The friend Washburne and Gratiot had gone to stay with at No. 18 Rue de Londres.

*we would walk to the heights of Montmartre to see what we could
see. From that point the whole surrounding country can be seen.
What was our surprise to find not even the sign of any military
operations. Our ambulance men returned this P.M. and reported
that nothing had been done today. All was a failure yesterday—
the army of 140,000 men accomplished nothing. They made one
attack on the battery at Le Bourget and were repulsed with the
loss of a thousand men. And on that plain that vast army stood
all day yesterday in the terrible cold and there they remained all
last night, still colder, without shelter and almost without food.
Gratiot, who was out both yesterday and today saw all, gives an
account of the dreadful sufferings of the troops. Tonight is much
colder than last night, and if the poor soldiers have to remain out
tonight, half of the army must be used up. All our ambulance
men who were out concur that there has never been anything more
wretched than these last two days.*

Diary—December 23, 1870

*96th day of the siege. A cold, bright, clear day. No military
movements, and the grand sortie has proved a grand fizzle,
resulting in nothing but loss to the French. One of their best
generals has been killed. I understand that their whole loss will
amount to fifteen hundred men, besides the vast number who
have been put hors de combat [out of action] by the excessive cold.
The situation is becoming daily much more grave here in Paris.
The suffering is intense and augmenting daily. The Clubs**

*Washburne is referring to the radical political clubs, which were publicly
criticizing the actions of the French government. Wickham Hoffman also
complained about the "rampant" existence of the clubs and some of their
outrageous claims. "Their orators advocated the wildest and most destruc-
tive theories amidst the applause of a congenial audience. Blasphemy was

have begun again to agitate. Hunger and cold will do their work. From the misery I heard of yesterday I begin to think it impossible for the city to hold out till the first of February, as I had predicted. They are killing off the horses very fast. I learn that the omnibuses will all stop running next week. At the present there are but very few cabs in the street and they will soon disappear. In passing across the Champs-Élysées the other day at noon, I could not count a half a dozen vehicles all the way from the Arch [of Triumph] to the Place de la Concorde. Without food, without carriages, without lighted streets, there is a pleasant little prospect ahead. The discouragement . . . which I feel creeping over me, as these long, dreary days and weeks run on. In the beginning no man was wild enough to imagine that the siege would last till Christmas.

Diary—December 24, 1870

97th day of the siege. Another cold, clear day and no military operations. The movements of this week have only proved simple ignoble fizzles and have only brought unheard of sufferings to the soldiers. A good many little bits of news have got in by the way of newspapers found on Prussian prisoners. There has evidently been a good deal of fighting on all sides and the Prussians have lost men as well as the French. The French must do a heap better outside than they do here [inside], or else nothing can come of it all. All this enormous force of 500,000 men now under arms for fourteen weeks have accomplished nothing and will not so long as Trochu is in command.

---

received with special favor," Hoffman wrote later. (Hoffman, *Camp, Court, and Siege,* 171.)

On Christmas Day, with no end to the siege in sight, Washburne's spirits were lower than ever. Throughout the city, desperate measures continued. Trees everywhere were being cut down for fuel, and horses of every kind were being killed for food—in the end some 65,000 would be butchered to feed the people of Paris.

Diary—December 25, 1870

Sunday [Christmas Day]—98th day of the siege. Never has a sadder Christmas dawned on any city. Cold, hunger, agony, grief, despair sit enthroned at every habitation in Paris. It is the coldest day of the season and the fuel is very short. The government has had to take hold of the fuel question and the splendid forests of Vincennes and Boulogne and the magnificent shade trees which have for ages adorned the beautiful avenues of this unrivalled city are all likely to go, in the vain struggle to save France. So says the Official Journal this morning. The sufferings of the last week exceed by far anything we have seen. There is scarcely any meat but horsemeat and the government is now seizing every horse it can lay its hands on for food. It carries out its work with remorseless impartiality. The omnibus horse, the cab horse, the work horse, the fancy horse, all go alike in mournful procession to the butcher's block—the magnificent blooded steed of the Rothschilds' by the side of the old "plug" of the cartman. Fresh beef, mutton, pork are entirely out of the question. A little poultry yet remains at fabulous prices. In walking through the Rue St. Lazare last night I saw a middling-sized goose and chicken for sale in a shop window and I had the curiosity to step in and inquire the price—rash man that I was. The price of the goose was twenty-five dollars and the chicken seven dollars . . .*

---

*Today those prices would be the equivalent of $431 for the goose and $121 for the chicken.

Elihu Washburne, Paris—to Secretary of State Hamilton Fish, Washington, D.C.—December 25, 1870

I hope you are having a "Merry Christmas" in Washington. I must confess it is not "jolly" here today. It is the coldest day of the season and all Paris is in one grand shiver. We have visions of roast turkey and cranberry sauce, plum pudding and mince pies, but they are in the dim distance. Passing through the Rue St. Lazare last night I saw a middling sized goose and a small chicken in the window of a shop for sale. The price of the goose was twenty-five dollars and the chicken seven dollars! If this siege continues much longer I do not know what is to become of many of our Americans who are here . . . I am doing all I can, but that is not much. But all seem to feel a sort of reliance upon me and I try to keep up their courage.

Diary—December 26, 1870

99th day of the siege. Quite a little dinner of ten covers yesterday evening at seven o'clock at seventy-five [75 Avenue de l'Impératrice]. I could not afford to let Christmas go entirely unrecognized. The cold was intense, but I managed to get the petit salon [parlor] and the salle à manger [dining room] quite comfortable by the time the guests arrived.

The dinner party was composed as follows:

Mr. Hüffer, Bowles, Durand of Chicago, Shepard of Chicago, McKean of Chicago, Col. Hoffman, . . . Dr. Johnston, Gratiot Washburne, Mr. Washburne.

Here is the bill of fare for the 98th day of the siege:

1. Oyster soup.
2. Sardines, with lemons.
3. Corned beef, with tomatoes and cranberries.

4. *Preserved green corn.*

5. *Roast chicken.*

6. *Green peas.*

7. *Salad.*

  Dessert.

  *Pumpkin pie and cheese, macaroni cakes . . . cherries,
  strawberries, chocolates, plums, apricots, café noir.*

*The cold is not as great as yesterday. The papers of this morning
speak of the awful suffering of the troops. Many have frozen to
death. I take it all military movements are at an end for the
present. The papers say that bad fortune pursues the French
everywhere. We are now getting long accounts from the German
papers of the fighting in the Loire and fearful work it must have
been. Yet the Prussians go everywhere, but they purchase their
successes at a dear price.*

  *There is now high talk in the Clubs. This last terrible fizzle has
produced intense feeling. Trochu is denounced as a traitor and
an imbecile. They say that he is now staying out in one of the forts
and [doesn't] care about coming back into the city. He cannot
fail more than once more without going to the wall. Never in the
history of the world has any army of half a million of men cut
such an ignoble figure. And it should not be said that the soldiers
are not brave, for they are. It is the want of a leader that has
paralyzed everything for fourteen mortal weeks . . .*

  *Evening . . . I did not leave the Legation till six P.M., having
been busy in getting my dispatches and letters ready for the bag
which leaves in the morning. A great many people of all nations
calling—a greater number of poor Germans than ever. The total
number I am feeding up to tonight is 1547, and more a coming.
It is now a question of fuel as well as of food and the wood riots
have commenced. The large square across the street diagonally*

*from our house was filled with wood from the Bois de Boulogne
which had been sawed up to burn into charcoal. At about one
o'clock this P.M. a crowd of two or three thousand women and
children gathered in the Avenue Bugeaud, the Rue Spontini, and
the Rue des Belles-Feuilles, right in our neighborhood and "went
for" this wood. Old Père, undertook to pass through the crowd in
an old cab, but they arrested him as an aristocrat, crying out,
"On ne passe pas." [They shall not pass.] Nearly all the wood was
carried off. This may be only the beginning . . .*

Diary—December 27, 1870

*100th day of the siege. And who would have thought it? It was
a cold, grey, dismal morning, spitefully spitting snow. Started
on foot for the Legation at eleven o'clock, nearly two miles. The
butcher's shops and the soup houses surrounded by poor half frozen
women. At the corner of the Rue de Courcelles and the Rue de
Monceaux the people had just cut down two large trees and were
cutting them up and carrying them off. Every little twig was
carefully picked up. At a wood-yard in the Rue Biot the street
was blocked up with people and carts. I hear that several yards
were broken into last night. The high board fences enclosing the
vacant lots on the Rue de Chaillot, near the Legation, were all
torn down and carried off last night. The news this evening is
that the Prussians commence this morning the bombardment of
some of the forts, but we don't learn with what success. The bag
came in at one o'clock P.M. bringing my official dispatches and
a very few private letters, and not a single newspaper. What an
outrage I can look for nothing more for a week. The Prussians sent
in news yesterday by parlementaire* that the Army of the North*

---

*An agent employed by commanders of belligerent forces in the field.

*had been beaten and dispersed—another "blessing in disguise" for
the French.*

By the end of December, Washburne and the American Legation staff were surviving on "our national pork and beans, and
the poetic fish-ball," as Wickham Hoffman would write. At
times like a "denizen of the rough West," the American Minister cooked his own pork over an open fireplace accompanied by
beans "à la mode Livermore."

Diary—December 28, 1870

*101st day of the siege . . . I made a requisition . . . today for some
provisions, more for others than for myself. Antoine got quite a
piece of pork and some beans. M. Jules Favre wrote to the mayor
of our arrondissement to do all he could for me to soften the rigors
of the times. For the last two weeks I have been having for my first
breakfast a piece of bread, a cup of coffee and sometimes one egg.
My second breakfast I have taken at the Legation consisting of
a piece of bread and a very small piece of cheese with a glass of
red wine. But we always have a good dinner at half past six. But
now that I have got my pork if you will come into my room at the
Legation at one o'clock P.M., you will see the Ministre des États
Unis cooking it for his breakfast on the end of a stick, before his
generous wood fire . . .*

Diary—December 30, 1870

*103rd day of the siege. Called to see my colleague, Dr. Kern,
the Swiss Minister, this morning . . . He says he now lives
almost entirely upon horse meat and macaroni, and when I
said to him that he would not be likely to starve he answered,*

'neigh.' *Rather dull at the Legation today. I have made a new arrangement for the poor Germans. They became too numerous for the Legation and so I hired a room on the street right under us to receive them. I put up a stove to warm it and have arranged some seats so that they can sit down and warm themselves when they come. I have arranged also that each woman shall have a glass of hot sangaree before she leaves. The poor creatures suffer so much from the intense cold. There is no news of any kind today. Some think the Prussians will have one of the forts soon and that the city will be bombarded. Trochu is universally denounced and the government seems to hesitate. They are bawling louder and louder at the Clubs every night. The situation becomes more and more critical. Wood is becoming more and more scarce. I paid day before yesterday forty dollars for less than a cord. I feel that I am becoming utterly demoralized. I am unfitted for anything. This siege life is becoming unendurable. I have no disposition to send anything. I merely skim the trashy French newspapers. I get no American or English papers any more. I am too lazy to do any work and it is an immense effort to write a dispatch once a week. It is at night that I attempt to jot down what has taken place during the day. I have full time to think of bygone days and to reflect upon the incidents of life now, alas! not a short one.*

Diary—December 31, 1870

[New Year's Eve]: Saturday evening. 104th day of the siege. Antoine came a little after midnight and opened "Sesame" [the dispatch bag]. A feast of letters and papers and read till three o'clock this morning. Remained in my room till 2 P.M. devouring the contents of the leather pouch. Then went to the Legation and at 5½ to see Mr. Jules Favre. Then G[ratiot] and I dined ...

So closed the last day of a sad and eventful year. A great deal of firing by the Prussians . . .

Diary—January 1, 1871

105th day of the siege. What a New Year's Day! With sadness I bid adieu to the fatal year of 1870 and with sadness do I welcome the new year of 1871. How gloomy and triste the day. A few calls only . . . It is rather a heavy burden for me to carry around all the news from outside which there is in Paris. I only made three calls today and then dined at Mr. Moulton's. And a good dinner for the 105th day of the siege.

4

DEFEAT

By mid-January 1871, provisions were running desperately short. Dog flesh was in high demand and the stocks of bread remaining in the city were described by *Galignani's Messenger* as "black as the Spartan broth of old and entirely without flavor."

With the unrelenting cold weather, Washburne reported to Washington that the "fuel famine" was "likely to become as severe as the food famine." The death rate in Paris from disease and starvation had risen to 4,000 a week, more than four times the rate before the siege. On January 5, Washburne received news of one German family "dying of cold and hunger." Although his own food stocks were running low, he immediately sent aid to the family.

That same day, in a final attempt to break the will of the French people, Bismarck began the bombardment of Paris. The Prussians fired some 300–400 shells each day, targeting mostly areas on the Left Bank. The Pantheon, Invalides, and surrounding neighborhoods were struck repeatedly. The beautiful ancient church of St. Sulpice was shelled as was the

Salpêtrière Hospital, leading many to believe that the Prussians were intentionally targeting hospitals during the bombardment to "intimidate the population."

Elihu Washburne, Paris—to Secretary of State Hamilton Fish, Washington, D.C.—January 2, 1871

The excessive and exceptional cold weather continues, and the suffering of the city is steadily increasing . . . Great discontent is now prevailing among the poorer classes, but yet there seems to be a disposition to hold out to the last extremity . . . The number of indigent Germans who are now calling on me for assistance is increasing fearfully. It amounts today to seventeen hundred and fifty-three. They are suffering severely, in spite of all I can do for them . . . but if the siege continues much longer, I really do not know what is to become of them, for the time is fast approaching when money cannot procure what is necessary to sustain human life. My position in this regard is becoming embarrassing to the last degree . . .

With the compliments of the season for yourself and for those gentlemen in the [State] department with whom I was associated, even for so short a time . . .

Diary—January 3, 1871

107th day of the siege. Tremendous firing all last night. Old Père says the house (75) trembled and the windows shook so much that none of them could sleep all night. I do not hear of any result today, however . . . [The] cold still continues—talk of another sortie. Hunger pinches; discontent increases, but nothing is said about surrendering. They think there ought to be more accomplished by the military . . .

On January 4, Washburne sent a hopeful note to Adele in Brussels.

Elihu Washburne, Paris—to Adele Washburne, Brussels—
January 4, 1871

[K]eep up your courage, be contented and happy as possible. Grack and I are well and cannot want. Our great trial is the separation from you and the children. I know how long and tedious the days must be to you, but it cannot last much longer . . .

Diary—January 4, 1871

108th day of the siege. Nix. It is cold still and more dreary than ever. I have been busy, however, with the current matters at the Legation and receiving calls. More people than ever seem to be coming to the Legation. Indeed, there are so many that it is almost impossible to do any work there. We seem to be the great centre as the only news that comes into Paris comes to me or through me. But as I can make no use of it, I am tired of receiving it. The newspapers lie like dogs. One says that it has news that comes through me. Another says I have got news, but as it is favorable to the French I won't let it out. And then they made an attempt yesterday to bribe Old Père. They offered him a thousand francs for the latest London paper. [But he stood firm.] . . . I have concluded that it is too much for me to have the news for two millions of people, and I don't care to bear the burden. Besides, it may get me into trouble and I have written Bismarck that I will have no more London papers sent to me.* I would rather be without them than to be bothered as I am. I will have the home papers however.

---

*Washburne wrote to Count Bismarck on January 4, 1871: "Some Paris papers represent that I have given out news; others say that I give out nothing, because the news is favorable to the French arms . . . I conclude the only safe way is to receive no more English papers. I shall expect to receive

Diary—January 5, 1871

*A case of terrible suffering of a German family, living in the
Avenue d'Italie, was brought to my notice yesterday. They were
literally dying of cold and hunger. I immediately sent Antoine
with a little wood, wine, chocolate, sugar, confiture, &c. He found
a family of seven persons, cooped up in a little attic about ten feet
square in the last stage of misery. No fire and no food. There was a
little boy some seven years old lying on a pallet of straw, so far gone
as to be unable to raise his head or to talk. I sent Antoine again
today to the family with a can of Portland sugar, corn, a very
small piece of pork—one half of my own stock and two herrings,
also one half of my own stock. I told Antoine to take the poor little
fellow to our house to be taken care of . . . but when he proposed it
he did not want to go.*

Diary—January 6, 1871

*110th day of the siege. 2nd day of the bombardment. The
bombardment of the forts seems to have stopped in a great measure
today, but occasional shells have been thrown into the city, but
with what results I do not know. It seems very strange that the
firing on the forts has ceased and nobody can tell why. The city
is very calm under the circumstances, but it is impossible to tell
what is coming next . . . I bought a peck of potatoes today for
four dollars in gold* and was glad to get them at that price.
I procured from the mairie [town hall of his arrondissement]
today some rice, some dry peas, some codfish and herring and some*

---

my home papers as usual and hope also to have permission to receive my
private letters."
*Approximately $71.00 in today's money.

Dutch cheese. With what I have already laid in I can keep the wolf from the door for a long time. Old Père informs me that all those beautiful shade trees in the Avenue Bugeaud have been cut down, and, what is worse, that magnificent tree right by our house which has been such an ornament. Quelle horreur! The cutting down of a shade tree is the next thing to the commission of murder. I just want to leave this town, taking a steamboat at the first wood yard. The weather has moderated very much, which will alleviate the sufferings of the people. Have not been away from the Legation today except to walk up to the American ambulance at night.

Diary—January 7, 1871

111th day of the siege. 3rd day of the bombardment. It was a mistake to say that the Prussians had moderated their firing yesterday. It was furious as ever, but the wind having changed we did not hear it. Today the bombardment has been very heavy all day and a good many shells have fallen in different parts of the city and quite a number of people have been killed and wounded. The great mass of the population has not been very much moved, but there is extreme violence in the Clubs. A revolutionary hand-bill was placarded yesterday, but it failed to affect anything. It was torn down as fast as put up, even in the most turbulent quarters. But I think the fuss will drive the government to make another sortie or another feint. The weather has been much more mild today and thawing considerably . . .

Diary—January 8, 1871

Sunday, 112th day of the siege. 4th day of the bombardment. One more week and we do not seem to be any nearer the end unless this bombardment shall affect something. It is so hard to get at the real truth as to what the Prussians have actually accomplished since they commenced bombarding the forts of the East eleven days ago . . . How long this thing can continue I cannot, of course, judge, but one thing is certain[:] the Prussians have fired away an immense amount of material. The carelessness and nonchalance of the Parisians in all this business is wonderful. No sooner does a shell fall than all the people run into the quarter to see what harm it does, and if it has not exploded they pick it up and carry it off. They have carried this thing so far that the government has had to forbid it. Ladies and gentlemen now make an excursion to the Point du Jour to see the shells fall. Twenty-four Prussian shells fell yesterday in precisely the same spot and not the least harm was done.

The change of the weather since last Sunday has done wonders in ameliorating the sufferings of the poor. The mayors are rationing the provisions to the poor, but when one has to buy outside[,] enormous prices have to be paid. Since I have got to housekeeping I have made provision against absolute want, and I will live well enough besides. I have now lots of American things like, succotash, green corn, tomatoes, cranberry sauce, and oysters. And then I have a little pork and a little ham, codfish, herring, nice dry peas and dry beans, chocolate. As to potatoes, there is the rub, but I have just bought half a bushel for which I have paid nine dollars in gold.* I can see my way clear till the first of March and now they can toot their horns. A good friend sends me enough milk for our coffee. Therefore, let there be no worrying on our account. Besides, we are in the way of having an ample supply of fuel . . .

---

*In today's dollars, equal to about $155.00.

Elihu Washburne, Paris—to Secretary of State Hamilton Fish, Washington, D.C.—January 9, 1871

There has been a good deal of discontent in the city during the past week. It has not, however, taken the direction of a cry for peace or surrender, but resulting in a sharp arraignment of the government for a failure to perform its whole duty . . . Although a great many people said the arraignment was partially just, yet but few were willing to accept the remedy proposed, by replacing the government of the National Defense by the revolutionary commune. They evidently adopted Mr. Lincoln's theory, that it was no time to swap horses while swimming a river . . .

On January 9, Washburne received word that an American, Charles Swager of Louisville, Kentucky, had been hit by a Prussian artillery shell.

Diary—January 9, 1871

113th day of the siege. 5th day of the bombardment. "Des canons, toujours des canons" [Cannons, always cannons]. The bombardment was furious all last night and all day today. The shells have come into the Latin Quarter thick and fast and many people killed and wounded. Among the number is a young American by the name of [Charles] Swager, from Louisville, Kentucky. He was sitting in his room in the Latin Quarter last night when a shell came in and struck his foot. He injured it to the extent that he had to have his leg amputated. He was taken to our American ambulance where the operation was performed by Doctors Swinburne and Johnston. [Despite the best efforts of the American ambulance corps, Swager died a month later.]

It has been snowing a little all day, but I have been very busy in my room writing dispatches and letters. A short time before my bag was ready to be closed I got word from the military headquarters that they could not send it out tomorrow morning on account of military reasons. It may now be detained a whole week. The French have some news this morning, the first from the outside government for three weeks. If to be credited, it is rather good and they are all "up a tree" today. Baked pork and beans for dinner today. I showed the cook how to prepare the dish, à la mode Livermore . . .

During the second week of January, the bombing of Paris continued with "undiminished intensity," as shells continued to strike in the neighborhood of the civilian hospitals on the Left Bank.

Diary—January 11, 1871

115th day of the siege. 7th day of the bombardment. Busy in reading the newspapers till two o'clock, P.M. Then went down town, and at six o'clock called on M. Jules Favre. He thinks the forts will hold out, and that the bombardment will not hurry the surrender. He spoke with much emotion of the barbarism of the bombardment without any notice whatever. He said he has just attended the funeral of six little children killed by a bomb. From the direction of the wind, or some other cause, we have heard but little firing today. I heard a few distant and random guns, as I wrote at ten o'clock this evening.

Diary—January 12, 1871

116th day of the siege. 8th day of the bombardment. Engaged pretty much all day on matters connected with the Diplomatic corps. This P.M. a full meeting of the corps at Dr. Kern's and the

form of a letter to Count Bismarck was agreed upon. I have
been very agueish all day—headache, cold feet, pains all over and
"not very well myself." Dr. Johnston to dinner—tomato and rice
soup, sardines, baked pork and beans, succotash, etc., very well for
a siege dinner. From what I can hear, I think the bombardment
has slackened a little today, but it is possibly only "getting off to
get on better." The city is filled with horror and indignation at
the bombardment of the hospitals, ambulances and monuments of
art, and if the city be not taken by bombardment or assault, they
will only hold out longer and suffer more. The weather has become
colder with the last two or three days and we have had snow
enough to just whiten the ground. It looks like young winter today.
They are now cutting down the big trees in the great avenues of
the city—on the Champs-Élysées and the [Avenue] Montaigne. It
made me sick to pass through the Avenue Bugeaud the other day,
that splendid avenue, with its magnificent shade trees, added so
much to the beauty of our neighborhood. How pleasant of a June
morning to be protected by their graceful shades. Not one single
tree left!*

Diary—January 14, 1871

*118th day of the siege. 10th day of the bombardment. This has
been a cold, dreary day. Our mild weather did not continue
long. Although my bag and papers came in last Tuesday night,
I have been so busy with matters connected with the Diplomatic
Corps, and other things, that I have not had time to read up the
papers. I therefore sat down to it this morning and did not leave*

---

*The next day, on January 13, 1871, a letter was drafted to Count Bismarck by Washburne and several "diplomatic agents formerly accredited to Paris" to protest the "bombardment of Paris, without previous notice."

my room till two o'clock this P.M. *I then walked down to Drexel,
Hayes & Co. [Washburne's banker in Paris] and witnessed the
horrible sight of two large and magnificent trees being cut down
on the Champs-Élysées. The Government seems to have no control
whatever. The people go where they please and cut down what
trees they please. The bombardment has been about as usual. In
those parts of the city where the bombs have not reached, there is
no change and everything goes on as usual. Codfish dinner today,
with "pork scraps."*

Diary—January 15, 1871

*Sunday. 119th day of the siege. 11th day of the bombardment.
The firing was heavy last night and I believe the French expected
an attack, for the official report this morning says that the most
vigorous measures had been taken to repress any attack. It is now
eleven days since this bombardment of the town and the forts of
the south commenced and it seems to me that it were high time
that some results were obtained. The Journal Officiel this morning
gives an account of the casualties by bombardment so far. They
amount to only 189—fifty-one killed and one hundred and
thirty-eight wounded and this in a population of two millions.
The number is not large considering there was no notice of
bombardment given. Of the whole number killed and wounded
there are* thirty-nine *children. The damage to the buildings has
not been very large as yet. It would not greatly surprise me if
things were culminating at the present writing.*

*A gentleman has just been in to say that there is a report that
the Prussians have made an attack this morning on the French
works this side of Le Bourget and the bombardment on the forts
of the South is tremendous, for the windows of my apartment
are trembling for the first time, as I write. An official from the*

*mairie has just been in to see me, and he says there are provisions
enough yet for* two months. *Another man will come in shortly
and tell me that the supply of bread will only last a week and that
the city must surrender. So to an outsider it is all guess-work. The
only thing I pretend to know is that the city . . . "Stands Firm."
But who can measure the horrors of this population. From what
I can gather from the outside world, I take it that all peoples of
the earth are looking in with utter indifference and saying, "Hit
him again . . ." The Diplomatic Corps sent out their document to
Bismarck yesterday morning.*

*Four o'clock P.M. A friend called and he and I took a walk out
to the Trocadero to see what we could see. Half the city seemed to
be going in the same direction and it was quite a sight to see such
a multitude standing in the cold, cutting, biting wind gazing
in the direction of the forts and the Prussian batteries. The firing
was tremendous, but nothing was really to be seen. It is almost
impossible to learn what is going on. A fort might be taken, or a
Prussian attack repulsed today, but we should hear nothing of it
till tomorrow morning when we should read a few stolid lines in
the official report.*

Diary—January 16, 1871

*120th day of the siege. 12th day of the bombardment. There
was so much firing and pounding away yesterday that I did
not know but something would actually take place, but the
military report shows nothing but a bitter combat between the
forts and the Prussian batteries, and perhaps rather more than
the usual number of shells thrown into the city. The sky is somber
this morning, but it is not quite so cold as yesterday. As I look
out of my window the city appears sullen and indifferent to
the constant thundering of the cannon. Nearly twelve days of*

furious bombardment has accomplished but little. The killing and wounding of a few men, women and children and the knocking to pieces a few hundred houses in a city of two millions is no great progress. But perhaps one of the French forts may fall. Then the Prussians may get a nearer range. If they do not accomplish [that] they will stay out some time yet. I dined last evening with a prominent French official, whose business it is to keep an account of the provisions of Paris, and he surprised us by saying that there was yet much to enable the city to hold out easily until the end of February. *The bread would not be of a good quality, but it would hold out; great quantities of rice, exhaustless quantities of wine, sugar, coffee, etc., etc., together with a good supply of horse meat. News comes in now by the German papers even as late as the 8th inst. [instant, i.e., January 8] and both sides appear to be claiming victories.*

Elihu Washburne, Paris—to Secretary of State Hamilton Fish, Washington, D.C.—January 16, 1871

I am today furnishing aid to twenty-two hundred and seventy-six destitute Germans, and I have had to employ three additional persons in my Legation to perform the service necessary to look after these people. Besides, it is necessary to consider the vastly-enhanced prices of everything which we have had to purchase, as incidents to the state of siege. For instance, I have had to pay at the rate of more than fifty dollars a cord of wood . . .

Diary—January 17, 1871

121st day of the siege. 13th day of the bombardment. The firing seems to have been less furious today. The people in the parts of the city bombarded are getting out of the way and are not

*exposing themselves so much. The consequence is that the number
of killed and wounded in the last few days has been much smaller
than before. Some few shells have nearly reached the Seine, but
the material damage is nowhere very great as yet, considering
the length of time the bombardment has been going on and the
amount of bombs thrown into the city. Old Moltke must put on
more steam if he expects to take Paris in this way . . . The weather
has become milder and military movements are spoken of, but
I have come to regard such movements as no more than "thistle
down and feathers . . ."*

Diary—January 18, 1871

*122d day of the siege. 14th day of the bombardment. Four months
of siege today and where has all this gone to? It seems to me as if I
had been buried alive. I have accomplished nothing and separated
from my family and friends, cut off from communication to a
great extent from the outside world, those dreary weeks might
as well be struck out of my existence . . . I am more and more
convinced that we can only be taken by starvation . . .*

In late December the government of National Defense discussed the possibility of one last big sortie to break the siege.
General Ducrot, still reeling from his defeat in the last major
battle, advised against such an offensive while General Trochu
pushed hard, proclaiming: "At the last hour, when hunger is
pressing on the population and all hope of outside assistance
has been abandoned, we will make the supreme effort." On
January 19, General Trochu led 100,000 members of the National Guard into battle. Despite a heroic charge against the
Prussian lines, they were once again pushed back. It was the
last great effort to break the Prussian siege.

Diary—January 19, 1871

123rd day of the siege. 15th day of the bombardment. This is the day of the great sortie. At this hour nothing is known of results, but it has undoubtedly been the bloodiest day yet seen around the walls of Paris. The great fighting seems to be between Saint Cloud and Versailles or rather to the north of St. Cloud. It is said, however, that other parts of the Prussian lines have been attacked also, but I hardly believe it. At half past two P.M. Col. Hoffman and myself went to the Château de la Muette in Passy . . . From the cupola of this château is the most magnificent view on that side of Paris, and it was there we went to look through the great telescope into the Prussian lines . . . We first looked at Mont Valérien, that now world-renowned fortress, standing in its majestic grandeur, overlooking and commanding this ill-fated city, and holding in awe its proud enemy for miles around. We then look at the Aqueduct . . . where we see the Prussian staff as plainly almost as we could see a group of men . . . from the balcony of our house. Then we turn to St. Cloud and see the ruins of that renowned palace for centuries the pride of France. Now we look right into the eyes of those terrible Prussian batteries which for two weeks have been vomiting fire and flame, death and destruction upon devoted Paris.

But strange to say they are comparatively silent—only now and then a gun from each battery. Other business to attend to besides killing innocent little children and women in the streets of this somber capital. One hundred thousand men are struggling to break through that circle of iron and of fire which has held them for four long, long months. The lay of the country is such that we cannot see the theater of the conflict which has been raging all day. The low muttering of the distant cannon & the rising of the smoke indicate, however, the field of carnage . . . From the château I

went to the American ambulance. The carriages had just returned
from the battlefield with their loads of mutilated victims. They had
brought in sixty-five of the wounded and all that they had room
for in the ambulance. The assistants were removing their clothes
all wet and clotted with blood and the surgeons were binding up
their ghastly wounds. The men who went out with the ambulance,
Dr. Johnston, Mr. Bowles, Dr. Lamson, and Gratiot represent
the slaughter of the French troops as horrible and they could
not see that they had made much head way. The whole country
was literally covered with dead and wounded and five hundred
ambulances were not half sufficient to bring them away . . .
All Paris is now on the qui vive *[alert] and the wildest reports*
circulate. The streets are full of people, men, women and children.
Who will undertake to measure the agonies of this dreadful horror!

6½ P.M. Gratiot has just come in from the ambulance. He had
charge of one of the wagons that went out to the battlefield and
he brought in seven of the wounded. He says the last reports are
bad for the French and that the left wing was giving way. My
own opinion is the day has been a failure for the French arms.
The government has today commenced rationing the bread. Each
adult person is to have ⅗ths of a pound per day and children
over five years of age one half of that amount. The quantity is
very small when it is considered that there is not much else to eat,
and the quality is horrible—black, heavy, miserable stuff, made
of flour, oat-meal, peas, beans and rice. The cook put a loaf into
my hands and I thought it was a pig of Galena lead smelted at
Hughlet's furnace.

Diary—January 20, 1871

124th day of the siege. 16th day of the bombardment. Results
of yesterday—blood, agony, tears, anguish, horror. I was not

mistaken last night as to the result of the fighting except that it is worse than I could have imagined. The troops have all come back into town. From what I can gather this sortie has been the most fatal of all to the French and has inflicted no great harm on their enemy. Everything has been so oppressive that I have been about but little today . . .

> *What fearful, fearful times we have fallen upon. Alas! we*
>   *are compelled:*
> *To dine on news of human blood*
> *To sup on the groans of the dying and dead,*
> *And supperless never will go to bed.**

Diary—January 21, 1871

125th day of the siege. 17th day of the bombardment . . . Only went out after dark for a little walk down the "Champs." It was about as dark and muddy as Main Street, Galena. There is talk of trouble in the city as the people are very much excited. Some people are accusing Trochu as being "crazy as a bed bug." Nobody knows anything of what actually took place at the sortie last Thursday. There are various estimates of the French losses running from 3,500 to 10,000. The weather has been very thick and foggy and quite warm.

As a result of the failed sortie, General Trochu was removed as head of the army and Governor of Paris. Trochu's removal

---

*Lines derived from a poem by Percy Bysshe Shelley titled "The Devil's Walk." The actual lines are: ". . . They dine on news of human blood; They sup on the groans of the dying and dead; And supperless never will go to bed . . ."

1

Representative Elihu Washburne of Galena, Illinois. First elected to Congress in 1852, he served eight consecutive terms.

President Ulysses S. Grant. A close friend and political ally from Galena, Grant appointed Washburne Minister to France in 1869.

2

3

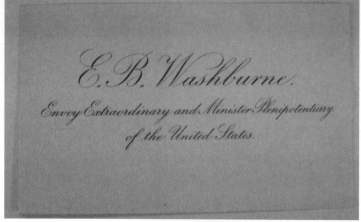

Washburne's calling card as Minister to France.

4

Daughter of one of Galena's most prominent families, Adele Washburne was charming, well educated, and "a fine conversationalist." The Washburnes were married for forty-two years.

5

The Washburne family home in Paris at 75 Avenue de l'Impératrice. Located off the Champs-Élysées and near the Bois de Boulogne, it had stables, a garden, and a little yard in front.

The American Legation in Paris at 95 Rue de Chaillot. After the outbreak of war, frightened Americans citizens and German nationals sought assistance from Washburne here. During a period of six weeks, Washburne helped over 3,000 Americans leave Paris.

6

7

Twenty-year-old Gratiot
(Grack), Washburne's oldest
son. Gratiot would remain
with his father throughout
the siege and the terror of the
Commune.

Panorama of Paris circa 1870.

Hôtel de Ville in 1870. All of Paris became one armed camp after the outbreak of war.

Napoléon III. Although ill and worn out, the reluctant Emperor led his subjects into battle against the mighty Prussian army. He was taken prisoner after the French defeat at the Battle of Sedan.

11

Secretary of State
Hamilton Fish.

12

Paris butcher selling dead rats, dogs, and cats for food during the siege. Some 65,000 horses and mules would also be slaughtered to feed starving Parisians trapped in the city.

[handwritten text]

Excerpt from a letter from Washburne to his wife, Adele, on December 8, 1870. Washburne quotes from Shakespeare's *Othello: "Horrors on horror's head accumulate."*

Raoul Rigault. Washburne described him as "one of the most hideous figures in all history." Rigault ordered the arrest of the Archbishop of Paris, Georges Darboy.

14

Onlookers examine the toppled Vendôme Column. On May 16, 1870, the column was pulled down before a crowd of 10,000 who shouted, "Vive la Commune."

16

Washburne visiting the doomed
Archbishop Darboy in his
prison cell for the last time.

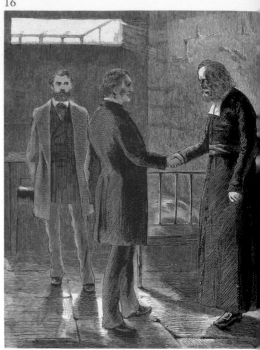

17

Ruins of the Hôtel de Ville. During the last week of May 1871, all of Paris was
"fire and battle" as government troops moved to crush the Commune.

was not wholly voluntary, later saying, "I am the Jesus Christ of the situation." He was replaced by the aging General Joseph Vinoy, a former senator and supporter of Napoléon III's Second Empire.* The siege had now lasted over four months and the bombardment almost three weeks. Daily rations were now down to a half pound of bread and an ounce of horseflesh per person. The bread was inedible, described as "black and bitter . . . [and] seems to have been made with the very last sweepings of the lofts."

Diary—January 22, 1871

Sunday morning. 126th day of the siege, 18th day of the bombardment. And yet another week has rolled round and the end seems to be no nearer. Always the same ill-fortune for France. The bombardment less effective . . .

At two this P.M. Col. Hoffman and myself went to a meeting of the Diplomatic corps at Dr. Kern's to consider Count Bismarck's answer to our letter in regard to the bombardment without notice.† We there learned of the great excitement in the

---

*The choice of Vinoy, a former supporter of the Second Empire, was seen as peculiar, but as Michael Howard noted in his book *The Franco-Prussian War*, ". . . the appointment [of Vinoy] was neither made nor accepted with a view to carrying on the war. Vinoy's task was to deal with the explosion within Paris which could not in anyone's view be averted any longer." (369)

†In a letter dated January 17, Count Bismarck responded to the letter of January 13 protesting the bombardment of Paris without previous notice. In his reply Bismarck took a hard, firm line dismissing all such accusations and blaming the French government for turning Paris into "a fortress and a battlefield." As a consequence, Bismarck argued, the city had now become a legitimate military target totally within the "recognized usages and principles" of international law. Bismarck continued: "Paris being the

*town—that a great crowd was at the Hôtel de Ville, yelling a bas
Trochu [Down with Trochu]—that the Belleville* battalions were
marching through the streets demanding the "Commune" etc.*

*Leaving [Dr. Kern's] at 4 P.M. we started for the hôtel to
see what was really going on. Everywhere on our way we saw
straggling companies and straggling squads of the National
Guard and great crowds of people in the streets. Descending to
the Rue Rivoli there were yet more people all moving towards the
Hôtel de Ville, or standing in groups engaged in earnest talk.
Within two squares of the hôtel the street was completely blocked up
by the crowd and our carriage could proceed no further. Beyond
us there was a dense mass of men, women and children and
still further on[,] the street and the great square were literally
blocked with soldiers, all standing in the mud. Here we met an
acquaintance, a young surgeon in the French navy, who was
profoundly agitated and profoundly depressed. He said the Breton
Garde Mobile had just fired on the crowd and killed five persons,
and that nobody knew what would come next, but that, at any
rate France was finished.*

*In returning, the street was filled with excited people all
making their way rapidly towards the hôtel. At the Place de
la Concorde a battalion of cavalry was drawn up in line and
batteries of artillery were passing. Up the Champs-Élysées large*

---

most important fortress in France, in which the enemy has concentrated
his principal forces, which, from their fortified positions in the midst of the
population, constantly attack the German armies by their sorties and by the
fire of their artillery, no good reason can be alleged why the German generals should give up the attack upon this fortified position, or conduct their
military operations in a manner which would be in contradiction with the
object they have in view."

*Alistair Horne in *The Fall of Paris* describes Belleville as one of the "solidly
proletarian and 'Red' arrondissements" of Paris. (26)

*numbers of the troops of the line and the Garde National were
drawn up. "Mischief there foot,"* in my judgment. The first
blood has been shed and no person can tell what a half starved
and exasperated Parisian population will do . . . To me it looks,
at the present writing, that we had reached the crisis, but in these
times it won't do to predict. It may turn out that nobody has been
killed after all. I am now going out to dine at the American
ambulance.*

Diary—January 23, 1871

*127th day of the siege. 19th day of the bombardment. Yesterday
was another dreadful day for Paris, and, as the Journal des
Debats says, "the most criminal that ever reddened the streets of
Paris with blood." On Saturday night the mob made an attack
on the Prison of Mazas. [Gustave] Flourens, [Félix] Pyat and
others of the revolutionists of the 31st of October were released.
Yesterday morning the insurrectionists seized the mairie of the
20th arrondissement and went to work to install the insurrection,
but they were soon driven out by some companies of the National
Guard. Along in the afternoon a crowd from Belleville of
men, women and children surged towards the Hôtel de Ville
crying, "Donnez nous du pain!" [Give us bread!] etc. and some
companies of the revolutionary National Guard. Some of these
went into the neighboring house and it was not long before a
regular attack was made on the hôtel. Many shots were fired
and explosive balls and bombs were hurled, particularly from
the windows. At this moment the gates and windows of the hôtel
were opened and the mobiles fired upon the mob, killing five and*

---

*A phrase derived from Shakespeare's *Julius Caesar*, Act III, scene 2: "Mischief, thou art afoot."

*wounding eighteen. And then such a scatteration—these wretches
flying in every direction, and crying, "Ne tirez plus!" [No more
firing!] and in twenty minutes it was all ended.*

Diary—January 24, 1871

*128th day of the siege. 20th day of the bombardment. A regular
London fog and a day for the "Blue Devils." I have never seen
such a gloom upon the city—hardly a person to be seen in the
streets except those persons who are cutting down the great trees
that adorn the avenues. Today for the first time there is real talk
about capitulation. The city is on its last legs for food and then
there are whispers of further disasters outside. All hope of relief
from the Provinces has finally died out and the question is seriously
asked what good now is all this suffering and destruction of
property. The bombardment of the forts of the east and the village
of St. Denis yesterday and last night was very violent and the
village and the great church, the burying place of the Kings, have
been knocked all to pieces. It is said there has been but little firing
today, at any rate, but little has been heard. Some interpret this in
the sense of a talk about capitulation which is going on. People are
beginning to prepare for the coming in of the Germans by hiding
their valuables. Antoine just tells me that thousands of the people
from St. Denis have been driven into Paris and that they are now
in the streets without shelter and without bread.*

Diary—January 25, 1871

*129th day of the siege. 21st day of the bombardment. According to
the military report there was a good deal of bombarding yesterday.
The atmosphere was so heavy we did not hear the guns. It is
probably the same way today for we have the same thick, heavy fog*

*as yesterday. We really miss this good old bombardment and we feel
that it [is now] quite dull and stupid. I am afraid that Bismarck
is failing in consideration for us. He ought to order the fog to lift
so that we could hear his guns and be jolly . . .*

*Many people at the Legation and only the one subject to talk
about: "When* will *the city surrender?" "What do you know?"
"What will the Prussians do when they come in?" And so on we
go, question after question and one caller after another, until I
finally get away and go down town, but nobody to see that I care
a fig about, yet I must circulate. I call to see the young Barons
Rothschild more frequently than anybody else, most agreeable,
intelligent, excellent gentlemen, and well posted in what is going
on.* *They appreciate the situation, and it is appalling enough.
Were I a Frenchman and a Parisian, I think I should call upon
the earth to open and swallow me up.*

Diary—January 26, 1871

*130th day of the siege. 22d day of the bombardment. Not only
"wars and rumor of wars,"† but wars and rumors of peace
today. Paris is as mild as new milk. All sorts of talk about peace
and armistice and every Frenchman makes things precisely as he
wishes or hopes. These trashy newspapers are teeming with the most
absurd reports, but I don't believe there is a man in the city that
knows anything about either peace or armistice. But something
must come soon, very soon . . .*

The day has been long and horrid. And what a dinner for a

---

*The Rothschild bank was handling funds that had been put in an account
by the Prussian government for Washburne to draw upon for expenses incurred in caring for the German nationals trapped in Paris.
†Matthew 24:6.

white man—a little piece of baked salt pork, saltier than Lot's
wife ever dared to be. One mouthful of it has made me so thirsty
that I have drank a carafe full of water this evening.

On January 27 relief finally came. It was announced that an
armistice had been reached and the siege would soon be lifted.
Although Washburne received the news with "a heart bowed
with grief," he knew surrender had become a "necessity" for
Paris to survive. In his diary, he proclaimed the news with joy.

Diary—January 27, 1871

131st day of the siege: "Hail mighty day." The Journal Officiel
this morning announces that we are to have an armistice upon
certain terms which it shadows forth, and I feel that a mountain
is lifted from my shoulders. The firing was to have ceased at ten
o'clock last night, but they could not stop it till half past eleven.
Not a gun is heard today—the most profound quiet reigns. My
bag came in at ten o'clock this morning, and I have been engaged
all day. We all want to know the terms of the armistice. I must
run up to Brussels at the earliest moment after the rail road is
opened. There is a poor prospect for living in Paris for sometime—
no provisions, no fuel, no horses or means of locomotion. If it can
only so fall out that peace can be made and we can remain here in
our house [No. 75], we will rejoice . . . The weather is again cold
and the sky is grey and dour. The people are on the very brink of
starvation, but I learn tonight the army will turn over some of its
bread to the starving. In eight days I hope we shall have something
to eat once more.

Diary—January 28, 1871

*132nd day of the siege. I was greatly disappointed this morning
in not finding the terms of the armistice in the Official Journal.
Nothing seems to have been signed, but we have, at any rate,
a suspension of arms. Paris is no longer bombarded and that
must be a great relief in the assailed quarters. People will now
be going back to their houses in the city. But to those people who
had their splendid houses in the numberless little villages that
surround Paris, what destruction and what horror. The houses
that have not been burned or torn to pieces by shells, have all been
broken open and robbed, furniture burned up or destroyed. It
will take a quarter of a century to repair the damage done. In
Paris proper, it is not so much. The Prussians utterly failed in
their bombardment—they have not hastened matters an hour,
but have subjected themselves to reproach for bombarding a great
city without notice. Having a slight cold, I have not been out of
my house today and have only seen a few persons. It seems that a
portion of the National Guard made a demonstration against
the armistice last night, but the cavalry charged upon them and
dispersed them. Some people say that there will now be no fooling
since General Vinoy has command of the Army of Paris. Trochu
was too weak for anything—weak as the Indian's dog which was so
weak that he had to lean against a tree to bark.*

*Voilà, the effects of the armistice, I have already a piece of fresh
beef, and the price of chickens has been reduced from eight dollars
to six dollars for a single chicken.*

5

——— ❖ ———

PEACE

Diary—January 29, 1871

Sunday evening. 1st day of the armistice. Though we have had a practical armistice since Thursday night, it was only signed last night. It appeared this morning in the Journal Officiel and it has been sought for and read by the whole town. It is an appalling document to the French, but, after all, what can they do. Paris has held out well and suffered much, but there is a great history to be written of this memorable siege. But after all Paris has ignobly failed. With a half million of soldiers, not one effective blow was struck in four months and a half. Trochu has undoubtedly proved himself the weakest and most incompetent man ever entrusted with such great affairs. It is a question how the people are going to take this armistice. The soldiers are coming into the city today and the streets have been full of them wandering about perfectly loose. I hear tonight that the people broke into the great central market today and seized everything they could lay their hands on.

*The market men were demanding the most extortionate prices
for everything that was eatable, and refused to make the least
concession to the poor starving people. The consequence was that
the said people "went" for them, and I am rather pleased than
otherwise. I took a walk this evening up to 75, and all the way it
was the desolation of desolations. How different from last June
when everything was so beautiful and lovely. This evening Gratiot
and I dined with the Moultons and had* roast beef *for dinner. In
a few days more I hope we shall have something from the outside to
eat. Still I have a "stock on hand" for a month yet, such as it is.*

Diary—January 30, 1871

*2d day of the armistice. I don't know yet whether or not I will
send out my bag tomorrow morning. I have sent Antoine to see
about the opening of the railroads. Unsealed letters are permitted
to go out and come in. People can go out on a permission
procured from the French authorities, their passes to be vised by
the Prussians. There is nothing said about the people coming in.
We are now entering upon a new and interesting phase of things
and the world will watch with anxiety the progress of events in
France. I have great apprehensions. The number of delegates [to
be elected] to the convention—730—is entirely too large, and the
time, seven days, entirely too short in which to do anything.* And*

---

*Under the terms of the armistice formally signed by France and Prussia
on January 28, 1871, France was allowed to convene an elected assembly
to decide whether to continue the war and, if not, what the final terms of
surrender and peace would be. On February 8, a nationwide election was
held to select delegates to this convention. To the dismay of the left wing
extremists, who demanded a continuation of the war, the candidates fa-
voring final capitulation to the Prussians won an overwhelming victory at
the polls. "News of the elections hit Republican Paris like a thunderbolt,"

*suppose peace is made, then what? What form of government is
to be ordained? Is there to be a republic, or will an Orleanist*
mount the throne? We must wait. Speculation is simply childish.
The papers this morning swallow the armistice, but with wry
faces. The government of the National Defense is denounced
without stint. They have commenced caricaturing the members of
the government the same as they caricatured the fallen dynasty.
We had a young snow storm last night and it is quite cold this
morning with a fog so thick that we can hardly see a single square,
and so dark as I write that I shall have to have the lamp lighted at
high noon.*

With an armistice in place, a desolate and suffering Paris
slowly came back to life. *Galignani's Messenger* reported that
snow and cold continued for a time, but by early February the
weather was "bright and mild." Regular mail service resumed,
the theaters reopened, train service was restored, and fresh provisions slowly made their way back into the bare city markets.
On February 1 a single cartload of food from Versailles arrived,
including a shipment of bread described as "white as snow and
beautiful to look on." Soon convoys of provisions were arriving
from England "as a gift to the people of Paris." The stalls of

---

historian Alistair Horne later wrote, "To the left wing . . . the elections, and
hence-forth the peace-seeking, conservative country squires would become
paired with the Prussian conquerors." (Horne, *Fall of Paris,* 256.) As a
dark harbinger of things to come, forty-three of the more radical delegates
elected in Paris resigned their seats to join the Communists.

One of the first acts of the newly elected convention was to name a new
government headed by Adolphe Thiers who immediately began negotiations with the Prussians to reach a final peace agreement.

*Washburne is referring to politically conservative constitutional monar-
chists who supported members of the Orléans branch of the house of Bourbon for the throne.

the central market were suddenly filled with mutton, salmon, "poultry in abundance," potatoes, parsnips, apples, artichokes, veal, and freshwater eels. On February 11, Minister Washburne received a donation of $30,000 from the people of New York City for "the distressed population" of Paris and a month later 200,000 francs from the people of New Orleans "in aid of the French wounded." With great hope Washburne wrote, "Paris is becoming quite Parisian and after a month of peace we will forget all the horrors we have seen."

Within days of the armistice Washburne made plans to leave for Brussels to be with his family. "Grack and I are very well," he wrote Adele on February 3, "I hope to start for Brussels next Tuesday." But he was cautioned by Dr. W. E. Johnston of the American ambulance about bringing his family back too soon. "All doctors are giving the same advice to absent families: not to return till we see a permanent improvement in the health of the city. It is usual to see pestilence follow a prolonged siege; we do not yet know what is to be our condition for a few weeks . . ."

Before departing for Brussels, Washburne sent a dispatch to Secretary of State Hamilton Fish in Washington.

Elihu Washburne, Paris—to Secretary of State Hamilton Fish, Washington, D.C.—February 5, 1871

Now that the siege is over I am thankful that I have remained through it all, for I believe that I have been of some service to the interests with which I have been charged. It is with pleasure that I am enabled to state that I have succeeded in protecting all American property in Paris, and that no harm has come to any of our Americans who have remained here. This statement must be qualified, however, so as not to apply to the young American,

Mr. Swager, who lost his life by having his foot torn to pieces by
a Prussian shell, and to the two young men whose property was
destroyed by the bursting of a shell in their apartment in the Latin
quarter . . .

A "good deal worn out" and anxious to see his family, Washburne left for Brussels on February 9. The journey by train was long and difficult. He arrived in Belgium after traveling "all night in a cold, cheerless car." For months he had dreamed of being reunited with his family, but it was a bittersweet and short-lived reunion. When word of his arrival in Brussels became known to the large colony of Parisian-Americans who had fled there after the war broke out, he was deluged with queries and requests for favors. Frustrated and distracted, he decided to return to Paris and have Adele and the children follow when conditions improved.

Once resettled in Paris, Washburne followed the progress of the peace negotiations between France and Prussia with a deep sense of anxiety. With the nation on its knees, Adolphe Thiers, now head of France, knew a just and reasonable peace for France was impossible. On February 26, after weeks of frustrating negotiations with a firm and unyielding Prussia, the new government signed a peace accord. Under the treaty, France would pay huge war reparations to Prussia in the amount of 5 billion francs; Alsace and Lorraine would be ceded to Germany; a portion of France would be occupied until the reparations were fully paid off; and the Prussian army would be allowed to march into Paris and occupy the city for two days.

The humiliating terms of surrender were received in Paris with "universal and violent" outrage. The lower classes and members of the National Guard felt a "sense of betrayal." Resentment spread throughout the city, and the radicals seized every opportunity they could to try to push the people to "anarchy and disorder."

On March 1, 1870, under the terms of the treaty, the Prussians entered Paris in triumph. Shops throughout every quarter of the city were closed, some posted with signs: FERMÉ POUR CAUSE DE DEUIL NATIONAL [CLOSED DUE TO NATIONAL MOURNING], and many statues throughout the city were covered in black crepe. As the victorious Germans marched in, Washburne was on hand to witness the humiliation of Paris.

Elihu Washburne, Paris—to Secretary of State Hamilton Fish, Washington, D.C.—March 1, 1871

> *They have come in. At 9 o'clock this A.M. three blue hussars entered the Porte Maillot, proceeded up the avenue of the Grand Army, and walked their horses slowly down the magnificent avenue of the Champs-Élysées, with carbines cocked and fingers upon the trigger. These hussars looked carefully into the side streets and proceeded slowly down the avenue. But few people were out at that early hour in the morning. Soon after, six more made their appearance by the same route, and every few minutes thereafter the number increased. Then came in the main body of the advance guard, numbering about one thousand men, consisting of cavalry and infantry, Bavarian and Prussian . . . By this time the crowd on the Champs-Élysées had increased and met the advancing Germans with hisses and insult. A portion of the German troops then halted and with great deliberation loaded their pieces, whereat the crowd, composed of boys and "roughs," incontinently took to their heels . . .*
>
> *From what I learn this evening the great body of the troops were reviewed by the Emperor of the new German Empire at Long Champs, before their entry into Paris. Instead, therefore,*

*of the great mass of the troops entering at ten o'clock, as had
been previously announced, it was not until about half past one
o'clock in the afternoon that the royal guard of Prussia, in four
solid bodies, surrounded the Arc of Triumph. Then, a company of
Uhlans, with their spears struck in their saddles, and ornamented
by the little flags of blue and white, headed the advancing column.
They were followed by the Saxons, with their light blue coats,
who were succeeded by the Bavarian riflemen, with their heavy
uniform and martial tread ... Now come the artillery, with
its pieces of six, which must have extorted the admiration of all
military men by its splendid appearance and wonderful precision
of movement. Next fell into line the royal guard of Prussia, with
their shining casques and glittering bayonets, which had been
massed around the world renowned Arc of Triumph, erected (and
with what bitter sarcasm it may now be said!) to the glory of the
grand army ... At first the troops were met with hisses, cat calls,
and all sorts of insulting cries, but as they poured in thicker and
faster and forming by companies, as they swept down the avenue
to the strains of martial music, the crowd seemed to be awed
into silence, and no other sound was heard but the tramp of the
soldiery and the occasional word of command ...*

*As I now write it is eleven o'clock at night. The day opened
cloudy and somber, with a raw and chilly atmosphere. A little
after noon the sun came out bright and warm, and the close
of the day was magnificent ... From the Boulevard du Temple
to the Arc of Triumph not a store or a restaurant is open, with
the exception of two of the latter on the Champs-Élysées, which
the Germans have ordered to be kept open. There are no excited
crowds on the boulevards, and, what is very remarkable and
without precedent in the memory of the "oldest inhabitant," not
an omnibus is running in the whole city ... Neither is there a
private or a public carriage to be seen ... Paris seems literally to*

have died out. There is neither song nor shout in all her streets. The whole population is marching about as if under a cloud of oppression. The gas is not yet lighted, and the streets present a sinister and somber aspect. All the butchers', and bakers' shops in that part of the city occupied by the Germans are closed . . . It is but just to say that the people of Paris have borne themselves today with a degree of dignity and forbearance which does them infinite credit . . .

Two days later, the Prussians left. Their departure began "in the midst of a thick fog" and when the last German left the "sun shone out brightly."

Elihu Washburne, Paris—to Secretary of State Hamilton Fish, Washington, D.C.—March 8, 1871

They have gone out. Consummatum est. [It is finished]* . . . The German troops commenced moving out at the appointed time, marching up the Champs-Élysées and passing under the Arch of Triumph, with great cheering. At eleven o'clock precisely the last German soldier passed through the gate of the Porte Maillot, and Paris breathed free . . . No sooner were the troops fairly on their way out of the city than the closed stores, cafés, restaurants, and hotels threw open their doors, and the avenue Champs-Élysées was swept and sprinkled, and the magnificent fountains in the Place de la Concorde began to play . . .

Washburne's trip to Brussels, the continued separation from his family, and the resumption of his diplomatic duties in Paris

---

*The Latin rendition of the last words of Jesus Christ as he was dying on the cross, according to John 19:30.

had all taken a toll on him. In mid-February, Doctors Johnston and Swinburne of the American ambulance had taken him under their care in Paris after he was "taken very suddenly and severely ill." By early March, Washburne was still weak, fatigued, and overworked, worn down by the "old attacks" he had battled for years.

Elihu Washburne, Paris—to H. H. Houghton, editor, *Galena* (Illinois) *Gazette*—March 6, 1871

> *I cannot get the ague out of my bones that I contracted in 1840 when we slept in the straw together in the old log building adjoining Larry Ryan's calf yard. I think I can hear those calves howl now. I have had an ugly attack lately and am not yet fully recovered . . . I got along through the siege as well as could have been expected, but it was a hard trial. My position has been a very awkward and trying one, but I have made the best of it. I believe all hands are satisfied . . .*

Praise for Washburne's efforts began to flow into the city including a dispatch from the Secretary of State on March 21, 1871.

Secretary of State Hamilton Fish, Washington, D.C.—to Elihu Washburne, Paris—March 21, 1871

> *Your government has sympathized deeply with you in the trials and privations and annoyances to which you were subjected during the long continued siege of the capital to which you were officially accredited, and where a high sense of duty, which is appreciated and commended, induced you to remain in the efficient and heroic discharge of the most difficult and delicate responsibilities that fall within the province of diplomatic service.*

> *The President recognizes that your continuance within the*
> *besieged capital after the discretionary permission given you . . .*
> *has been from the promptings of your own conviction that the*
> *interests committed to you required the very great sacrifice of*
> *comfort; of the separation from your family; isolation from the*
> *intercourse of friends, personal discomforts, and risk of health and*
> *life. This sacrifice and these trials you have endured, and I desire*
> *officially to record the high appreciation and warm approval of*
> *your government. You have done your duty faithfully and ably,*
> *and the President tenders you his thanks for the manner in which*
> *you have discharged the delicate duties devolving upon you, and*
> *have, on all occasions, maintained the dignity of your position*
> *and the rights of your government.*
>
> *An acknowledgment is also due to Mr. Hoffman . . . for his*
> *faithful and able service during this long period of trial. You will*
> *please express to him the sense of the Department of his conduct . . .*

Washburne dismissed all such tributes to his own conduct, telling a friend in Illinois: "I fear I am too much praised. It is always perilous to be too popular."

Washburne suspended his diary during the month of February, reflecting a brief respite from the suffering and horrors of the siege. But by the middle of March political and social discontent among the lower classes and radical political clubs—which had simmered ominously beneath the surface since October—broke out in an "orgie of crime, incendiarism, ruin, cruelty, desolation . . . [and] blood." For the next two months the streets of Paris would be filled with the "most horrible events and consequences ever recorded in history." Now trapped again in Paris under a reign of terror, Washburne would resume his diary, recording the events of one of the most savage periods in the history of France.

6

REIGN OF TERROR

It all began on the heights of Montmartre in the north end of Paris.

In late February a group of "die-hard" National Guard insurgents—"tinctured with [a] revolutionary and insurrectionary spirit"—seized some 200 cannon and hauled them to a strategic outpost overlooking the city. At first the insurrectionists were viewed as an "amusing comedy" in the aftermath of war, but matters soon turned serious and deadly. For weeks the new government, led by Adolphe Thiers, failed to take any determined action against the insurgents, allowing the "rabble in arms" to gain strength and confidence daily. "The officers with broad, red belts, high boots and long swords, paraded with cigars in their mouths and seemed almost overpowered with the importance of the high mission which had so suddenly devolved upon them," wrote Elihu Washburne with disdain.

The insurgents resisted any attempt at negotiation and refused to give in, recognizing "no authority than that of their own fancy, and . . . ready to defend themselves against any power that may venture to be of a different opinion." Washburne was angered and bewildered at the government's refusal to take swift action, knowing that each day its "weakness encouraged all elements of discontent."

As these "grave incidents" unfolded, Washburne could clearly foresee "the storm which was soon to break upon Paris."

Diary—March 18, 1871

> *I had seen Mr. Jules Favre last night in regard to certain official matters, and in taking leave of him I asked him how long the scandal of Montmartre was to continue. He said they would have it under control in two or three days—that it was a great outrage and shame that such a state of things should exist. However, it would all be ended soon. Yet, I was struck by the idea that it was still three days that the Government was to tolerate their defiance. This morning in going to the Legation I met an American in the Avenue Joséphine who told me that there was trouble and that many cannon had been heard in the direction of Montmartre . . .*

That same day the government finally acted, mounting an assault against the insurgents on the "Butte Montmartre." In announcing the operation, Adolphe Thiers proclaimed: "Evilly-disposed men . . . have taken control of a part of the city. You will approve our recourse to force, for it is necessary, at all cost . . . that order, the very basis of your well-being, should be re-born."

When the attack was launched, Washburne was in the Office of Foreign Affairs, meeting with Jules Favre.

Diary—March 18, 1871 (continued)

*I found the court of the Hôtel of Foreign Affairs filled with
carriages and the horses of military men. On entering the
building I was told the government was in council. I sent in word
to Favre that I must see him for a moment. He at once came
out into the ante-room which I found full of officers . . . While
waiting to deliver my message, Thiers . . . came out into the ante-
room. I had no idea of the gravity of the situation and I do not
believe the Government had. At about noon . . . I saw a member
of the National Guard who told me that the Government had
got the cannon away from the insurgents and that all was over.
He therefore went off feeling quite easy . . . As we approached
the Place de la Bastille we found the circulation interdicted in
the main streets and we were turned into the bye streets. We soon
found ourselves impeded in our way by barricades improvised in
the streets. After being stopped several times we finally made our
way out of the obstructed quarter and got safely home. I heard
various wild rumors of the shooting of the Generals &c, but paid
no attention to them. After dinner Gratiot and I walked down
to the Legation, but the streets were all deserted, not a carriage
or scarcely a person to be seen. We heard no news however and
returned home about half past nine.*

The government's attempt to recapture the cannons on
Montmartre had actually failed miserably. Although they had
seized the cannon, the attack stalled when horses needed to
haul them away did not arrive on time. As the regular forces
waited, the insurgents mobilized a hostile antigovernment
crowd composed of "the worst riff-raff from the Montmartre
slums." Now surrounded and threatened by the unruly mob,
the government force sent to subdue the insurrectionists surrendered, reversing their weapons and raising their rifle butts

in the air. Chaos filled the streets and the mob turned ugly. "It was a strange sight to see the women and children all coming into the streets, taking part with the insurrectionary forces and howling like a pack of wolves," Washburne later wrote.

The rumor he had heard about the shooting of two French generals was soon confirmed. The drunk and angry crowd had grabbed General Claude Martin Lecomte, in command of a part of the attack force, and General Jacques Léon Clément-Thomas, a despised ex-Commander of the National Guard, who had the misfortune to be recognized as he passed by the scene. Both prisoners were dragged away to a nearby house for interrogation and a "mock tribunal." Afterward, they were taken outside, stood up against a garden wall, and summarily executed. Worked into a "frenzy," the bloodthirsty executioners continued to riddle the dead bodies with bullets and then stood aside as a group of women urinated on the corpses—all under the watchful eye of children perched on the garden wall. As the mob went wild, Georges Clemenceau, then Mayor of Montmartre, saw the crowd "shrieking like wild beasts . . . dancing about and jostling each other in a kind of savage fury. It was one of those extraordinary nervous outbursts, so frequent in the Middle Ages, which still occur amongst masses of human beings under the stress of some primaeval emotion."

Diary—March 19, 1871

I heard nothing till about ten o'clock this morning when Mr.
[Joseph Karrick] Riggs* called at the house and said rumors

---

*After the receipt of the donation of $30,000 to the people of Paris from the City of New York, Riggs, a friend of Washburne's and longtime resident of Paris, had been appointed to a commission to oversee the distribution of the funds in Paris.

were prevailing that were of the most sinister character—that the National Guard and the troops of the line had fraternized and the authority of the Government had been overcome and two Generals killed. He hardly believed the rumors though the papers confirmed them. But the killing of such a man as General Clément-Thomas who was such an old Republican, seemed so absurd that I discredited the whole story. Therefore Mr. Riggs and Gratiot having left, I went to reading my newspapers very quietly.

Soon at eleven o'clock, two ladies called in a great fright. One, an American-born lady and the wife of a French General, wanted my aid to get out of town. She then told me all that had happened the day before and the last night—that the National Guard had affected a revolution—that the troops of the line had fraternized with the Guard and that Thiers and all the members of his government had been chased from Paris—that General Clément-Thomas and General Lecomte had been murdered by the troops the afternoon before and in fact that the government of the mob was in the "full tide of successful experiment."* I then started to the Legation with the ladies and though I could not get the wife of the French General any passport, I gave her a great big paper covered all over with seals asking protection for her. I then started for the Foreign Office to see what was the situation there, though I was warned I had better keep out of the way. I could not, however, see the least shadow of danger. At the Foreign Office, I found . . . not another soul in that magnificent palace, which Mr. Thiers had adopted as his official residence. They told me that Thiers, Jules Favre and the whole concern had left the night before, at half past nine, for Versailles. At four o'clock in the afternoon before a battalion of the vagabond National Guard had marched in the front of the building yelling "à bas Thiers, à bas Jules Favre." As

---

*A line from Thomas Jefferson's First Inaugural Address, March 4, 1801.

there was no force to oppose these blood thirsty ruffians, I supposed
it was deemed necessary in the interests of personal safety to get out
of the way as soon as possible . . .

"Paris was in full revolt," wrote Washburne. The flight of the Thiers government to Versailles was seen as an act of cowardice. "There never was a more cowardly and disgraceful surrender than the retreat to Versailles," wrote Wickham Hoffman. "It discouraged the respectable citizens, and abandoned to the mob all the advantages of position, immense war material, and the unbounded wealth of the capital."

The insurgents were emboldened by their victory. "They saw at their feet one of the largest, richest, most beautiful, and most attractive cities in the world," wrote Washburne, "with all the departments of the government, the Treasury, the War, the Navy, the Interior, the Prefecture of Police, and the Hôtel de Ville . . . With no restraint and amenable to no power, the position of the insurgents was something never before seen or even dreamed of."

Meanwhile, Washburne received word that Adele and the family were on their way to Paris by train from Brussels. Pressed by events in the streets and demands at the Legation, Washburne sent his "faithful messenger" Antoine to the train depot to meet them. However, on the way he was seized by a group of insurgents and "forced to carry stones to build a barricade." When Adele and the family failed to arrive home at 75 Avenue de l'Impératrice that night, Washburne feared for their safety. Totally "in the dark in regard to their movements" and unable to obtain any information about their whereabouts, Washburne spent an anxious and "very uneasy" night. The next afternoon, however, Adele and the family arrived safely at home. An American banker friend, Max

Hellman, had recognized them at the station and brought them to his apartment for the night, until he could safely escort them home the following day.

With events in Paris spinning out of control, Washburne regretted that he had permitted his family to return to Paris so soon. "We are in a pretty mess here and no one knows what next," he wrote to his brother. A few days later he admitted to a friend, "I should not have had them come back could I have foreseen all that has happened."

That night, with the government in flight and the insurgents on the rise, Washburne hurried off an "unofficial" dispatch to Secretary of State Fish in Washington.

Elihu Washburne, Paris—to Secretary of State Hamilton Fish, Washington, D.C.—March 19, 1871, 8 P.M.

There seems today a culmination of every horror . . . I hope, however, that the worst has been reached, but God only knows. Some say organized plunder & pillage will commence soon, but I doubt it. Unfortunately, my family has returned today to find Paris in a far worse . . . position than ever.

Once the National Government moved, Washburne spent several busy days trying to find suitable accommodations for a temporary American Legation at Versailles.

Diary—March 20, 1871

I have been out to Versailles today to look the land over and see about moving my Legation. The National Assembly had met about one o'clock P.M. and a very full attendance . . . I went out in my own carriage and found a great many troops of the line

on the other side of the Seine . . . But everything seemed to be a
state of confusion, no confidence anywhere and no head nor tail to
anything . . .

On March 21 a group calling themselves the "Amis de l'Ordre" [Friends of Order] staged a protest outside the headquarters of the National Guard at the Place Vendôme. They were quickly dispersed after a Guard commander threatened to open fire. However, the next day a group of some 1,500 protesters returned, this time refusing to disperse. The local commander ordered the National Guard to open fire on the crowd, killing 30 unarmed people. Washburne called it a "massacre," telling a friend, "Blood has this day flown in the streets and there is everywhere intense excitement."

Diary—March 22, 1871

An eventful and terrible day. The peace and order demonstrations
yesterday enraged the insurgents and encouraged the good
citizens. A good deal of alarm is being felt by the Americans in
Paris and many have called for advice. At noon I started again
for Versailles—ten miles—in my own carriage. I went to two
gates and found them closed and began to think we were shut in.
But on going to another gate and being closely questioned by a
brutal and serious looking soldier, he let me through. On arriving
at V[ersailles] I went at once into the Diplomatic Tribune of the
National Assembly where I found many of my colleagues . . . I
then went out to find a place for my Legation and engaged for . . .
lodging and eating, one *room, which must sustain the dignity of*
the great republic. Just as I was starting to return at half past five
the news of the fight, or rather the murders, had reached Versailles
and groups were everywhere eagerly discussing it . . .

The accommodations leased by Washburne were located at No. 7 Rue de Mademoiselle in Versailles. He described them as "thoroughly republican in simplicity," consisting of "one room well-lighted, quite well-furnished, with a good bed in one corner, and presenting quite a cheerful appearance."

. . . but when it comes to the question of getting something to eat, *hic est opus hic labor est.** The scramble in the restaurants would put a western steamboat in the shade in emigration times. After a brisk skirmish of an hour, I succeeded in obtaining a plate of soup, a slice of cold veal, and a piece of bread for my dinner. The worst of it is, one does not know how long this thing is to last; but I know of no other way than to take it as it comes, and to make the best of it.

Elihu Washburne, Versailles—to Secretary of State Hamilton Fish, Washington, D.C.—March 25, 1871

It would be difficult to convey to you an adequate idea of the condition of things existing in Paris. In some portions of the city all is quiet and orderly; but in other parts we see nothing but "grim-visaged war," barricades, regiments marching and counter marching, the beating of the rappel, the mounting guard, the display of cannon and mitrailleuses,† and the interdiction of circulation in the streets. Then there are the numerous arrests, the mock trials, and the executions . . .

Everybody inquires what is next? The disorganization of Paris is complete. There is no power to be appealed to for protection of life, liberty or property. Anarchy, assassination, and massacre hold high carnival . . .

*Loosely translated, "This is the problem. This is the hard task."
†Rapid-fire weapons of rifle caliber.

That same day, in the midst of the chaos, Washburne once again took a moment to write to his son's teacher in London urging Pitt's attention to certain matters at school.

Elihu Washburne, Paris—to Paul Hedler, London—March 25, 1871

He wants more time for arithmetic and for penmanship. In this last respect, nothing improves the student more than letter writing. The more letters he writes the better. Always have the spelling corrected and the letter re-written carefully. All talk about engineering, as a profession, is premature. I should prefer he would be a doctor . . .

In the present terrible condition of things here, I would advise no one to come. It is impossible to speak of the future of Paris. All is now anarchy and terror. It must be a long time before things are settled.

On March 26, the insurrectionists ordered an election to secure political legitimacy for its actions. Washburne dismissed the results as a "put up job . . . without the pretense of legality." But the insurgents declared a great victory, proclaiming themselves the "Commune of Paris" with absolute power over the entire city.

Washburne knew that dark days lay ahead. "It is difficult to conceive what were the sensations of those wretched creatures, who found themselves the depository of an insurrectionary and lawless power which was to end in lighting up Paris in flames, and the commission of every crime of which the imagination could conceive."

Elihu Washburne, Versailles—to Secretary of State Hamilton Fish, Washington, D.C.—March 27, 1871

The election for the commune which took place in Paris yesterday was a perfect farce. It was ordered by the comité central *without the shadow of authority, and the acquiescence in it at the eleventh hour by nearly all the mayors, and some ten members of the National Assembly representing Paris, gave it no legality. Yet if the people had generally voted there would have been a certain moral force in the result. But that was not the case. There are some five hundred and fifty thousand voters in the city. On yesterday there were not more than one hundred and eighty thousand votes cast . . . Notwithstanding all this, the insurgents will claim an advantage from the election, and assume that they have been endorsed by the people of Paris. The election will bring no change for the better, but, on the other hand, the situation will become more threatening . . .*

The government here [at Versailles] evidently does not feel strong enough to cope with the Paris insurgents, and is waiting to get up other and more reliable troops . . .

Diary—March 27, 1871

Left Paris to come to Versailles in my own carriage. The election yesterday in Paris was simply a burlesque. Of the persons elected I have never heard of but few of them and those I have heard of are the worst men in Paris. The election complicates matters. The situation is more and more grave. Nothing done in the Assembly except the declaration of M. Thiers that the government would stand by the republic, which declaration was accepted. Weather magnificent.

Diary—March 28, 1871

> *Lord Lyons* made an early call on me. He considers the situation
> as bad as possible. The truth is the Government here has no force,
> no decision, no courage and no energy. Thiers told his Lordship
> last night that it would be* two weeks *before they would have force
> enough to attack the insurgents. Jules Favre thinks when they get
> that force, the insurgents in Paris will* cave in. *He is mistaken.
> Let them look out for the insurgent and revolutionary spirit which
> will be diffused all over France . . .*

Later that day, before a crowd of some one hundred thousand people, the Commune held a ceremony at the Hôtel de
Ville publicly proclaiming itself the legitimate authority in
Paris. Two days later Washburne reported to Washington that
"events are marching apace."

Diary—March 29, 1871

> *Came in from Versailles yesterday P.M. sick with a cold and went
> right to bed. I am down to the Legation this morning . . . The
> Commune and the Red Flag everywhere.*

**Elihu Washburne, Paris—to Secretary of State Hamilton Fish—
Washington, D.C.—March 30, 1871**

> *The election of members of the commune was proclaimed with
> great ceremony at the Hôtel de Ville . . . All the national guards
> were invited to be present. At about four o'clock they commenced
> to arrive from every direction, drums beating and flags flying.*

---

*Lord Richard Bickerton Pemell, British ambassador to Paris.

Upon a platform in front of the hôtel there was placed a large
square table, which was surrounded by some members of the
comité central *in citizens' dress, and many officers of the national*
guard, all distinguished by a red scarf. The proceedings are
opened by a display of flags, by repeated salvos of artillery, followed
by great applause and cries of "Vive la commune!" "Vive la
république!" &c . . . At a given moment the soldiers place their
caps upon the point of the bayonet and raise their muskets in the
air. M. Ranvier, the president of the central committee, read to
the multitude the list of members elected to the commune . . . The
military bands placed at the foot of the balcony then struck up
the Marseillaise, *the* Chant du Depart *. . . the entire assemblage*
joining in the chorus. The ceremony of the proclamation of the
Commune having been finished, all the battalions which had
been massed upon the place of the hôtel defiled before the balcony
to the cry of "Vive la Commune!" . . . All the windows of the
neighboring houses were well filled with spectators, the barricades
were covered with people, and the gamins *perched themselves in all*
the trees of the avenue Victoria . . .

The Commune may be said to be complete masters in Paris to
day, as there is no force to oppose them . . .

Diary—March 31, 1871

Was at the Legation all day yesterday and very busy. The
Commune is looming up and "means business." Everything has a
more sinister look. Before I left my house this morning I had word
that all the trains were stopped and the gates closed. I have sent
out to see what the real situation is and to get a pass, for I must go
to Versailles today. The Post Office is bust—the Commune seized
the whole concern and all the employees have left. Everything now
will have to go to Versailles . . . There never was such a hell upon

*earth as this very Paris. I don't know how soon I shall be obliged
to take the family away. The Americans now begin to be alarmed
and if the gates continue closed that alarm will increase in a
regular panic. "How long. Oh, how long."*

Diary—March 31, 1871

*Have just returned from a reception of M. Thiers. He lives at the
Prefecture [of the Department of the Seine-et-Oise], which is really
a beautiful palace. It was the residence of the King of Prussia
when he was in Versailles. There was quite a large number of
people there, nearly all gentlemen. Only about half a dozen ladies.
Madame Thiers is a respectable looking person. Everybody seemed
desirous of talking with Thiers and to give him advice. Nobody is
satisfied with his policy. He answers complaining that he did not
seek his position and would be glad to give it up, but while he holds
it he shall act according to his own judgment. He says he is doing
his best in his own way—that he works twenty hours a day. I guess
he stretches that a little, but he has always been a great worker.
For a man of 74 he is wonderfully bright and smart—tough as a
pine-knot. He always gets up at four o'clock in the morning but
then he sleeps an hour before and an hour after dinner. He has his
own theories and is impatient under any criticism. He asked me
about Paris and I told him that things were growing worse and
worse there all the time, a proposition which he warmly contested
and declared that they were getting better and better all the time.
When a man is struck with such blindness it is but little use in
talking to him and less use in expecting much from him. There
are seventy thousand troops in and around Versailles and the
government persists that they cannot be depended upon and they
are waiting for other troops to come up. If any man wants to be
disgusted come to Versailles . . .*

Washburne would later write, "And now it was in the last days of March that the hopes of so many of the best people of Paris almost died within them . . . And the spirit of insurrection and revolution seemed to be spreading over all France."

Within days, however, Thiers and the government at Versailles were finally ready to act. At a gathering of his secret council Thiers announced, "The organization of one of the finest armies possessed by France has been completed at Versailles; good citizens can thus reassure themselves and hope for the end of a struggle which will have been painful, but short."

On Palm Sunday, the attack began. Washburne and his family watched the commencement of the battle from the upper windows of their residence. "It was a singular sight . . . to watch . . . the progress of a regular battle under the walls of Paris," Washburne wrote, "and to hear the roar of artillery, the rattling of musketry, and the peculiar sound of the mitrailleuses."

Diary—April 3, 1871

Awakened at 5½ this morning by discharges of artillery . . . Go to the Legation at 9½ and Antoine comes in with wild reports. Some say that in the night two bodies of insurgents met and fired into each other, others that they have gone out beyond the fort and are moving on Versailles . . .

Diary—April 4, 1871

The greatest quiet has prevailed in the city all day. It is impossible to get at the truth in regard to anything, but the impression everywhere is that the Reds have been thrashed out of their boots.

The insurgent papers are perfectly furious. The Commune has impeached all the members of the Government and confiscated their property.

Diary—April 5, 1871

All last night the cannon thundered on the side of Vanves and Issy forts. It was a regular artillery duel between these forts and the Versailles batteries and nobody hurt . . . Indeed, we will not be likely to get at the truth in regard to operations as the Commune will suppress every paper that tells the truth . . . The day has been beautiful. We have watched the artillery all day from our window at the Legation. It brought back the days of the siege.

Elihu Washburne, Paris—to Secretary of State Hamilton Fish, Washington, D.C.—April 6, 1871

We still have here a large number of Americans, and while I hope that they may not be molested or have their property injured, yet no one knows what may happen from hour to hour. Under such circumstances I deem it my duty to remain in Paris as much as possible, going or sending to Versailles to transact business with the government there . . .

There has been almost constant fighting ever since outside walls of the city, and in the direction of Versailles. The results have been uniformly unfavorable to the insurgents, who have lost large numbers in killed and wounded, and a great many prisoners. It seems to be understood that all of their forces are to be brought into the city under the pretext of reorganization. The greatest discouragement exists among the insurrectionary population of the city, and the most desperate things are not only proposed but are being accomplished . . .

Diary—April 6, 1871

There is intense excitement in the city today. There is the decree
of the Commune for the establishment of a Revolutionary
tribunal—vast numbers of the best citizens are seized as hostages
and cast into dungeons . . . All Frenchmen prohibited from
leaving Paris. The Legation crowded all day with Americans
seeking passports and advice . . .

Despite furious fighting between the Communards and Government forces outside the walls of Paris, inside the city the Commune was still the "complete master of Paris," as Washburne would later write. "Day after day was passing, and nothing was being done. Paris continued to be left at the mercy of the Commune."

When the Commune had first come to power, Washburne had seen it as a strange and sinister collection of "utterly unknown" men who had "emerged from total obscurity." But now, firmly in control of the city, they became infamous to the world, embarking upon a savage and bloodthirsty reign of terror.

One of the most sadistic and treacherous of the lot was Raoul Rigault, a young political agitator of middle-class origins who had grown up detesting any form of civilized authority. In his youth he had been fascinated by books about the French Revolution and the bloody terror that gripped Paris during the 1790s. Although only twenty-five years old, he had already been imprisoned three times and once, while incarcerated, had tried to spark a prison revolt with "blood-curdling shouts of 'Vive la Guillotine!'"

Lillie Moulton, the young and beautiful daughter-in-law of Washburne's friend Charles Moulton, described Rigault as "short, thick-set, with . . . a bushy black beard, a sensuous mouth, and a cynical smile." He wore tortoiseshell glasses, but even those could not mask the "wicked expression of his cunning eyes." His beliefs were fueled by a passion for political destruction and personal debauchery. He advocated "sexual promiscuity" and viewed concubinage as a "social dogma."

Rigault had a bizarre fascination with police tactics and undercover espionage, spending hours peering through a spyglass into the offices of the Prefecture of Police while perched on a Seine bookseller's stall. After the rise of the Commune, he demanded and received the post of Prefect of Police. Once in power, he set about arresting anyone he deemed an enemy of the Republic.

Washburne himself described Rigault as "one of the most hideous figures in all history . . . Bold, energetic and cynical, he was consumed by the most deadly hatred of society and the most intense thirst for blood. All his associate assassins bowed before his despotic will. No one opposed him, for his gesture was the signal of death. He held in his hand the life of every man in Paris and he wrought his vengeance on every one for whom he took a dislike."

Washburne would later find a "method" in Rigault's madness, accusing him of using countless acts of violence to "keep up terror" in the city. Above all, Washburne would come to realize that Rigault "took devilish pleasure in tormenting his victims."

On April 4, Rigault ordered the arrest and imprisonment of the Catholic Archbishop of Paris, Monsignor Georges Darboy.

Elihu Washburne, Paris—to Secretary of State Hamilton Fish, Washington, D.C.—April 6, 1871

> *The Archbishop of Paris, Monseigneur Darboy, was arrested the night before last and carried to prison, while his palace was*

*plundered . . . The Abbé Deguerry, the curé of the Madeleine, was
also arrested and sent to prison on Tuesday night . . . Four priests
were also arrested during the same night and carried to Mazas
[prison]. As you may well imagine, the greatest terror prevails
among all these people who are now being hunted down. Their fate
seems hard indeed. All of them remained here during the siege,
suffering unheard of privations of cold and hunger, visiting the sick
and wounded, and upholding the courage of the people of Paris . . .*

From the moment Adele and the children had arrived from
Brussels, Washburne had regretted allowing them to return.
Increasingly concerned about his family's well-being, Washburne decided to move them from the house at 75 Avenue de
l'Impératrice to a friend's home further downtown and out of
harm's way.

Diary—April 8, 1871

*Thursday there was a good deal of fighting in all directions and
great uneasiness everywhere felt. The arrest of the Archbishop
of Paris . . . and scores of priests has created the greatest alarm
among all classes. The center of interest on that day was the
Avenue of the Grand Army and the Porte Maillot. Constant
artillery firing from both sides. Yesterday, Friday, still more firing
in the same quarters and an immense crowd of people looking
from the neighborhood of the Arch de Triomph. I left the Legation
at a quarter before five to come to the house and I stopped there
on my way. I should think there were ten thousand people in the
Grand Army Avenue watching the firing. I reached the house
at five . . . Sue* then ran down and told me that three shells had*

*His daughter Susan, who would have been twelve years of age at this
time.

struck right near the house—one not more than fifty feet off.
Rather too close to be agreeable and so I made up my mind that
Adele and the children had better leave the house and go down
town . . .

Grack was in the Avenue of the Grand Army about 6 P.M.
yesterday when a shell went over the heads of the crowd and struck
the Arc de Triomph. He says he never saw such scampering in all
his life—men, women and children, running, tumbling, yelling
like mad.

Diary—April 9, 1871

Heavy cannonading all day yesterday between the Versailles
batteries and the Porte de Neuilly and the insurgent batteries
at the Porte Maillot. A good many shells came into the city and
many persons killed and wounded. Big firing this morning and
shells coming in fast—two fell in the Rue de Chaillot not far from
the Legation. Adele and the children are still at Miss Ellis', but
they may have to move from there as the shells are falling not far
from them . . .

Elihu Washburne, Paris—to Secretary of State Hamilton Fish, Washington, D.C.—April 9, 1871

It is one week ago today since actual fighting commenced between
the Versailles troops and the insurgents . . . There has been but
little cessation of the fighting during the week. The successes have
been invariably on the side of the government troops, and the
Commune forces are now strictly on the defensive . . . [A] large
number of shells have fallen in that part of the city in which the
Arc de Triomphe is situated, and in which locality a great many
of the apartments are occupied by the Americans. One shell fell
in the Avenue Joséphine, half a square distant from the Legation

and the Champs-Élysées. On going to my house at five o'clock on Friday afternoon last I found that three shells had exploded in the immediate vicinity, one of them striking within fifty feet of my parlor window. Considering it no longer a safe place for my family, I lost no time in removing my wife and children to a less-exposed situation. Coming to the Legation this morning I saw two shells burst at the Arc de Triomphe. I do not know how long this business is to continue, but the communists are evidently expecting an attack, for they have great numbers of soldiers in all the streets running out from the Champs-Élysées. It is estimated that the losses of insurgents in the last week amount to more than seven thousand . . .

Diary—April 10, 1871

I started downtown to the Legation. The shells were just hissing through the air and exploding in the neighborhood of the Porte Maillot and the Arc de Triomphe. I got within about two hundred yards of the Arc when pop went the weasel—a shell struck and burst against the Arc. A piece of shell fell in the street, which a National Guard picked up, all warm and smoking, and sold to me for two francs.* Up to three o'clock P.M. the shells were falling in all that part of the city. I took a ride in the P.M. to the Grand Boulevard and Rue de Rivoli—great many people out. They had just commenced building a barricade where the Rue de Rivoli enters into the Place de la Concorde. Not much firing today and things are more quiet than they have been for several days. I have just

---

*Wickham Hoffman would later write how some enterprising Parisians would do a "large business . . . in these fragments after the siege, as well in the exploded shells. They were sold as relics; and the Parisian shop-keepers mounted them as clocks, fenders, inkstands, penholders, and other *articles de Paris*." (Hoffman, *Camp, Court, and Siege*, 275–276.)

come from Miss Ellis to 75. The folks are still at Miss E's, but I have to stay in my own house or else the servants will clear out. I will not leave them where I will not stay myself. Down town this P.M. and the streets are somber enough. The day has been blue and chilly.

Even during the constant shelling of the city from the Versailles troops, the rabble of the Commune commenced stripping Paris of its riches. The streets were filled with "violence, blackguardism, vulgarity, indecency," wrote Washburne. More and more people began to flee, including many of the remaining Americans, all increasingly alarmed at the state of affairs in Paris. Washburne wrote of the dire situation facing the people as the Commune became more and more desperate:

People were in a state of panic at the atrocities and robberies and burnings of the Commune, and were leaving Paris as fast as possible. In the first half of April it was estimated that the number who left was three hundred thousand. Everybody was concealing or carrying away capital. All the sources of labor were dried up. There was neither trade, commerce, traffic, nor manufacturing of any sort. All the gold and silver that had been found in the churches and all the plate belonging to the government, found at the different ministries, had been seized by the Commune to be converted into coin. The Catholic clergy were hunted down. The priests were openly placarded as thieves, and the churches denounced as "haunts where they have morally assassinated the masses, in dragging France under the heels of the scoundrels, Bonaparte, Favre and Trochu."

Washburne and the Legation were now swamped with throngs of people "from morning till night seeking passports and 'protection papers' for their property."

To make matters worse Washburne himself was facing possible retribution. The Commune had formed a "bureau of de-
nunciation" to which anyone could simply denounce another
as a "Versailles sympathizer," resulting in the accused being immediately arrested or, in some cases, executed. One Commune
gathering denounced Washburne and issued a threat to hang
him and destroy the American Legation. Fortunately, nothing
ever came of the threat, but he was now increasingly concerned
about the danger the Commune posed to his family. He finally
decided it was time to remove them from Paris.

Diary—April 12, 1871

*Versailles . . . Mr. Berand an American was arrested in coming
out here yesterday by the Versailles troops . . . and treated most
infamously. He was searched and sent under a guard here and
put in prison. It was one o'clock this morning before I got him out.
He came to my room and slept on the floor. He was arrested on the
old charge of being a "spy." I had hoped the spy business was played
out, but it seems I was mistaken.*

Diary—April 13, 1871

*. . . was sick yesterday at V[ersailles] with a most horrid cold and
hardly went out of my room. Today at 10 A.M. attended a great
funeral ceremony of the Generals Clément-Thomas and Lecomte.
How strange in regard to Clément-Thomas. He was a splendid
man and a life-long Republican and was a long time in exile on
account of his principles. And he was the first man murdered by
these savages . . .*

*As we come to the Legation Antoine tells me that the shells
have been raining in the neighborhood of the Legation. A piece of*

shell struck the Legation building and a piece fell in a yard right opposite Miss Ellis where the family is now stopping. I am more and more discouraged every time I go to Versailles and I must confess I see now no immediate end of the troubles and I fear the worst. The insurgents claim recent advantages. The Versailles people are making great preparations to attack, but they seem afraid. The thing may end suddenly and by chance, but the look now is that there will be bloody fighting and terrible times. I am afraid I will have to send the folks away again. The stampede from the city is tremendous . . .

Diary—April 17, 1871

I have been confined to my house since Friday with a bad cold. As there were less shells bursting about the house the folks came up from Miss Ellis on Saturday. But the firing is going on all the time, both cannonading and musketry, so near that it seems almost under the windows. Bang, bang, crack, crack, crack, now the whizzing of a shell . . . And we are all getting used to it. For two weeks we may be said to have been right in the midst of a battle. For more than four weeks, in anarchy and insurrection. Every day makes things worse. Domiciliary visits, arrests, incarcerations . . . pillage. The houses of Thiers and Favre have been sacked, all the ministries robbed . . . The house adjoining ours was entered and sacked the night before last. The same fate would have attended ours had we not been occupying it. The insurgents boast of their successes, but it is all boast. The look to me now is that the city will be besieged by the Versailles people. I must send the family somewhere—perhaps to Germany, perhaps to Fontainebleau. I hardly know what to do. There never was a more horrible condition of things than there is here at present and I see no immediate end to it all. All pretty well except myself.

Diary—April 19, 1871

It is almost always the same that I have to write; always war and worse . . . All is one great shipwreck in Paris. Fortune, business, public and private credit, industry, labor are all in "the deep bosom of the ocean buried."* The physiognomy of the city becomes every day more sad. All the upper part of the Champs-Élysées is completely deserted in fear of the shells. Immense barricades are going up at the Place de la Concorde. The great manufactuaries and workshops are closed . . . The cafés close at 10 o'clock and Paris is not Paris when the cafés are shut up. Where I write, at 75, always the roar of cannon, the whizzing of shells and the rattling of musketry. When I came home at 6½ this evening the noise was terrific. Two shells burst not a great distance from me. It seems that it must have been a regular battle, but I suppose it was only a skirmish. Gratiot went to Fontainebleau today to find a place for the family, but was unsuccessful.

Elihu Washburne, Paris—to Secretary of State Hamilton Fish, Washington, D.C.—April 20, 1871

I am certain that I never believed that it would fall to my lot to live, with my family, in a city of two millions of people in a state of insurrection for such a length of time as the present one has already lasted. I should be too happy if I could advise you that I could see any prospect of a termination of the terrible state of things existing here. Nothing comes to us from Versailles, that can be relied on, to show that effective measures are soon to be taken to expel the insurgents from power and to re-establish the authority of the government in Paris. To be sure, we hear rumors of attack and

---

*From Shakespeare's *Richard III*, Act I, scene 1.

assault in great and overpowering force, and then other rumors of another siege; but day after day passes away without particular results further than heating still hotter the blood and inflaming still further the existing hatreds and animosities . . .

On Thursday, April 19, 1871, Washburne was approached by the Papal Nuncio in Paris, Flavius Chigi, to help secure the release of the imprisoned Archbishop Georges Darboy. Earlier efforts to enlist the assistance of the British envoy at Versailles had failed. Now Chigi was turning to the American Minister as his only hope, appealing to him "in the name of the right of nations, humanity, and sympathy" to do what he could to save the life of the Archbishop.

Washburne knew the Archbishop to be "a man eminently beloved by all who knew him, sincerely devoted to the interests of his church and distinguished for his benevolence and kindness of heart." Washburne had also admired the fact that the Archbishop had remained in Paris throughout the war and siege to help protect and aid those suffering from hunger and cold. When he first heard of the Archbishop's arrest, he "considered it among the most threatening events that had taken place" since the rise of the Commune.

Three days later, on April 22, Washburne met with the Papal Nuncio at Versailles to discuss the case. There were indications that Darboy had been taken hostage by the Commune to be offered in an exchange for political prisoners held by the government. Sensing the urgency of the Archbishop's plight, Washburne agreed to help at once. "I fully sympathized with the Nuncio," Washburne wrote, "and had no hesitation in telling . . . [him] . . . that I was at his disposal to do everything in my power."

Diary—April 23, 1871

Sunday evening. The Pope's Nuncio, the Friar General of Paris and some other high dignitaries of the Catholic Church, having made a strong appeal to me to interpose my good offices in behalf of the Archbishop of Paris, cast into prison by the Commune, I went this morning to see General [Gustave-Paul] Cluseret* on the subject. He could give me no encouragement in regard to the Archbishop, as he was held as a hostage. I then told him I must see the Archbishop to satisfy myself in regard to his treatment in prison, the state of his health and his wants. He said that was reasonable and that he would immediately go with me to the Prefect of the Police and get the permission. So we all started off (Mr. McKean† was with me) and made our way to the Prefecture. And what a horrid place that, even in the best times. So immense, so somber, so frowning with its dark and crooked ways, its damp and dismal cells. Now all filled with the National Guard with their dirty and sinister look. We go upstairs and downstairs, through dark passages, turning this way and that way. What mysteries within these walls, what stories of suffering, torture and crime. We at last reach the sanctum and Mr. [Raoul] Rigault. The prefect signs a pass to permit me and my secretary to freely visit the Archbishop. Then McKean and I start for Mazas and without difficulty are admitted. We are ushered into a visitor's cell and soon the Archbishop is sent in. Poor old man, with his slender form, bent person, long beard and countenance haggard with disease. He was very glad to see us, for up to the

---

*A member of the Commune's Ministry of War. Washburne initially sought his assistance because, as he noted in a letter to Secretary of State Fish, he seemed "at present time, to be the directing man in affairs here." (Washburne to Fish, April 23, 1871.)

†J. A. McKean was Washburne's private secretary.

*day before he had been a prisoner in secret and he had seen no
person from the outside before us since his imprisonment. Though
fully appreciating his dangerous position, he was wonderfully
cheerful and charming in his conversation. He said he was
simply awaiting the logic of events and prepared for any fate
that might await him. He uttered no word of complaint against
his persecutors, but he was disposed to consider the mob as bad
as the world generally thought them to be . . . No man was ever
more beloved for his liberality, generosity and kindness . . . He
is confined in one of the ordinary cells of the prison designed for
malefactors, about ten by six with one little window. His furniture
consists of one little wooden chair, a little table and a prison bed.
As a political prisoner he is permitted to get his food outside. I
offered him any assistance he might want, but he said he had no
need of anything. I shall try and send some newspapers to him and
will visit him every few days. There are forty other priests in the
same prison of Mazas.*

Washburne was deeply touched by seeing the Archbishop in
such a state:

I shall never forget the naiveté with which he introduced me
into his dismal little cell, describing it all at once as his "parlor," his "sitting room," his "sleeping room," and his "dining
hall" . . . Never before had I seen such resignation and such a
Christian spirit in any man and never a person so raised above
the things of earth.

After his visit to the Archbishop's "gloomy and naked little
cell," Washburne was convinced the Archbishop was in great
peril. After the arrest of Darboy one of the Commune newspapers had written: "The dogs will soon not be satisfied with

looking at the bishops . . . but will bite them . . . and not a voice will be raised to curse us on the day in which we shall shoot Archbishop Darboy."

"I could not conceal from myself the real danger that he was in," Washburne later wrote, "and I hoped, more and more strongly that I might be instrumental in saving him from the fate that seemed to threaten him."

While struggling to save the Archbishop, Washburne was also preoccupied with finding a secure house for his family outside Paris. On April 24, with shells falling "thick and fast," Washburne learned of a safe house in a small town just outside the city. He moved his family there at once. He described it to a friend in Galena as a "little French village four hundred years old. We occupy a cottage near an old château, and we have a splendid yard, garden etc. It is very healthy and pleasant, and Mrs. Washburne and the children are very well."

Diary—April 25, 1871

> *The folks left this morning for the country. The morning was bright and pleasant. Mr. McKean went out with them, as it was impossible for me to leave. All the Alsatians and Lorrainians are coming to me to claim my protection as Germans and get passes to leave Paris. At one time yesterday there were no less than 500 of them waiting and blocking up the street near the Legation. Bismarck ought to have sent his minister here before this time to relieve me. He seems, however, to be satisfied with me and is not disposed to let me off . . .*

That same day Washburne received a letter from the Papal Nuncio thanking him for his visit to the Archbishop.

**The Papal Nuncio, Versailles—to Elihu Washburne, Paris—
April 25, 1871**

Sir and Dear Colleague:

*Truly, I do not know how to thank you for all you have had the
kindness to do to aid the worthy Archbishop of Paris. You have
done more than I could have hoped for, notwithstanding the
confidence with which I was inspired, knowing the sentiments
of humanity and of pity of your heart, and the generous nation
you represent so worthily in France, and I am sure that the steps
you will take with the men into whose hands lies the fate of the
Archbishop, will not fail to produce the most favorable result
which it is possible to hope for under present circumstances . . .*

As the army of Versailles pounded away at Paris, the Communards became more desperate and more depraved.

Diary—May 2, 1871

*Fighting going on all the time all about the city, but without
perceptible results . . . There is great fury among the insurgents
now, and last night they formed a fearful committee—the
Committee of Public Safety—which in the first revolution [1789]
was a committee simply to legalize butchery. This new committee
has full powers and the reign of terror may now commence in
earnest any day. I fear for the life of the good old Archbishop. A
lot of drunken National Guard broke into the prison Sunday
clamoring for his blood and threatening to shoot, but a member of
the Commune happened to be there and stopped them.*

Washburne would write that the middle of May was "the darkest time in the Commune." Weeks earlier a decree had been issued ordering the destruction of the Vendôme Column* and on May 10 the Commune ordered the destruction of Adolphe Thiers's home at the Place St. Georges. The decree, Washburne noted, "was scrupulously carried out." For days fanatics set loose by the Communards tore the house apart stone by stone and stripped it of Thiers's priceless collection of art, rare books, and manuscripts. An indignant and overwrought Washburne would later write, "Such vandalism was without a parallel in all the history of civilization."

Despite the worsening conditions in Paris, Washburne found time to visit his family, now safely housed outside the city. During one visit on May 7 he was taken ill with a "bilious attack" of nausea, stomach pains, cold sweats, and vomiting. Although confined to bed for a day, he was back at his duties the next afternoon issuing urgent dispatches to Washington about the rapidly changing affairs in Paris. Throughout the siege and reign of terror, Washburne "always rebounded more elastic than ever after a relapse . . ." wrote an observer who knew him in Paris. "His courage kept up the courage of those around him."

---

*According to historian Alistair Horne, the Column "had been erected by Napoléon I on the site where, in 1792, the mob had destroyed an equestrian statue of Louis XIV." The political left wing of France had long "detested" the Column because it represented everything it most despised "about militarism and imperialism" in French politics and government. (Horne, *Fall of Paris,* 349.)

Elihu Washburne, Paris—to Secretary of State Hamilton Fish, Washington, D.C.—May 11, 1871

The crisis seems to be really approaching. You will have seen the announcement of the capture of the fort of Issy by the Versailles troops, and the report this evening is that the fort of Vanves has also fallen. The government, having apparently completed the preparations, is now attacking Paris with great fury . . .

The insurrectionary force are said to have been withdrawn from these positions, and the resistance that will be made by the insurgents will be in other parts of the city. I thought a week ago that the opposition would be greater than I am now satisfied it will be . . .

The desperate wrangles in the Commune, and the quarrel between that august body and the central committee, which were all well known to the public, added to the general excitement . . . Signs of demoralization are everywhere visible. The National Guard is being weakened every day, not only by its losses in actual combat and in prisoners, but by the vast numbers of desertions. Almost every man who has the chance to do so with any degree of safety to himself is slipping out of the service, and instead of an army of sixty or eighty thousand, as claimed a week ago, I do not believe one-half that number can be counted on today. A good many think that, in the present feeling of discouragement, the government troops could enter and retake Paris without any serious resistance; but others, of an equal number, look upon a desperate contest and the shedding of a great deal of blood as inevitable. The worse things grow, the more desperate the Commune becomes . . .

The Archbishop is still in prison, and his situation is becoming daily more and more dangerous. I am interesting myself

officiously in endeavoring to have him exchanged for Blanqui,*
who is under sentence of death . . . for his . . . part in the
attempted insurrection of the 31st of October last. The Commune
has once agreed to make the exchange, which M. Thiers declined,
but the Archbishop, whom I saw in prison yesterday, thinks he may
now agree to it, in view of the increasing dangers to which he is
exposed . . .

Diary—May 11, 1871

Quite an exciting day yesterday . . . The Versaillais are pounding
away very hard and there is an evident demoralization in the
Commune. It really looks as if the end were coming. Called
yesterday to see the Archbishop again . . . The National Guard are
deserting fast and things are getting desperate . . . They are still
working on the Column Vendôme and hope to get it down before
the city is taken . . .

Diary—May 12, 1871

The Commune is more and more desperate and now has a regular
revolutionary tribunal in working order . . . Six more papers
suppressed this morning, making in all twenty-one. What a
splendid republic we have here.

---

*Auguste Blanqui (1805–1881) was one of the oldest and most revered
leaders of the French revolutionary movement. After his involvement in
the failed October 31, 1870, insurrection, he was arrested and sentenced
to death by the government. As the Commune began to splinter apart,
Raoul Rigault saw Blanqui's leadership as the only hope for the Commune.
"Nothing can be done without the Old One," Rigault proclaimed, hoping that a hostage exchange for the Archbishop would free Blanqui from
prison.

Diary—May 16, 1871

*The Commune is getting more and more outrageous. The Column
Vendôme still stands, but they give out that it is going to fall every
day. The consequence is that thousands and thousands of people
stand watching it all day long . . . Thiers refuses to exchange the
Archbishop of Paris for Blanqui . . .**

Later that day the Vendôme Column was toppled at last. For
weeks those in charge of bringing it down had stalled and
delayed its demolition. Finally, after strong threats from the
leaders of the Commune, May 16 was set as the date for its
destruction. It was to be a day of great festivity, with special
invitations issued for the event. To prepare for the tremendous
shock which would come from the fallen column, tons of ma-
nure and straw were piled at its base and "shop-windows within
half a mile were pasted over with strips of paper to prevent their
being broken," wrote Wickham Hoffman.

At 3 P.M. on May 16, a crowd of some 10,000 heard a band
strike up the "Marseillaise." Moments later the column was
pulled down with a "mighty crash." Amid the shattered ruins
of the memorial, people shouted "Vive la Commune."

Diary—May 16, 1871 (continued)

*5:30. The act of vandalism has been accomplished. The grand
Column Vendôme has this moment fallen, the greatest infamy of*

---

*It was reported that Adolphe Thiers was "very angry" at Washburne for
trying to meddle in a proposed exchange of Blanqui for the Archbishop,
calling Washburne's actions *"conduite très singulière"* ("very peculiar behav-
ior"). (Stewart Edwards, *The Paris Commune, 1871.* Chicago: Quadrangle
Books, 1973, p. 213.)

modern times and a blot upon the civilization of the age. I did
not see it fall and did not want to. I rode down the Boulevard at
half past two and I should think there were 20,000 people . . . to
see it come down.

In the midst of the outrages and atrocities of the Commune,
Washburne received a personal letter from his old Galena friend
President Ulysses S. Grant.

President Ulysses S. Grant, Washington, D.C.—to Elihu Washburne,
Paris—May 17, 1871

I have not written to you whilst shut up in Paris because I did not
know that anything but purely official dispatches were proper, or
would be so considered by the Prussians, to send through the lines. I
thought none the less frequently of you however, and the relief from
care and anxiety which you sought in a foreign Mission. Your
time will come I trust for relief. Already you have the reward of
your services in the gratitude and pride the American people feel
for the glorious course you pursued in standing at your post which
all others, like situated, had deserted . . .

In the middle of May, Raoul Rigault issued a general order re-
voking any permission to see prisoners held by the Commune,
including Washburne's pass to see the Archbishop. On May
18, Washburne sent his private secretary to Rigault protesting
the order and requesting special permission to visit Darboy in
prison. At first Rigault denied the request, telling the secretary
he was "very much indisposed to give" what Washburne de-
sired. However, after repeated protests, Rigault relented and
Washburne was once again granted leave to see the imprisoned
Archbishop.

Diary—May 19, 1871

> *Fighting and banging away all the time most furiously, but
> yet the troops don't get in and we are almost worn out with
> waiting and waiting. The Commune gets every day more furious
> and outrageous. Today they threaten to destroy Paris and bury
> everybody in the ruins before they will surrender . . . I have also
> just seen the Archbishop in prison and he is feeble and I do not
> believe he can live long in that miserable hole . . .*

That same day, he wrote Secretary of State Fish in Washington informing him that the French government in Versailles had refused to exchange Blanqui for the imprisoned Archbishop.

**Elihu Washburne, Paris—to Secretary of State Hamilton Fish,
Washington, D.C.—May 19, 1871**

> *Since I have commenced writing this dispatch, I have again
> visited the Archbishop, to communicate to him that it was
> impossible to effect his exchange for Blanqui. I am sorry to say I
> found him very feeble. He has been confined to his pallet for the
> last week with a kind of pleurisy; is without appetite, and very
> much reduced in strength. He is yet cheerful, and apparently
> resigned to any fate that may await him . . .*

On May 20, while working at the Legation, Washburne received news that a squad of National Guard was attempting to seize his house at 75 Avenue de l'Impératrice. "They pounded away vigorously at the great door which entered the courtyard, while the servant held a parley with them," Washburne later reported:

The leader of the squad said to her that they had been sent to take possession of the house, and that they intended to do so. She told them that it was the house of the Minister of the United States, and that they had no right to enter. They answered that they did not care to whom the house belonged, or who lived there, and that they intended to enter: and further, that if she would not open the door (which was a very heavy one, and securely fastened), they would go back to their post and procure reinforcements and then break in.

Washburne immediately dispatched a letter to Paschal Grousset,* the Commune's Delegate for External Affairs, demanding protection. Grousset agreed and sent a force which intercepted the "brigands of the National Guard" before they invaded Washburne's home. Washburne would later write that "never before had matters in Paris looked so dark and threatening to me as on that day."

The next day, Washburne paid another visit to the Archbishop:

I no sooner got inside than I saw there was a great change in affairs. The old guardians whom I had often seen there were not present, but all were new men, and apparently of the worst character, who seemed displeased to see me. They were a little drunk, and were disputing each other's authority. I asked to see the Archbishop, and expected to be permitted to enter his cell, as I had hitherto. The request was somewhat curtly refused, and

---

*Grousset was a twenty-six-year-old former journalist known as a "fiery, dapper little Corsican, so carefully groomed" that his nickname was "the ladies' hairdresser." Washburne evidently liked and trusted Grousset, calling him someone of "intelligence, education, and genteel personal appearance." (Horne, *The Fall of Paris*, 299.)

they then brought the unfortunate man out of his cell into the corridor, to talk with me in their presence. The interview was, therefore, to me very unsatisfactory, both from the surroundings and from the condition of distress in which the Archbishop seemed to be. It was impossible to talk with him freely, and I limited myself to saying that while I regretted that I had nothing encouraging to communicate to him, I had taken pleasure in calling to see him in order to ascertain the state of his health and if it would not be possible for me to render him some further personal service. Such was the situation that I thought proper to bring my interview to a speedy close, then it was, for the last time, I shook the hand of the Archbishop and bade him what proved to be a final adieu.

The next day, May 22, 1871, the government at Versailles launched its final all-out assault on the Paris Commune. The Communards had sworn that if Paris were taken they would "bury everything in a common ruin."

Diary—May 22, 1871

This day will always live in the history of France. For more than nine weeks I have lived here in a reign of terror and matters have gone on regularly from bad to worse. And it seemed as if it would never end. The last days have been most anxious ones as the brigands of the Commune have become utterly desperate. Every day for the last two weeks had I hoped to hear in the morning of the entry of the Government troops, but every morning I have been disappointed. I dined out last night and returned to my lodgings about eleven o'clock and I saw no more signs of the troops coming in than I had seen for the last two weeks. Yet at that moment they had . . . entered at the Porte St. Cloud.

*The entry was a complete surprise both to the troops and the
insurgents [Communards]. I awoke at 6 this morning and heard
a good deal of talking in the house and I thought something
might possibly be up and so I rang for the servant who came and
told me nothing had taken place. In a few minutes, however, the
same servant returned and said that the tricolour floated on
the Arc de Triomph. Gratiot and I dressed very hurriedly and
I went at once into the Avenue Joséphine and sure enough there
was the tricolour waving in triumph on the top of the Arc. The
concierges and the few people in the avenue were out and they
all met me with congratulations upon their deliverance from
the reign of terror. Gratiot and I then hurried down the avenue
and immense bodies of troops were advancing along the route of
Versailles . . . towards the Place de Concorde. An attack had been
made on the barricades at the latter point and the cannonading
and firing of the mitrailleuse and musketry was very heavy. Soon
all came to a halt and after remaining with the troops till half
past seven we returned to Miss Ellis' for our coffee. After coffee
I went to the Arc de Triomph and passed the barricades into the
Avenue of the Grand Army. As the troops entered the city, in
their rear that whole quarter had been suddenly abandoned at
4½ this morning and what a wreck! The houses on that splendid
avenue are all riddled, the streets torn up, the trees cut off by
shells and presenting altogether a most dreadful aspect. The
barricade near the Arc is a monstrous one, twenty feet high and
nearly fifty feet wide. But it proved of no earthly use.*

*Since nine o'clock and up to this hour I have been down with
the troops expecting every hour that the Place de la Concorde
would be taken. I got tired of waiting at two o'clock and came
back to the Legation. At about nine o'clock the insurgents began to
bombard our part of the city from their batteries at Montmartre
and the shells came thick and fast. They have stopped for some time*

and the report is that the troops have taken that battery. If that
prove true, the business may be over before tomorrow morning,
for with the immense number of the troops coming in, said to be
80,000, they can soon surround the Place Vendôme, the Place de
la Concorde and the Hôtel de Ville. The Commune have been
completely surprised and they are now fighting for dear life, under
great disadvantages. There are a good many deserters in the
National Guard and the moment one is taken, he is shot at sight.
There are a good many sailors manning the insurgent gunboats
on the Seine . . . The day is magnificent and thank Heaven we
are safe in our quarter as it is all in the possession of the troops.
I can now go back to my house and we will have no more bombs.
I have no time now to express my detestation and abhorrence of
the Commune and the National Guard and the whole gang of
brigands and assassins who have held this city by the throat for
so long a time. A week longer all the great monuments would
have been destroyed, all foreigners pilloried. The wretches had
just got matters into working order. The Column had fallen,
Thiers' house had been demolished . . . Friday I saw myself the
scoundrels cutting out the great bas relief of Henry the 4th at
the Hôtel de Ville. It is a mistake—Montmartre is not taken,
for a shell from there has this instant burst right across the street
from the Legation. Everywhere the troops have been received with
enthusiasm by the few people remaining, and with the cry of 'Vive
la Ligne!' . . .

5:45 P.M. Have just taken a long ride . . . The havoc has been
dreadful—the houses are all torn to pieces, cannon dismantled,
dead rebels, &c, &c. One could hardly conceive such destruction.
We saw immense numbers of troops coming in and all through
the streets of Passy. Our house has escaped wonderfully. The piece
of shell that entered it did but little harm further than smashing
some windows. Returning to the Legation we find the fighting still

going on at the Place de la Concorde and it would seem this is to
be a long business . . .

Elihu Washburne, Paris—to Secretary of State Hamilton Fish,
Washington, D.C.—May 23, 1871

Tuesday morning. It seems difficult to get at anything reliable
this morning. The fight continues, and always in the same
neighborhood. The firing was terrific all last night. Shells from
Montmartre were continually falling in our quarter, but it is
extraordinary how little the damage has been. We can see from the
top of the Legation building that the red flag, *the hated emblem*
of assassination and pillage, anarchy, and disorder, still flies from
the Tuileries and from the Ministry of the Marine. The insurgents
are evidently making a desperate resistance . . .

Diary—May 23, 1871

The battle raging in the central part of the city. The troops have
made progress, but have not yet got the Place Vendôme and the
Concorde . . . A battery has been shelling this neighborhood from
the Tuileries for the last twelve hours.
   9:30 P.M.—The building of the Legion of Honour was on fire
at dinner time. Have just returned from Passy when I went to see
Marshal MacMahon at his headquarters about getting possession
of the prison of Mazas in order to save the life of the Archbishop
of Paris. He hopes they will be there in a day or two. At 4 this P.M.
Antoine and I went into the Avenue Montaigne and two shells
exploded not far from us.

In the midst of brutal street-to-street fighting, the desperate Communards finally embarked on what historian Alistair

Horne called a "scorched-earth policy," wickedly intent on burning the city to the ground. The Tuileries, part of the Palais-Royal, the Palais de Justice, and, finally, the Hôtel de Ville were all set ablaze. Wickham Hoffman would later write that in the last days of the Commune "petroleum became the madness of the hour," with wild rumors circulating about mobs of men, women, and children roaming the streets with petroleum-filled bottles trying to set all of Paris on fire.

Diary—May 24, 1871

What a horrid night. At one o'clock this morning I was awakened to see the Tuileries on fire. Dressing hastily I went into the street and then to the house of Dr. Samson where I got a very full view of it. We then thought we would go down nearer the scene and off we started down the Rue François Premier. We soon found difficulty in passing the sentinels and as the abuses were flying and the balls whistling we did not go farther than the foot of the Rue Bayard. We then returned to the Legation and went to the 6th story of the building which completely overlooks the city. The sight was literally awful. The lurid flames from the Tuileries lighted up half the Heavens. There were other fires also—the palace of the Legion of Honour, the Ministry of Finance, the État Major, had been burning since nine o'clock last night. At a little after two o'clock this night it seemed as if the Hôpital des Invalides was on fire and our hearts all sunk within us to think that that grand old home of the soldiers of France was also to be destroyed to gratify the rage and hatred of the demons whose crimes were appalling the world. But as the night wore [on] and daylight appeared it turned out that the fire was farther off . . .

9:30 A.M. Came to the Legation at half past eight. The morning is beautiful, but the thick smoke in the city obscures the

sun a little. We have the most terrible accounts of the fire. I will
try and get down town to find out something.

10 o'clock evening—Went down town at eleven o'clock and I
can give no adequate description of what I saw. All the fighting in
all the revolutions which have ever taken place in Paris, has been
mere child's play as compared with what has taken place since
Sunday and what is now going on. The fighting heretofore has
been confined to limited quarters in distant parts of the city, but
these battles for these days have been right in the heart of the city
and have been desperate to the extreme. You can scarcely imagine
the appearance of the streets where the barricades were and where
the fighting took place. The biggest sight was at the barricade
at the foot of the Boulevard Malesherbes and it lasted two days.
It was the key of the insurgent's position. The sidewalks of that
magnificent Boulevard were all covered with horses, baggage
wagons, cannon, caissons &c. The houses all riddled and battered,
the trees all torn to pieces and the branches in the street. Very near
was the dead body of a National Guard . . . Went as far as the
burning Tuileries, the front all falling in and the flames bursting
out in another part of the building. The whole appearance
dreadful. Fires in all directions raging—many of them under the
guns of the insurgents so that they cannot be put out.

That night Washburne scribbled a painful note to his twelve-
year-old daughter, Susan.

Elihu Washburne—to Susan Washburne, Vieille Église—May 24,
1871, Wednesday afternoon, 3½ o'clock

This has been a horrible night. I was awakened at one o'clock to see
the Tuileries on fire. At this moment the building seems entirely
consumed and the fire appears to be spreading to the Louvre.

*Several other buildings have been burned and others are still on
fire—the palace of the Legion of Honour, the Ministry of Finance,
the État Major. I have been watching from the top story of the
Legation Building. The horrid flames, the raging battles, the
roar of the cannon . . . have all contributed to make this a historic
night. The insurgents have had a battery at the Tuileries which
has been sending shells to our neighborhood all the time for the last
twenty-four hours. It has not fired now for an hour and I guess it
has been silenced. Tremendous firing in another part of the city
and the windows of the Legation shake. I think the Place de la
Concorde and the Place Vendôme have been taken. I fear that the
buildings on the Rue de Rivoli are on fire. I shall hope to get out
on Saturday. Kissings and blessings for you all.*

As the government troops battled their way into the city, they
arrested anyone suspected of being a Communard. On the
Place de l'Opéra, Washburne saw a group of some 500 men,
women, and children indiscriminately arrested and forced to
march to Versailles. Others were shot on sight. Wickham Hoffman recalled "wholesale butcheries committed by the troops,"
who believed that every insurgent was "an incarnate devil."
Young children suspected of carrying petroleum to burn buildings were executed on the spot.

**Elihu Washburne, Paris—to Secretary of State Hamilton Fish,
Washington, D.C.—May 25, 1871**

*When I closed my dispatch last night it was fire and battle. It is
the same this morning. There were frightful burnings all night.
The great Hôtel de Ville, with all its traditions and souvenirs
of history, exist no longer . . . All has been the work of organized
incendiarism, and the insurrectionists have done everything in*

their power to destroy Paris. If the entry of the troops had been delayed much longer, they would certainly have succeeded . . .

The state of feeling now existing in Paris is fearful beyond description. Passing events have filled the whole population opposed to the Commune with horror and rage. Arrests are made by the wholesale, of the innocent as well as the guilty. Last night four Americans—two gentlemen and two ladies— innocent as yourself of all complicity with the insurrection, were seized, while dining at a restaurant, and marched through the streets to one of the military posts. They sent word to me as soon as possible of their arrest, and I lost no time in going to their relief . . .

I went down in the city this afternoon to see for myself what was the progress of events . . . I passed up the Rue de Rivoli by the smoking ruins of the Tuileries, and had the inexpressible pleasure of seeing for myself that the Louvre, with all its untold and incalculable treasures, had been preserved. As I continued up the street, it seemed as if I were following in the track of an army . . .

I have not time now to speak more fully of the scenes of carnage, fire, and blood of which Paris has been the theater for the last four days. They are without parallel in all its history . . . The fighting has been long, desperate, and persistent. The insurgents have fought at every step with the fury of despair. Even as I write, at the hour of midnight, the contest is not yet ended, for I hear the booming of the cannon beyond the "Place de la Bastille." The government troops have displayed great bravery, and have never for a moment recoiled before the formidable and deadly barricades of the insurgents. They have shown the spirit of the old French army . . .

That same night Washburne sent a "private" note to Secretary Fish with a souvenir of the Commune.

Elihu Washburne, Paris—to Secretary of State Hamilton Fish, Washington, D.C.—May 25, 1871, Midnight

I have neither been excited, nor frightened during all these shocking events, but my time has been completely taken up by the constant calls upon me. When at the smoldering ruins of the Hôtel de Ville this afternoon, I tore from the wall of a house in the neighborhood the enclosed handbill, which is the last note, not of the "dying swan" but the dying Commune. It will have a historic interest.

On May 26, Washburne drafted another dispatch to the Secretary of State with this dire report.

Elihu Washburne, Paris—to Secretary of State Hamilton Fish, Washington, D.C.—May 26, 1871

The fighting is still going on this forenoon in the remote parts of the city, and new fires have broken out. I have no news of the fate of the Archbishop, but the general belief is that all the hostages have been shot . . .

As the final savage battles continued throughout the city, Raoul Rigault was as defiant and sadistic as ever, rushing everywhere and demanding his "assassins" carry out his last-minute "bloody decrees" of death. "His activity in these moments in the work of blood was something amazing," Washburne would recall.

Rigault was determined that if the Commune were destroyed, the hostages should perish with it. Only days earlier, on May 22, and unbeknown to Washburne, Rigault had ordered the execution of the Archbishop and sixty-three others held at La Roquette prison.

Diary—May 28, 1871

*Sunday morning. Yesterday I went out to Versailles and returned
late in the afternoon. I first went to the headquarters to ascertain
the fate of the Archbishop, but they knew nothing . . . The fighting
went on all day yesterday . . . the insurgents holding desperately,
but always driven back. There was firing all last night and it
continues this morning showing that the insurrection is not
suppressed. As soon as I came to the Legation this morning I sent a
messenger to General MacMahon to enquire after the Archbishop
and he has this moment returned with the horrible news that he
was shot yesterday at the prison. Oh! Heavens, what horror! No
language can characterize the acts of these barbarians . . . Were
there ever such atrocities heard of in the history of civilization as
Paris has been the theater of for the last eight days? They make
the blood curdle. I had become intensely interested in the fate of
the good old Archbishop and had prayed that his life might be
spared . . . I saw him at half past four or five o'clock last Sunday
afternoon. I had been to see him on Friday and found him so
feeble that I thought I would go again on Sunday to see how he
was. The Versailles troops had already entered the gate of St.
Cloud on the other extreme of the city, but of course no one knew
it where we were. The National Guard delegated to the prison
was drunk and everything was very disagreeable inside. They
would not let me enter the cell of the Archbishop as I had been
in the habit of doing, but insisted he should come out to see me
in a vacant cell. I regretted that for I knew how weak and feeble
he was. But he soon came in, looking very badly, but with the
same pleasant countenance and the same warm thanks. I told
him I was sorry I could bring him no news, but that I had felt so
anxious about his health that I had come to see how he was. He
replied that he was a little better. We talked of the situation and*

*of the probabilities of the speedy delivery of Paris. I told him I
thought the end was near and that I hoped I should soon have the
pleasure of seeing him at liberty. He replied that I was always so
amiable and so kind and that if it were the will of God that he
should be spared that it would be his greatest pleasure to tell the
world of all I had done for him . . . I think he had a prescience of
his coming fate.*

**Elihu Washburne, Paris—to Adele Washburne, Vieille Église—
May 28, 1871**

*The insurrection is suppressed but alas! The poor old Archbishop
was shot on Tuesday night last with some 70 priests. The horrors
have been shocking beyond expression. There is great prejudice here
against the Americans and indeed all foreigners but it will soon
blow over. The Versailles people don't like very much that I stayed
here during the insurrection. But I cannot help that. I had to do
my duty . . .*

Diary—May 29, 1871

*After eight of the most horrible days the world has ever known,
the . . . suppression of the insurrection was finished yesterday
afternoon. The whole thing has been awful beyond description
and perhaps human belief. There has been nothing but a general
butchery since Wednesday last: men, women and children,
innocent and guilty alike. The rage of the soldiers and the people
knows no bounds. No punishment is too great, or too speedy, for
the guilty, but there is no discrimination. Let a person utter a
word of sympathy, or even let a man be pointed out to the crowd
as a sympathizer and his life is gone. In fact let a cry be raised
against any man no matter how strong he may be against the*

*Commune and his life is in danger. A well dressed, respectable
looking man was torn into a hundred pieces . . . by the crowds
yesterday, for expressing a word of sympathy for a man who was
a prisoner and being beaten almost to death. Mr. Carter, an
American merchant here, a thoroughly peaceable and inoffensive
man, had a cry raised upon him yesterday in the Boulevard
Haussmann, was set upon by the crowd who yelled* a mort, a mort
*and struck him and beat him. His life was only spared by some
line officers who surrounded him and rescued him from the very
jaws of death.*

**Elihu Washburne, Paris—to Secretary of State Hamilton Fish,
Washington, D.C.—May 31, 1871**

*After an insurrection of seventy-one days, such as has never been
known in the annals of civilization, Paris was finally delivered
on Sunday, the 28th instant; the last positions held in the city by
the Commune having been taken, and their last troops captured
at four o'clock on the afternoon of that day . . . The reign of
the Commune for ten weeks, pursuing its career of murder,
assassination, pillage, robbery, blasphemy, and terror, finally
expired in blood and flame . . . The incredible enormities of the
Commune, their massacre of the Archbishop of Paris and the other
hostages, their countless murders of other persons who refused to
join them in their fiendish work, their horrid and well organized
plans of incendiarism intended to destroy almost the entire city,
and which resulted in the destruction of so many of the great
monuments of Paris, are crimes which will never die . . .*

That same day he sent a dispatch to fellow diplomat George
Bancroft, the American Minister to Germany.

**Elihu Washburne, Paris—to Honorable George Bancroft,
May 31, 1871**

*I remained here during the whole period of the infernal
insurrection and I saw it go out in fire and blood and amid
scenes which have no parallel in the history of civilization. No
consideration on earth, except one of the highest, that of the
discharge of a sacred public duty, could ever induce me to go
through [that] which I have passed through for the last nine
months, and more particularly the last ten weeks. But it is a
pleasure for me to know that I have been able to protect the lives
and property of all the Americans and I believe all the Germans
in Paris, but it has been at a fearful risk . . .*

*The suppression of the insurrection brings with it a military
rule (perhaps necessary) of terrible severity. No persons are
permitted to leave Paris at present and I do not know how long
people are to be shut in . . .*

Two days later a worn and distraught Washburne visited the
empty prison cell of the Archbishop of Paris.

Diary—June 2, 1871

*Things are greatly quieted down. The indiscriminate killing
and shooting has stopped. All Paris has come out of doors, the
streets are crowded. The smoldering fires are being extinguished
and the tottering walls pulled down. The shops are being opened
and omnibuses and carriages are moving. I made a long trip
yesterday—went to the prison La Roquette, saw the cell from
which the Archbishop was taken to be shot—saw the very spot
in the prison yard where he was shot, standing against a wall.
His abdomen was then ripped open by the fiends and his body*

with others thrown into a common ditch at Père la Chaise
[Cemetery] . . .

Ten days earlier—just after he had ordered the execution of the
Archbishop of Paris—Raoul Rigault had taken to the streets,
directing and rallying the Communards in their final desperate
struggle against the government troops. But as the Commune
disintegrated, Rigault fled the scene, hiding out in a hotel
under a false name until hunted down by the Versailles troops.
After being seized and dragged into the streets, he cried out,
"Vive la Commune!" Moments later he was executed on the
spot, shot through the head several times. He was dumped
in a nearby gutter and, for two days, Rigault's body lay there,
kicked, stripped, and spat on by disgusted passersby.

EPILOGUE

On the morning of June 7, 1871, Elihu Washburne attended the funeral services of Archbishop Darboy at Notre-Dame Cathedral. At ten o'clock the Archbishop's cortege, drawn by six horses, made its way to the church. Cannons fired in tribute from the Invalides and spectators, overcome with "regret and pity," lined the streets. At Notre-Dame the Bishop of Versailles and the Papal Nuncio, Monsignor Chigi, presided at the service. Washburne was deeply moved by the ceremony, describing it as "one of the most emotional and imposing funeral services that I ever attended."

Afterward, letters from Catholic organizations everywhere expressed thanks to the American Minister for his efforts to save Darboy's life. The Catholic Union of New York wrote:

> You beheld around you God's temples desecrated, and the ministers of His Holy religion hunted down like wild beasts, by an infuriated rabble. Eminent among the victims was the venerable Archbishop of Paris. He was "sick and in prison,"

and in obedience to the divine commandment, you visited him;
sympathized with him in his sufferings, consoled him in his af-
fliction, and endeavored, at no small risk to yourself, to save his
precious life.

Although Washburne knew those responsible for Darboy's
execution would "excite eternal execration," such messages
of support did little to comfort him. For years afterward he
would still feel the pain of the Archbishop's death. "Alas!
Could such efforts at all times have been successful," he wrote
in 1875, "the world might not have been called upon to witness one of the most tragic and fearful events in history, the
foul murder of the Archbishop of Paris."

That same day Count Bismarck sent a letter to Minister
Washburne thanking him for all he had done on behalf of the
trapped German nationals in Paris:

> His Majesty has commanded me to convey to your Excellency
> the grateful acknowledgment for the zeal and kindness you have
> devoted to the interests of the German residents under circum-
> stances of extraordinary difficulty, and with corresponding sacri-
> fice of time and personal comfort.

For weeks after the end of the reign of terror, generous
praise about Washburne poured into Paris. One American
paper noted:

> Paris was deserted by the titled and great. It witnessed starva-
> tion and death, and all manner of disaster . . . Mr. Washburne
> still remained at his post, throwing himself between the ranks of
> arrayed Frenchmen, fighting in a horrible death struggle, saving
> all that he could save . . .

The *New York Tribune* wrote: "We do not recall an instance in our diplomacy of a more brilliant and successful performance of duty in circumstances of such gravity and delicacy . . ."

Perhaps the finest tribute came from one who had stayed by his side throughout the siege and terror. Months after the fall of the Commune, Frank Moore, Washburne's Assistant Secretary for the Legation, wrote to his wife:

> Hasn't our Minister in Paris done splendidly? By the use of common sense, a kindly generous disposition and a true appreciation of the right, he has during the past year brought more credit to our government and people at home than they can ever reward him for. His name is on every tongue and I am sure that he will not escape the fate of other honest men for whom thousands of boy babies have been and will affectionately and admiringly be named.

"We have been through fire and blood here," Washburne wrote to friends in mid-June. "I hope now Paris may have some peace and quiet."

The city was in ruins. "Paris, the Paris of civilization, is no more," wrote the *Times* of London. "Dust and ashes, tottering walls, twisted or molten ironwork, smolder and stench are all that remain . . . [T]he terrible end of this chapter may be only the beginning of one sadder still. Time alone can tell."

But miraculously, within days the city came back to life. "There has been a marvelous change in Paris," Washburne reported to Secretary of State Fish on June 2. "[T]he whole city is alive with people . . . the smoldering fires have been extinguished and the tottering walls pulled down. Nearly all the barricades have disappeared."

As Paris sprung back to life, Washburne rejoined his family out at Vieille Église, experiencing great joy in spending time with Adele and the children once again. "It is a healthy spot and the children are in perfect health and growing like pigs," he wrote a friend.

Now, with the turmoil in Paris at an end, Washburne himself was ready for an extended rest. "I am a good deal used up and run down," he wrote a friend. "From 193 [pounds] I am down to 176." In early July he left Paris, on his way to the curing springs of Carlsbad. He was thrilled to be away, and by late August the "wonderful waters" of Bohemia had restored him to health. "I have not been as well for five years," he proudly told a friend. And by the fall he was pleased to report back to America that life in Paris was pleasant once again. "All is quiet on the banks of the Seine," he told an old colleague in Washington.

On October 8, 1871, the city of Chicago was consumed by fire. For two days the "Great Fire" raged through the city killing some 300 people, leaving nearly 100,000 homeless, $222 million in property destroyed, and nearly 4 square miles of the city in ruins.

When Washburne received word in Paris about the "awful calamity" that had struck Chicago, he was devastated:

> Our great and beautiful city, to which we have been allied by so many associations, is literally in ashes [he wrote a friend]. It is such destruction as has never been recorded in human annals. Nearly all our mutual friends must be ruined. It has made Mrs. W[ashburne] and myself nearly sick . . . Indeed, it is impossible for us to comprehend the long train of horrors and suffering that must follow that awful tragedy.

Washburne immediately called a meeting of Americans in Paris to solicit funds for the suffering in Chicago. He raised

$30,000 in contributions* which he immediately transferred by telegraph to Chicago.

Despite these successful efforts in Paris, Washburne still hoped he could do more, telling friends back home he wished he could be there "to put my shoulder to the wheel" to help in the rebuilding of Chicago.

A month later Washburne's American friends in Paris held a dinner in his honor for the "valuable services" he had provided during the siege and Commune. The dinner was held at Washburne's home, which was "brilliantly lit up for the occasion and tastefully decorated with American flags." In attendance were Dr. Thomas Evans, Charles Moulton, and many others from the American colony who gathered to pay tribute to their friend. He was presented with a "superb service of silver plate"—some 213 pieces in all—manufactured by Tiffany & Company in New York.

Over the next several years Washburne watched Paris steadily come back to life. By late 1872 work began on restoring the Vendôme Column, toppled during the Commune; the Grand Opera House was reopened; repairs were under way on the Palais-Royal; and some forty swans were scattered about the city's public parks to replace those eaten during the siege.

Meanwhile, Washburne spent time with his family traveling about Europe—making trips to Nice and Bonn—and attending to his ceremonial duties as Minister to France. He hosted a number of formal dinners in Paris, including one in August of 1872 for the famous British explorer Henry Morton Stanley, who only ten months before had successfully located Dr. David Livingstone in the tropical forests of Tanganyika. He also helped

*The equivalent of nearly $500,000 in current dollars.

promote a bold and ambitious idea by French sculptor Frédéric-Auguste Bartholdi to design and create a "Statue of Liberty" as a gift to America from the people of France.

In the fall of 1872, Washburne returned to America for the first time since leaving to serve in France. He traveled briefly to Galena, where he was met at the train station by a huge crowd of old friends who stood for hours to greet him. Days later he made the long journey to Livermore, Maine, to see his eighty-seven-year-old father. Washburne found him to be "blind, a little deaf, but [his] intellect, bright and disposition cheerful."

It was the last time Washburne would see his father alive. Four years later, on September 1, 1876, Israel Washburn, Sr., passed away. During the dark days in Paris, Washburne had thought often of his father, and now he was gone. "The hour has come finally to strike. Celestial spirits at last beckoned our kind, good father to a brighter and better world," he told Adele. Though his father's death brought "a pang of grief" to the entire family, he told his brother Cadwallader:

> In dying he has left to his children the most priceless legacy of an honored and well spent life . . . Well will it be for his children if, when they should be called hence, they can leave to those that survive and come after them, as clear a record and as spotless a name.

In the fall of 1877 after Rutherford B. Hayes had succeeded Ulysses S. Grant as President, Elihu Washburne stepped down from his post in Paris. In accepting his resignation on behalf of the President, Secretary of State William Evarts expressed to Washburne an "appreciation of the faithful manner" in which he had performed his duties and a recognition that those "services . . . must ever remain on record as among the most important rendered by the diplomatic representatives of this Government."

Upon his departure from Paris, a large group of friends bade farewell to Washburne at the train station.

> The passengers on the train . . . took off their hats as a mark of respect and many of them, who had never seen or known him, asked to be presented and shake his hand [reported the *Chicago Tribune*]. Mr. Washburne and family . . . received, not without some emotion, these marks of attention . . . As the train moved out of the depot, there was a general raising of hats and waving of handkerchiefs, and groups stood watching the train until it was out of sight . . .

He and his family traveled by way of Le Havre to Southampton, where they boarded the steamer *Neckar* for New York. Upon Washburne's arrival, the press noted with pride the return of the American Minister:

> Mr. Washburne has returned from France . . . [He] is not a scholar, but a plain Western man who . . . has an unusual amount of that practical every day common sense for which the American character is distinguished. There is no flummery about him, no pretense, no palaver. He wore no beads, nor ribbons, and [had] no coat-of-arms painted on his carriage. He talked the plainest sort of English, and took off his coat and worked in his shirt-sleeves, doing the thing that most needed to be done . . .

Washburne had served his nation faithfully for twenty-six years, and now he was private citizen Washburne, heading home to the little town he had left nearly nine years before.

Washburne and his family arrived by train in Galena, Illinois, on October 16. An immense crowd stood in heavy rain to greet them at the station. That evening a formal welcome was staged at Turner Hall attended by a packed gathering of "all classes of . . . citizens irrespective of nationality and politics." The stage in the hall was decorated with American, French, and German flags, and a huge banner overhead proclaimed, "Galena honors the man who honors the nation."

As Washburne entered the hall, a band struck up "La Marseillaise." Speeches in tribute followed and then Washburne rose to speak. After thanking the people of Galena for the "hand of friendship which [had] never been withdrawn," he recounted his memories of first arriving in Galena and the struggle he had endured to make a go of it.

He concluded by saying:

I have long looked forward to the period of my return home with feelings of pleasure, but all my anticipations have been far more than realized by the goodwill and hearty friendship with which I have been welcomed back. While I guard so many pleasant souvenirs of my official residence in Paris, and while I severed with regret so many agreeable associations formed with the Americans abroad and with the French people whom Dr. Franklin once so justly described as being, "A pleasant people to live among," I hailed the approaching day when I could turn my face towards my own country and home . . . I pray that you will believe me that wherever I am, and whatever fate may betide me, all my aspirations will go up for the happiness and prosperity of all the people of Galena . . .

When Washburne had accepted the post as Minister to France, he was thrilled to be leaving the rough-and-tumble life of Washington politics. In fact, many times he expressed deep regret in ever giving up his law practice. "That little old law library I had in Galena has been pretty well-scattered since the time I was fool enough to abandon a noble profession and enter into political life," he wrote an old colleague in 1871.

However, in 1880, out of loyalty to an old friend, he was once again dragged into politics and, to his deep regret, ended up destroying one of the most cherished friendships of his life.

Beginning in 1873, while Washburne was still Minister to France, rumors had circulated about him as a future candidate for President or Vice President. Such speculation continued for the next several years until, in 1876, he flatly told a reporter, "I am not vain enough to suppose that my name can ever figure seriously in that direction." However, as the 1880 presidential campaign approached, newspapers and politicians throughout the country pushed once more for him to accept the nomination of the Republican Party for President. The *Boston Herald* noted that he had "elements of political strength not possessed by any other man in the United States." The *New York Sun* touted him as "by far the strongest man" that the party could pick.

Another paper, in an obvious slight to former President Ulysses S. Grant and his scandal-ridden administration, wrote of Washburne: "He is one of the few American politicians who stands before the public pure and undefiled . . . With Washburne as the standard bearer . . . we would have a character needing no whitewash and an easy walk over any leader the Democrats could put forth."

Meanwhile, Grant himself, who had just returned from a triumphant world tour, was hinting that he might be interested in seeking a third term as President. (He was President from 1869 to 1877.) Although there was an initial surge of support for his candidacy, many in the party were adamantly opposed to his nomination.

Washburne himself thought his old friend was making a grave mistake and would be defeated. He knew many would oppose a third term as a matter of principle—seeing it as a "menace to our form of government"—but he also felt his old friend was simply being used by old cronies in an attempt to regain power in Washington.

Once Grant signaled his desire for the nomination, Washburne nevertheless agreed to support his bid, helping to direct the Grant campaign in Illinois and offering advice and counsel to the candidate. However, as the convention grew nearer, Grant's candidacy began to lose steam. Anti–third-term groups mounted opposition to him and many party leaders pulled away from his campaign. One Republican Party leader told Washburne: "I shall vote the Republican ticket down to the last constable, but I shall never vote for Grant electors." The *Philadelphia Telegraph* declared: "The people have had enough of him."

As support for Grant began to dwindle, there were "scattered voices" heard around the country once again pushing Washburne for the nomination and promoting him as a "dark horse" candidate. Washburne, however, dismissed all such encouragement and remained loyal to Grant. In May 1880, only weeks before the convention, Washburne told a reporter that under no circumstances was he a candidate for President and that he was "for Grant, first last and all the time."

Some in Grant's inner circle, however, grew suspicious of the talk about a Washburne candidacy, hinting that he was "guilty of duplicity" and secretly seeking the nomination himself. In fact, the *St. Louis Globe-Democrat* openly "accused Washburne of plotting his own candidacy while avowing support" for Grant.

As voting at the convention got under way, Grant was at home in Galena. On the first ballot he received 304 votes—the most of any candidate—but not enough to secure the nomination. For days the convention was deadlocked, shifting back and forth between Grant, James G. Blaine, John Sherman, and others, until finally James A. Garfield secured the nomination on the thirty-sixth ballot. During the balloting, Washburne had received a total of 40 votes "in spite of his own repeated declaration that he was not a candidate."

After his defeat Grant was "deeply disappointed" and, astoundingly, allowed family and advisors to convince him that his old friend Washburne had been "guilty of a kind of personal treason" in the campaign. Grant's son, Fred, publicly proclaimed that Washburne was "a God damned liar and fraud."

Grant himself would never speak of Washburne without "bitterness," and the two old friends from Galena would never talk to each other again.

In 1880, Elihu Washburne was sixty-four years old. Despite occasional bouts of ill health, he was still as active and strong as ever:

> Washburne's face and form call up the idea of granite-cliffs and clear-sky—not of wool-bags on a wet day [noted one Chicago reporter]. He . . . knows just what he wants to say, and says it; just where he wants to go, and goes there by the most direct-route, without waste of nervous force. His voice [has] the ring of perfect self-control and consequent command.

Since returning from Paris, he had spent a great deal of time busying "himself with the pen," delivering lectures throughout the country, mostly about his years in Paris, and publishing articles about many great figures of the past, including Thomas Paine and Abraham Lincoln. He also began work on his memoir, *Recollections of a Minister to France, 1869–1877,* which was initially published in *Scribner's Magazine* during the winter and spring of 1887.

He and Adele eventually bought a house in Chicago, but Washburne used it mostly as "his headquarters, a place to which he returned from time to time from his frequent journeys." But being in the city also put them near their son Hempstead, who had become a prominent lawyer in Chicago and who, like his father some three decades before, would eventually enter politics.

On December 17, 1886, Washburne's oldest son, Gratiot, died in Louisville, Kentucky. He was on business as Secretary of the American Exposition in London and died suddenly from a stroke. He was only thirty-seven years old.

In his diary Washburne wrote, "Our hearts are all broken." He was devastated and "prostrate" with grief at the death of the son who was by his side in Paris throughout the bloody days of 1870–1871. "The world is nothing to me anymore," he told one of his daughters. "The light of my life has gone out . . ."

Just three months later on March 20, 1887, his beloved wife, Adele, died in Chicago. Days earlier she had suffered a sudden attack of "gastric fever" and never recovered. She was sixty-five years old. After a memorial service in Chicago, she was taken to Galena and buried in the family plot at Greenwood Cemetery.

Washburne was "crushed into the earth" by her death and was in deep agony for months afterward. Feeling alone and adrift, he told his daughter Marie: "Where I shall go and what I shall do it is impossible for me to tell. I sometimes think I will take a sea voyage in order to get away from myself, but I know nothing further than that I am the most miserable man on the face of the earth. Pray write me oftener and try and lift me out of the despair which overwhelms me . . ." Grief-stricken and with his own health deteriorating, Washburne moved in with Hempstead and his wife at their home on Maple Street in Chicago.

That fall, on the afternoon of September 21, only seven months after Adele's death, Washburne was found in his room "lying on the bed unconscious [and] breathing heavily." Diagnosed with "congestion of the brain," for days Washburne passed in and out of consciousness.

After several weeks Washburne's condition improved and, as he regained strength, the doctors became hopeful that he might soon make a full recovery.

On the morning of October 23, Washburne rose from bed, dressed himself, and called for one of his servants to give him a shave. Once seated in the chair, Washburne felt a sharp pain in his chest and had to be helped back to his bed. Surrounded by members of his family, Washburne died a short time later. He was seventy-one years old.

The next day, the Department of State in Washington, D.C., suspended all business and the department's building was "draped in mourning." President Grover Cleveland ordered all American diplomatic and consular offices around the world to exhibit similar "expressions of sorrow" for the former Minister.

In Chicago an immense funeral service was held in Washburne's honor at the Unity Church. The building was "crowded to overflowing, [with] a large number of people being obliged to stand in the aisles and vestibule." Washburne's casket was plain and black, "draped with a United States flag." Facing the congregation was a platform bearing a huge American flag in the center and, in tribute, the tricolor of France to the right and the black eagle of Germany to the left. On an arrangement of flowers near the altar were the words, "Washburne, Finis."

After the service Washburne's casket was drawn through the city by "four jet black horses" with the "muffled drums" of a band signaling its approach to the train depot. The procession was an "impressive and imposing pageant," led by a "platoon of police" and members of various local German societies carrying torches in Washburne's honor.

At the Illinois Central station, Washburne's coffin was placed on a train bound for Galena.

Sixteen years earlier, as Minister to France, Elihu Washburne had been trapped in Paris, caught in the midst of insurrection, bloodshed, and a savage civil war. One night, while overcome with despair about the brutality and inhumanity all about him, he sat down to write an entry in his diary. As he began, his thoughts wandered back to memories of Galena, Illinois, and the day he first arrived with no friends or money and only a few items of clothing packed by a "careful mother."

Diary—April 1, 1871

It is thirty-one years this day since I arrived in Galena. I was a passenger on the little steamwheeler "Pike," Capt. Powers. We arrived on the little levee before daylight and when I got up in the morning it was bright and clear—and looked out upon the town [and] I shall never forget the impression made upon me. The mud in the streets knee deep, the log and frame buildings, all huddled together. The river full of steamboats, the discharging of freight, busy men running to and fro and the yelling of the draymen. Those were the high days of old Galena . . .

With nothing "to aid him . . . except hard experience and a high resolve" to succeed, he had always cherished the "hand of friendship" extended to him by the people of Galena.

Now, nearly fifty years later, he had returned.

Washburne's casket arrived at the Galena train station early on the morning of October 27 and was taken to lie in state at Turner Hall, where he had spoken many times during his long public career. The hall was "elaborately decorated," with the flags of America and Germany once again flanking the coffin.

After the service his casket was drawn through town followed by the longest funeral procession Galena had ever seen. He was taken to the family plot at Greenwood Cemetery, just outside of town, to join Adele and Gratiot. He was buried there on a small hill overlooking that "little, rugged, great-hearted" town he had come to know as home.

ACKNOWLEDGMENTS

First, and foremost, I would like to thank David McCullough. For nearly thirty years, I have had the honor and great pleasure to work as his research assistant on a variety of projects. In that time he has been a true mentor, a guiding spirit, a fellow adventurer, and, above all, an inspiration and true, steadfast friend. The idea for this book originated while David was writing his book *The Greater Journey,* which includes chapters on Washburne's life and his heroic years in Paris. I shall always be grateful to him for suggesting the book to Simon & Schuster and for his guidance and encouragement along the way.

I also want to thank David's wife, Rosalee, who during my three decades of research adventures with David has always been kind, thoughtful, and of unending good cheer.

My editor at Simon & Schuster, Bob Bender, and publisher Jonathan Karp deserve special thanks as well. When David McCullough first approached them about publishing the Washburne diary, they welcomed the idea without hesitation, despite my being a novice writer. Throughout the entire process, Bob has been patient and has provided wise counsel.

To Michael Korda, my good friend, mentor, and patron, I also owe a special thanks. For years he has provided me with encouragement, invaluable assistance, and, most important, the gift of friendship.

Jeffrey Flannery, archivist extraordinaire and good friend, helped unravel the mystery of the Washburne diary at the Library of Congress. He is a resourceful, indefatigable, and keen-eyed archivist. I am also thankful to Gerard Gawault and Patrick Kerwin at the Library of Congress, who were both extremely helpful to me while working with the Washburne Collection.

At the Washburn-Norlands homestead and archives in Livermore, Maine, many kind people opened the doors to the research facilities, allowing David and me to dig deeper into the Washburne story. Sheri Leahan and Jennifer Colby-Morse have been especially helpful. Unfortunately, the joy of this project was tempered by the sad loss of Nancey Drinkwine, who passed away before this book was completed. Her support at Norlands during the early part of this project was a special delight.

Terry Miller and Jamie Dimke were especially kind and helpful during a research visit to Washburne's hometown, Galena, Illinois. I can't thank them enough for the time they took to show my wife, Rebecca, and me around town, and to provide insight and valuable background information about the history of Galena, the Washburne family, and the relationship between Grant and Washburne.

Throughout the drafting and editing process, there were countless people who reviewed and helped with manuscript drafts, providing invaluable guidance and suggestions along the way. They include: Nathaniel Philbrick, Dorie Lawson, James Eastwood, Richard Moe, Bryson Clevenger, Celeste Walker, Simon Watts, and, particularly, Keith Wamsley and Jonathan Levin, who both provided counsel, advice, and editorial criticism, all of which helped shape the final work. I would also like to thank Johanna Li and Gypsy da Silva at Simon & Schuster for all their help in finalizing the book.

I must also express my sincere gratitude and joy to all those individuals who have allowed me, through good luck and good fortune, to be a part of their own creative works, whether books or films, over the last thirty years. Each of them, in his or her own way, has taught me the thrill and joy of archival and historical research and a deep respect for their craft, especially the hard work, patience, and long hours that are essential to any creative process. They include: David McCullough, Michael Korda, Ken Burns, Evan Thomas, Nathaniel Philbrick, Michael Beschloss, Dorie Lawson, George Englund, Jeff Shesol, Mark Salter,

Sally Bedell Smith, Geoffrey C. Ward, Jeff Nussbaum, Richard Moe, and Caroline Kennedy.

Finally, I would like to thank my father and mother, Clarence and Mary Hill, who early on instilled in me a love of history and books. And, above all, to my wife, Rebecca Purdy, who stood by me while I struggled to tell the story of Elihu Washburne's heroic life and was always there with invaluable guidance, suggestions, love, and support throughout.

ILLUSTRATION CREDITS

NOTES

Prologue

PAGE

1 *During the worst days:* Hoffman, *Camp, Court, and Siege,* 227.

2 *Reminiscent of the brutal Commune de Paris:* Horne, *The Fall of Paris,* 293.

3 *During the final bloody week:* Ibid., 15.

3 *"The gaudy butterflies":* Undated article, *Chicago Journal,* Scrapbooks, Washburne Papers, Library of Congress.

3 *"This is my place where duty calls me":* Hunt, *Israel, Elihu, and Cadwallader Washburn,* 250.

3 *Despite all the hardships and dangers:* Hoffman, *Camp, Court, and Siege,* 271–272.

4 *"With no experience in such matters":* Hunt, *Israel, Elihu, and Cadwallader Washburn,* 252.

4 *"a denizen of the rough west":* Undated article, Scrapbooks, Washburne Papers, Library of Congress.

5 *His hair was "iron gray":* Hunt, *Israel, Elihu, and Cadwallader Washburn,* 194.

5 *His eyes were "large and full":* Ibid.

5 *"The model is Yankee":* Ibid., 191–192.

5 *Although "without fortune in dollars":* Undated news article, Scrapbooks, Washburne Papers, Library of Congress.

5 *Elihu later added the* e: Hunt, *Israel, Elihu, and Cadwallader Washburn,* 155.

5 *The family, he would recall:* Ibid., 158.

5 *His father, Israel:* Ibid.

6 *Elihu, twelve years old by now:* Ibid., 157.

6 *"With me memories are awakened":* Elihu Washburne to Adele Washburne, Sept. 2, 1876, Washburne Papers, Library of Congress.

6 *Although of little education:* Hunt, *Israel, Elihu, and Cadwallader Washburn,* 158.

6 *She could be "firm and resolute":* Ibid.

6 *"When I think of her labors":* Ibid.

6 *"I dug up stumps":* Ibid., 159.

6 *"I was called up every morning":* Ibid., 158.

7 *His grandfather:* Ibid., 156.

7 *He would never forget:* Ibid.

7 *"The sad and heavy months":* Ibid.

7 *"Witnessing the poverty":* Ibid., 159.

7 *"I determined to shift for myself":* Ibid.

7 *During the next several years:* Ibid., 161.

8 *More than just a teacher:* Ibid., 164.

8 *"A fellow who comes":* Ibid., 314.

8 *I was a passenger:* Ibid., 172.

8 *He was a "green Yankee boy":* Elihu Washburne to Miss Clarke, March 18, 1872, Washburne Papers, Library of Congress.

8 *In Galena, Washburne found:* Hunt, *Israel, Elihu, and Cadwallader Washburn,* 176.

9 *He took a room:* Ibid., 172.

9 *At night he would be kept awake:* Elihu Washburne to H. H. Houghton, March 6, 1871, Washburne Papers, Library of Congress.

9 *Washburne soon set to work:* Hunt, *Israel, Elihu, and Cadwallader Washburn,* 172.

9 *Galena was a "horrid rough place":* Ibid.

9 *Her father, Colonel Henry Gratiot:* Marsh, *Galena, Illinois,* 25, 55.

9 *Adele was ten years younger:* Hunt, *Israel, Elihu, and Cadwallader*

Washburn, 182; undated article, Scrapbooks, Washburne Papers, Library of Congress.

9 *An early biographer wrote:* Hunt, *Israel, Elihu, and Cadwallader Washburn,* 179.

9 *Above all, she believed:* Ibid., 181.

10 *I made a canvass:* Washburne, *Recollections of a Minister to France,* Vol. I, 283.

10 *I called one afternoon:* Diary of Elihu Washburne, Dec. 28, 1870, Washburne Papers, Library of Congress.

12 *Finally, on November 2, 1852:* Washburne, *Recollections of a Minister to France,* Vol. I, 284.

12 *At the end of the day:* Ibid.

12 *The next day Washburne:* Hunt, *Israel, Elihu, and Cadwallader Washburn,* 173.

12 *Three other brothers:* Ibid., 174; McCullough, *The Greater Journey,* 275.

13 *Later, as chairman of the Committee on Appropriations:* Hunt, *Israel, Elihu, and Cadwallader Washburn,* 174.

13 *He was "one of the ablest":* Undated editorial, Scrapbooks, Washburne Papers, Library of Congress.

13 *"He steadily set his face":* Ibid.

13 *Others found him:* Welles, *Diary of Gideon Welles,* Vol. I, 234.

13 *At first, Washburne was hardly impressed:* Hunt, *Israel, Elihu, and Cadwallader Washburn,* 228.

13 *He delivered a speech:* Ibid., 190.

14 *In Baltimore, as his train:* Donald, *Lincoln,* 278.

14 *"The door of the President's house":* *Chicago Tribune,* Oct. 27, 1887.

14 *Washburne first met Ulysses S. Grant:* Hunt, *Israel, Elihu, and Cadwallader Washburn,* 231.

15 *"I can assure you":* Ibid., 233.

16 *Washburne, in the middle of the battle:* Ibid., 201.

16 *Never before had I such feelings:* Ibid.

16 *They jumped out and tried:* Ibid., 202.

16 *"A more sober set":* Ibid.

16 *"We will whip the traitors yet":* Ibid., 203.

17 *"We are in the midst":* Ibid., 219.

17 *"Such a long and awful":* Ibid., 220.

17 *After Lee surrendered:* Ibid., 222–223.

17 *As the rebel prisoners:* Ibid., 223.

17 *The news of Lincoln's death:* Ibid., 225–226.

17 *Selected as one of Lincoln's pallbearers:* Ibid., 227. A copy of Washburne's ticket designating him as one of Lincoln's pallbearers still exists in the Papers and Journals of Elihu Washburne, Washburn-Norlands Living History Center, Livermore, Maine.

18 *But soon, like Grant:* Ibid., 236–237.

18 *Let him be impeached:* Speech by Representative Elihu Washburne, delivered on the floor of the House of Representatives, Washington, D.C., Feb. 22, 1868.

18 *As the machine ticked away:* Hunt, *Israel, Elihu, and Cadwallader Washburn,* 242.

18 *"The little old library":* Ibid.

19 *"We felt pretty foxy":* Ibid.

19 *In one of his first Cabinet appointments:* As with most decisions of political leaders throughout history, there are inevitably varied voices and various versions of what actually occurred. It is no less true regarding the appointment of Elihu Washburne as Secretary of State. Chroniclers of the lives of Grant and Washburne suggest a host of scenarios regarding the rumors, events, and "contradictory statements" surrounding the appointment. For instance, some historians question whether the appointment was a complete surprise to Washburne, or whether he had some persuasive hand in the selection by his old friend Ulysses S. Grant. William McFeely, for instance, in his biography of Grant, raises the possibility that a "snap promise" to make Washburne Secretary of State was made "in a moment of exuberance and gratitude" to Washburne on the night of the election, a promise, McFeely suggests, which Grant soon regretted and then spent days before his inauguration persuading Washburne to "relinquish." (William McFeely, *Grant: A Biography.* New York: W. W. Norton, 1981, 295.) Others, however, suggest that Washburne and Grant actually discussed the appointment and that Washburne knew all along he would be selected. "The construction of a cabinet is an elaborate process involving discussion and consultation," argued Gaillard Hunt in his biography of the Washburns, "and it is improbable that Washburne did not know that he was to be Secretary of State." (Hunt, *Israel, Elihu, and Cadwallader Washburn,*

243.) Still others suggest a more elaborate scenario: that Washburne actually coveted the post of Minister to France because of a "desire to please his wife who was of French descent, his fondness for all things French, and the need to be near the hot springs of Carlsbad for health reasons." A temporary appointment as Secretary of State, some suggest, would greatly enhance his prestige in Paris after becoming Minister, and Washburne asked Grant to appoint him Secretary for a few days as a "personal favor." (See Jean Edward Smith, *Grant*. New York: Simon & Schuster, 2001, 470–471.) McFeely, however, rejects this theory. "The proposition . . . that Washburne was given the senior position in the cabinet in order to enhance his prestige for the Paris post is silly. One does not go downward in a hierarchy to gain prestige." (See McFeely, *Grant: A Biography*, 294–295.) Above all, however, there is no dispute that Washburne's health played a major role in his decision to give up the post at State and accept the position in France. Many primary sources provide ample support for the fact that Washburne was ill and in a fragile state of health during the early part of 1869. (See Washburne, *Recollections of a Minister to France*, Vol. II, 1–2; Hunt, *Israel, Elihu, and Cadwallader Washburn*, 243, 245; letters of Elihu Washburne to Hamilton Fish, April 5, 1869, and Gratiot Washburne to his father, March 12, 1869.)

19 *The* New York World: Dec. 12, 1868.

19 *Gideon Welles:* Welles, *Diary of Gideon Welles*, Vol. III, 551.

19 *"No other idea":* Hunt, *Israel, Elihu, and Cadwallader Washburn*, 246.

19 *Throughout the winter Washburne:* Ibid., 241.

19 *Once he had sought medical treatment:* Elihu Washburne to Adele Washburne, March 11, 1871, Washburne Papers, Library of Congress.

20 *Knowing he would "not be able":* Hunt, *Israel, Elihu, and Cadwallader Washburn*, 246.

20 *Washburne's eldest son:* Washburne, *A Biography of Elihu Benjamin Washburne*, Vol. III, 369–370.

20 *"The last few years":* Elihu Washburne to H. S. [Townsend?], Dec. 25, 1869, Washburne Papers, Library of Congress.

21 *Dear Mother: And did she roll:* Elihu Washburne to Adele

Washburne, May 13, 1869, Papers and Journals of Elihu Washburne, Washburn-Norlands Living History Center, Livermore, Maine; Washburne, *A Biography of Elihu Benjamin Washburne,* Vol. III, 383–386.

22 *On May 17 he told the children:* Elihu Washburne to his children, May 17, 1869, Papers and Journals of Elihu Washburne, Washburn-Norlands Living History Center, Livermore, Maine.

22 *"I have my teacher":* Elihu Washburne to Adele Washburne, May 20, 1869, Papers and Journals of Elihu Washburne, Washburn-Norlands Living History Center, Livermore, Maine.

22 *The Minister's room:* Fowler, *Reminiscences,* 33; Washburne, *A Biography of Elihu Benjamin Washburne,* Vol. IV, 13–14.

23 *"Gratiot is a good boy":* Elihu Washburne to Judge Lathrop, June 2, 1870, Washburne Papers, Library of Congress.

23 *Washburne told friends back home:* Elihu Washburne to R. H. McClellan, Jan. 1, 1870; Elihu Washburne to Cadwallader Washburn, Sept. 5, 1879, Washburne Papers, Library of Congress.

23 *The Emperor:* Washburne, *Recollections of a Minister to France,* Vol. I, 2–3.

24 *While the wealthy benefited:* Horne, *The Fall of Paris,* 25.

24 *Washburne himself noticed:* Washburne, *Recollections of a Minister to France,* Vol. I, 6.

24 *"There have been great riots":* Hunt, *Israel, Elihu, and Cadwallader Washburn,* 248.

24 *George Sand:* Horne, *The Fall of Paris,* 21.

25 *The Paris press teemed:* Washburne, *Recollections of a Minister to France,* Vol. I, 29–30.

25 *"My . . . health is quite wretched":* Elihu Washburne to Cyrus Woodman, March 4, 1870, Washburne Papers, Library of Congress.

26 *A reluctant Napoléon III:* Hoffman, *Camp, Court, and Siege,* 142.

26 *"Thus by a tragic combination":* Howard, *The Franco-Prussian War,* 57.

Chapter 1: War and Revolution

PAGE

27 *It was "like a clap of thunder":* Washburne, *Recollections of a Minister to France,* Vol. I, 31.

27 *"The excitement was something prodigious"*: Ibid., 32.

27 *"The streets, the Boulevards"*: Ibid.

27 *Many German nationals:* See *Galignani's Messenger,* Sept. 22, 1870.

27 *A proclamation by the French government:* Ibid.; Hoffman, *Camp, Court, and Siege,* 147. See also *Galignani's Messenger,* Aug. 29–30, 31, 1870.

28 *You will see I am back:* Elihu Washburne to Adele Washburne, July 19, 1870, Washburne Papers, Library of Congress.

28 *You see we are in troublesome times:* Elihu Washburne to Israel Washburn, Jr., July 21, 1870, Washburne Papers, Library of Congress.

29 *Washburne reported to President Grant:* Grant, *The Papers of Ulysses S. Grant,* Vol. 20, 257.

29 *"Frenchmen!"*: Washburne, *Recollections of a Minister to France,* Vol. I, 55.

29 *"He is the great I am"*: Elihu Washburne to Adele Washburne, April 9, 1867, Washburne Papers, Library of Congress.

29 *Émile Zola warned:* Horne, *The Fall of Paris,* 43.

30 *"The two nations"*: Washburne, *Recollections of a Minister to France,* Vol. I, 58.

32 *When news arrived:* Ibid., 64.

33 *He found her "in great distress".* Washburne, *Recollections of a Minister to France,* Vol. I, 67.

34 *All of Paris was "paralyzed"*: Elihu Washburne to Secretary of State Hamilton Fish, Aug. 8, 1870, Washburne Papers, Library of Congress.

34 *With the Emperor on the field:* Washburne, *Recollections of a Minister to France,* Vol. I, 73.

34 *"shared the legislative function"*: William E. Echard, *Historical Dictionary of the French Second Empire, 1852–1870* (Westport, Conn.: Greenwood Press, 1985), 130.

35 *France is on the brink:* Elihu Washburne to Israel Washburn, Jr., Aug. 9, 1870, Washburne Papers, Library of Congress.

37 *I was so tremendously used up:* Elihu Washburne to Adele Washburne, Aug. 1870, Papers and Journals of Elihu Washburne, Washburn-Norlands Living History Center, Livermore, Maine.

38 *Since the breaking out of the war:* Elihu Washburne to Secretary of

State Hamilton Fish, Aug. 15, 1870. Washburne, *Franco-German War and the Insurrection of the Commune,* 32.

38 *I have just received your letter:* Adele Washburne to Gratiot Washburne, Aug. 19, 1870, Papers and Journals of Elihu Washburne, Washburn-Norlands Living History Center, Livermore, Maine.

39 *I shall be glad when we go back:* Susan Washburne to Elihu Washburne, Aug. 22, 1870, Papers and Journals of Elihu Washburne, Washburn-Norlands Living History Center, Livermore, Maine.

39 *During a period of six weeks:* In *Camp, Court, and Siege,* 149, Wickham Hoffman writes: "In six weeks we issued eleven hundred passports. Allowing an average of three persons to a passport, thirty-three hundred Americans passed through Paris in those six weeks. To these may be added another thousand who had passports from the State Department."

39 *An additional 1,000:* Hoffman, *Camp, Court, and Siege,* 149.

39 *The greater part of the German population:* Elihu Washburne to Secretary of State Hamilton Fish, Sept. 2, 1870; Washburne, *Franco-German War and the Insurrection of the Commune,* 56.

40 *I am depressed and sad:* Elihu Washburne to Adele Washburne, Sept. 2, 1870, Washburne Papers, Library of Congress.

41 *"A great misfortune":* Galignani's Messenger, Sept. 3, 1870.

41 *The people of Paris were "alarmed":* Washburne, *Recollections of a Minister to France,* Vol. I, 100.

41 *With this latest defeat:* Ibid.

44 *Republic proclaimed:* Elihu Washburne to Secretary of State Hamilton Fish, Sept. 5, 1870, Washburne Papers, Library of Congress. See also *Galignani's Messenger,* Sept. 5, 1870.

45 *It affords me great pleasure:* Elihu Washburne to Mr. Jules Favre, Sept. 7, 1870, in Washburne, *Franco-German War and the Insurrection of the Commune,* 65.

45 *You see all that has happened:* Elihu Washburne to William Washburn, Sept. 7, 1870, Washburne Papers, Library of Congress.

46 *At 2 o'clock P.M. yesterday:* Elihu Washburne to Secretary of State Hamilton Fish, Sept. 9, 1870. There were two different dispatches on the same day relaying information about events in Paris, in Washburne, *Franco-German War and the Insurrection of the Commune,* 65, 66. See also reports of Washburne's actions in *Galignani's Messenger,* Sept. 9, 11, 1870.

47 *I would like to see you:* Grant, *The Papers of Ulysses S. Grant,* Vol. 20, 257.

47 *I am very sorry:* Elihu Washburne to Pitt Washburne, Sept. 9, 1870, Washburne Papers, Library of Congress.

48 *After the proclamation of the new republic:* Horne, *The Fall of Paris,* 59.

48 *Wickham Hoffman, the Legation Secretary:* Hoffman, *Camp, Court, and Siege,* 173–174.

49 *After France's crushing defeat:* Horne, *The Fall of Paris,* 53.

49 *The French army was in full retreat:* Galignani's Messenger, Aug. 17, 1870.

49 *They were thronged:* Hoffman, *Camp, Court, and Siege,* 180.

Chapter 2: Siege

PAGE

51 *For two days:* Horne, *The Fall of Paris,* 75.

51 *Paris was fortified:* Ibid., 63.

51 *This chain:* Ibid.

51 *To succeed:* Ibid.

51 *Twelve thousand laborers:* Ibid.

51 *Signal semaphores:* Ibid., 64, 65; *Galignani's Messenger,* Sept. 8, 12, 1870.

51 *Artillery camps:* Horne, *The Fall of Paris,* 64.

51 *Throughout the city:* Ibid., 68.

51 *Provisions were set aside:* Ibid., 67.

52 *"As far as ever the eye can reach":* Ibid., 65.

52 *For the next four and a half:* Washburne, *Recollections of a Minister to France,* Vol. I, 133.

52 *The Ambulance corps:* See Hoffman, *Camp, Court, and Siege,* 222–226.

56 *By a German who is to be sent out:* Elihu Washburne to Adele Washburne, Sept. 28, 1870, Washburne Papers, Library of Congress.

58 *Washburne himself would later write:* Washburne, *Recollections of a Minister to France,* Vol. I, 133.

58 *The French live from hand to mouth:* Hoffman, *Camp, Court, and Siege,* 208.

58 *I think it very likely:* Elihu Washburne to Israel Washburn, Jr., Oct. 2, 1870, Washburne Papers, Library of Congress.

59 *I am afraid we are in:* Elihu Washburne to Cadwallader Washburn, Oct. 3, 1870, Washburne Papers, Library of Congress.

60 *On October 7:* Washburne, *Recollections of a Minister to France,* Vol. I, 180; *Galignani's Messenger,* Oct. 7, 1870.

60 *He was accompanied:* McCullough, *The Greater Journey,* 281.

61 *On October 2, American General:* Washburne, *Recollections of a Minister to France,* Vol. I, 154.

63 *On October 10, 1870:* Bismarck to Washburne, Oct. 10, 1870, in Washburne, *Franco-German War and the Insurrection of the Commune,* 81.

63 *Washburne had been hopeful:* Washburne, *Recollections of a Minister to France,* Vol. I, 205.

64 *"Not an ounce":* Hoffman, *Camp, Court, and Siege,* 196.

64 *Colonel Wickham Hoffman would write:* Ibid., 198.

64 *A few newspapers:* Elihu Washburne to Lizzie, Oct. 12, 1870, Washburne Papers, Library of Congress. It appears this is a letter to his sister-in-law Elizabeth Muzzy, the wife of his brother William Drew Washburn.

65 *This is really terrible:* Elihu Washburne to Adele Washburne, Oct. 13, 1870, Washburne Papers, Library of Congress.

67 *Many of our countrymen:* Elihu Washburne to Secretary of State Hamilton Fish, Oct. 18, 1870, in Washburne, *Franco-German War and the Insurrection of the Commune,* 83.

69 *As Wickham Hoffman later wrote: Camp, Court, and Siege,* 203.

70 *Finally, on October 24:* Washburne, *Recollections of a Minister to France,* Vol. I, 203.

71 *When I am prostrated:* Elihu Washburne to Israel Washburn, Jr., Oct. 27, 1870, Washburne Papers, Library of Congress.

76 *The government survived:* Horne, *The Fall of Paris,* 120.

77 *I am so happy to find:* Elihu Washburne to Adele Washburne, Nov. 3, 1870, Papers and Journals of Elihu Washburne, Washburn-Norlands Living History Center, Livermore, Maine.

78 *I think the large vote:* Elihu Washburne to Secretary of State Hamilton Fish, Nov. 7, 1870, in Washburne, *Franco-German War and the Insurrection of the Commune,* 93.

81 *This terrible isolation:* Elihu Washburne to Adele Washburne, Nov. 13, 1870, Papers and Journals of Elihu Washburne, Washburn-Norlands Living History Center, Livermore, Maine.

81 *All is gloom:* Elihu Washburne to Secretary of State Hamilton Fish, Nov. 14, 1870, Washburne Papers, Library of Congress.

84 *the weather was "exceedingly wet":* Galignani's Messenger, Nov. 19, 21, 1870.

84 *Markets were nearly out of food:* Galignani's Messenger, Nov. 23, 1870.

85 *This is the eighty-sixth birthday:* Washburne, *Recollections of a Minister to France,* Vol. I, 226.

90 *All the London papers:* Pitt Washburne to Elihu Washburne and Gratiot Washburne, Nov. 28, 1870, Papers and Journals of Elihu Washburne, Washburn-Norlands Living History Center, Livermore, Maine.

90 *By the end of November:* See Horne, *The Fall of Paris,* 147–161.

91 *Reports circulated:* Galignani's Messenger, Nov. 28, 1870.

92 *Inside Paris:* Ibid., Nov. 29, 1870.

94 *That day a hard, severe frost:* Ibid., Dec. 1, 1870.

94 *The streets were cluttered:* Ibid.

Chapter 3: Desperation and Despair
PAGE

95 *The "great sortie" had failed:* Elihu Washburne to Secretary of State Hamilton Fish, Dec. 5, 1870, in Washburne, *Franco-German War and the Insurrection of the Commune,* 105.

95 *The Seine was filled:* Galignani's Messenger, Dec. 23, 24, 1870.

95 *During Christmas week alone:* Ibid., Dec. 24, 31, 1870.

99 *I hope you approve:* Elihu Washburne to Secretary of State Hamilton Fish, Dec. 4, 1870, Washburne Papers, Library of Congress.

100 *I have the honor:* Elihu Washburne to Count de Bismarck, Dec. 5, 1870, in Washburne, *Franco-German War and the Insurrection of the Commune,* 106.

103 *Your last letter:* Adele Washburne to Gratiot Washburne, Dec. 7, 1870, Papers and Journals of Elihu Washburne, Washburn-Norlands Living History Center, Livermore, Maine.

104 *It looks to me darker:* Elihu Washburne to Adele Washburne, Dec. 8, 1870, Papers and Journals of Elihu Washburne, Washburn-Norlands Living History Center, Livermore, Maine.

105 *There is universal approbation:* Secretary of State Hamilton Fish to Elihu Washburne, Dec. 8, 1870, Washburne Papers, Library of Congress.

107 *The government of the National Defense:* Elihu Washburne to Secretary of State Hamilton Fish, Dec. 12, 1870, Washburne Papers, Library of Congress.

110 *Wickham Hoffman would recall entering:* Hoffman, *Camp, Court, and Siege,* 210.

111 *No bag & no nothing:* Elihu Washburne to Adele Washburne, Dec. 17, 1870, Papers and Journals of Elihu Washburne, Washburn-Norlands Living History Center, Livermore, Maine.

111 *"Star by star":* Washburne is quoting a speech by Edmund Burke in Parliament on May 9, 1788.

116 *Trees everywhere:* Horne, *The Fall of Paris,* 178.

117 *I hope you are having a "Merry Christmas" in Washington:* Elihu Washburne to Secretary of State Hamilton Fish, Dec. 25, 1870, Washburne Papers, Library of Congress.

120 *By the end of December:* Hoffman, *Camp, Court, and Siege,* 210.

Chapter 4: Defeat
PAGE

123 *Dog flesh was in high demand: Galignani's Messenger,* Jan. 13, 14, 1871.

123 *With the unrelenting cold weather:* Elihu Washburne to Secretary of State Hamilton Fish, Jan. 2, 1871, in Washburne, *Franco-German War and the Insurrection of the Commune,* 118.

123 *The death rate in Paris:* Hoffman, *Camp, Court, and Siege,* 227.

124 *The excessive and exceptional cold:* Elihu Washburne to Secretary of State Hamilton Fish, Jan. 2, 1871, in Washburne, *Franco-German War and the Insurrection of the Commune,* 118.

125 *[K]eep up your courage:* Elihu Washburne to Adele Washburne, Jan. 4, 1871, Papers and Journals of Elihu Washburne, Washburn-Norlands Living History Center, Livermore, Maine.

129 *There has been a good deal:* Elihu Washburne to Secretary of State Hamilton Fish, Jan. 9, 1871, in Washburne, *Franco-German War and the Insurrection of the Commune,* 121.

130 *During the second week: Galignani's Messenger,* Jan. 9, 1871.

134 *I am today furnishing aid:* Elihu Washburne to Secretary of State Hamilton Fish, Jan. 16, 1871, in Washburne, *Franco-German War and the Insurrection of the Commune,* 125.

135 *"At the last hour":* Kranzberg, *The Siege of Paris,* 138.

139 *"I am the Jesus Christ":* Howard, *The Franco-Prussian War,* 369, n. 1.

139 *The bread was inedible: Galignani's Messenger,* Jan. 31, 1871.

144 *Although Washburne received the news:* Washburne, *Recollections of a Minister to France,* Vol. II, 3.

Chapter 5: Peace

PAGE

147 *"stock on hand":* It appears as if the Moultons (as did Washburne and Hoffman) made provision to stock up before the siege. Specifically, Lillie Moulton writes in her memoir, *In the Courts of Memory* (1912; pages 255–256), how they came to have beef and other food on hand:

"The family had not eaten cats and dogs during the siege as, according to the newspapers, other people had done.

"Mr. Moulton having been in Paris at the time of the revolutions, had the forethought to lay in a stock of provisions, such as ham, biscuits, rice, etc. and all sorts of canned things which he deemed would be sufficient for their requirements . . ."

In addition, Lillie said the French government had given the Moultons permission to bring into their Paris residence "one or two cows . . . a calf, a sheep and some chickens . . ." from their estate, Petit Val, located just outside Paris. "The cows and the sheep," she wrote, "shared the stables with the horses, while the chickens were let loose in the conservatory into a sort of kitchen garden . . . So you see the family took good care that it should have enough to eat, the mice and rats only appeared on the table after the repasts."

148 *With an armistice in place: Galignani's Messenger,* Feb. 1, 1871.

148 *On February 1:* Ibid.

148 *Soon convoys of provisions:* Ibid., Feb. 5, 1871.

149 *The stalls of the central market:* Ibid., Feb. 2, 3, 4, 1871.

149 *On February 11:* Ibid., Feb. 11, 1871.

149 *With great hope:* Elihu Washburne to General Read, Feb. 25, 1871, Washburne Papers, Library of Congress.

149 *But he was cautioned:* Letter of Dr. W. E. Johnston to Elihu Washburne, Feb. 8, 1871, Papers and Journals of Elihu Washburne, Washburn-Norlands Living History Center, Livermore, Maine.

149 *Now that the siege is over:* Elihu Washburne to Secretary of State Hamilton Fish, Feb. 5, 1871, in Washburne, *Franco-German War and the Insurrection of the Commune,* 141.

150 *A "good deal worn out":* Washburne, *Recollections of a Minister to France,* Vol. II, 5. See also Hoffman, *Camp, Court, and Siege,* 241–242.

150 *The journey by train:* Washburne, *A Biography of Elihu Benjamin Washburne,* Vol. IV, 374–375.

150 *When word of his arrival:* Hoffman, *Camp, Court, and Siege,* 241–242.

150 *Under the treaty:* McCullough, *The Greater Journey,* 303; Wawro, *The Franco-Prussian War,* 310.

150 *The humiliating terms of surrender:* Horne, *The Fall of Paris,* 261.

151 *On March 1, 1870:* See accounts by Elihu Washburne in letter to Secretary of State Hamilton Fish, March 1, 1871, in Washburne, *Franco-German War and the Insurrection of the Commune,* 148; *Galignani's Messenger,* March 10, 1871.

151 *many statues: Galignani's Messenger,* March 10, 1871.

151 *They have come in:* Elihu Washburne to Secretary of State Hamilton Fish, March 1, 1871, in Washburne, *Franco-German War and the Insurrection of the Commune,* 148.

153 *Their departure began: Galignani's Messenger,* March 10, 1871.

153 *They have gone out:* Elihu Washburne to Secretary of State Hamilton Fish, March 8, 1871, in Washburne, *Franco-German War and the Insurrection of the Commune,* 152.

154 *In mid-February:* Washburne, *A Biography of Elihu Benjamin Washburne,* Vol. IV, 375.

154 *I cannot get the ague:* Elihu Washburne to H. H. Houghton, March 6, 1871, Washburne Papers, Library of Congress.

154 *Your government has sympathized deeply:* Secretary of State Hamilton Fish to Elihu Washburne, March 21, 1871, in Washburne, *Franco-German War and the Insurrection of the Commune,* 161.

155 *"I fear I am too much":* Elihu Washburne to Horace Rubel, Feb. 3, 1871, Washburne Papers, Library of Congress.

155 *But by the middle of March:* Washburne, *Recollections of a Minister to France,* Vol. II, 27.

155 *For the next two months:* Ibid.

Chapter 6: Reign of Terror

PAGE

156 *In late February:* Washburne, *Recollections of a Minister to France,* Vol. II, 34.

156 *At first the insurrectionists:* See Horne, *The Fall of Paris,* 277–281.

156 *"The officers with broad":* Washburne, *Recollections of a Minister to France,* Vol. II, 35.

157 *Washburne was angered:* Ibid., 34.

157 *As these "grave incidents" unfolded:* Ibid., 27.

157 *In announcing the operation:* Horne, *The Fall of Paris,* 269.

158 *As the regular forces waited:* Ibid., 271.

159 *"It was a strange sight":* Washburne, *Recollections of a Minister to France,* Vol. II, 37.

159 *The rumor he had heard:* Horne, *The Fall of Paris,* 271.

159 *Afterward, they were taken:* Ibid., 272.

159 *As the mob went wild:* Ibid., 273.

161 *"Paris was in full revolt":* Washburne, *Recollections of a Minister to France,* Vol. II, 44.

161 *"There never was a more cowardly":* Hoffman, *Camp, Court, and Siege,* 247.

161 *"They saw at their feet":* Washburne, *Recollections of a Minister to France,* Vol. II, 34.

161 *Pressed by events:* Ibid., 33.

161 *However, on the way:* Ibid.

162 *"We are in a pretty mess here":* Elihu Washburne to his brother, March 21, 1871, Washburne Papers, Library of Congress.

162 *A few days later:* Elihu Washburne to Madame Erlanger, March 26, 1871, Washburne Papers, Library of Congress.

162 *There seems today:* Elihu Washburne to Secretary of State Hamilton Fish, March 19, 1871, Washburne Papers, Library of Congress.

163 *On March 21 a group calling themselves:* Washburne, *Recollections of a Minister to France,* Vol. II, 49.

163 *Washburne called it a "massacre":* Ibid.

164 *He described them:* Ibid., 58.

164 *but when it comes to the question:* Ibid.

164 *It would be difficult:* Elihu Washburne to Secretary of State Hamilton Fish, March 25, 1871, Washburne, *Franco-German War and the Insurrection of the Commune,* 167.

165 *He wants more time:* Elihu Washburne to Paul Hedler, March 25, 1871, Washburne Papers, Library of Congress.

165 *Washburne dismissed the results:* Washburne, *Recollections of a Minister to France,* Vol. II, 61.

165 *"It is difficult to conceive":* Ibid., 62.

166 *The election for the commune:* Elihu Washburne to Secretary of State Hamilton Fish, March 27, 1871, Washburne, *Franco-German War and the Insurrection of the Commune,* 168.

167 *Two days later:* Elihu Washburne to Secretary of State Hamilton Fish, March 30, 1871, ibid., 171.

167 *The election of members:* Ibid.

170 *"And now it was in the last days":* Washburne, *Recollections of a Minister to France,* Vol. II, 54–55.

170 *"The organization of one of the finest":* Horne, *The Fall of Paris,* 307.

170 *"It was a singular":* Elihu Washburne to Secretary of State Hamilton Fish, April 4, 1871, in Washburne, *Franco-German War and the Insurrection of the Commune,* 176.

171 *We still have here a large number:* Elihu Washburne to Secretary of State Hamilton Fish, April 6, 1871, ibid., 178.

172 *One of the most sadistic:* Horne, *The Fall of Paris,* 334.

172 *Although only twenty-five:* Ibid.

172 *Lillie Moulton:* Ibid., 335.

173 *He advocated:* Ibid., 334.

173 *Rigault had a bizarre fascination:* Ibid., 335.

173 *Washburne himself described:* Washburne, *Recollections of a Minister to France,* Vol. II, 192–193.

173 *Washburne would later find:* Ibid., 194.

173 *Above all, Washburne:* Ibid., 196.

173 *On April 4, Rigault ordered:* Horne, *The Fall of Paris,* 337.

173 *The Archbishop of Paris:* Elihu Washburne to Secretary of State Hamilton Fish, April 6, 1871, in Washburne, *Franco-German War and the Insurrection of the Commune,* 178.

175 *It is one week:* Elihu Washburne to Secretary of State Hamilton Fish, April 9, 1871, ibid., 180.

177 *The streets were filled:* Washburne, *Recollections of a Minister to France,* Vol. II, 92.

177 *People were in a state:* Ibid., 88–89.

177 *Washburne and the Legation:* Ibid., 88.

178 *To make matters worse:* Hoffman, *Camp, Court, and Siege,* 271–272.

180 *I am certain that I never believed:* Elihu Washburne to Secretary of State Hamilton Fish, April 20, 1871, Washburne Papers, Library of Congress.

181 *Earlier efforts to enlist:* Hunt, *Israel, Elihu, and Cadwallader Washburn,* 258.

181 *Washburne knew the Archbishop:* Washburne, *Recollections of a Minister to France,* Vol. II, 163–164.

181 *When he first heard:* Ibid., 164.

181 *"I fully sympathized":* Ibid., 166.

183 *I shall never forget:* Elihu Washburne to Dr. Henry James Anderson, Jan. 31, 1873, Washburne Papers, Library of Congress.

183 *After his visit:* Washburne, *Recollections of a Minister to France,* Vol. II, 169.

183 *After the arrest of Darboy:* Elihu Washburne to Dr. Henry James Anderson, Jan. 31, 1873, Washburne Papers, Library of Congress.

184 *"I could not conceal":* Washburne, *Recollections of a Minister to France,* Vol. II, 170.

184 *He described it to a friend:* Elihu Washburne to [unknown], May 14, 1871, Washburne Papers, Library of Congress.

185 *Truly, I do not know:* The Papal Nuncio to Elihu Washburne, April 25, 1871, in Washburne, *Franco-German War and the Insurrection of the Commune,* 216.

186 *Washburne would write:* Washburne, *Recollections of a Minister to France,* Vol. II, 125.

186 *Weeks earlier:* Horne, *The Fall of Paris,* 349.

186 *The decree, Washburne noted:* Washburne, *Recollections of a Minister to France,* Vol. II, 114.

186 *An indignant and overwrought:* Ibid., 115.

186 *During one visit:* Washburne, *Recollections of a Minister to France,* Vol. II, 113.

186 *Throughout the siege and reign of terror:* "Over Land and Sea: Father Washburne Abroad," undated news article, Washburne Scrapbooks, Box 7, Papers and Journals of Elihu Washburne, Washburn-Norlands Living History Center, Livermore, Maine.

187 *The crisis seems to be really approaching:* Elihu Washburne to

Secretary of State Hamilton Fish, May 11, 1871, in Washburne, *Franco-German War and the Insurrection of the Commune,* 195.

189 *Later that day:* Horne, *The Fall of Paris,* 349.

189 *It was to be a day:* Ibid., 350.

189 *To prepare for the tremendous:* Ibid.; Hoffman, *Camp, Court, and Siege,* 254.

189 *At 3 P.M.:* Horne, *The Fall of Paris,* 350.

189 *Amid the shattered ruins:* Ibid., 351.

190 *I have not written to you:* Grant, *The Papers of Ulysses S. Grant,* Vol. 21, 364–365.

190 *In the middle of May:* Washburne, *Recollections of a Minister to France,* Vol. II, 172.

190 *At first Rigault:* Ibid.

191 *Since I have commenced:* Elihu Washburne to Secretary of State Hamilton Fish, May 19, 1871, in Washburne, *Franco-German War and the Insurrection of the Commune,* 200.

191 *"They pounded away":* Washburne, *Recollections of a Minister to France,* Vol. II, 133.

192 *The leader of the squad:* Ibid., 133–134.

192 *Washburne immediately dispatched a letter:* Ibid., 134.

192 *Grousset agreed:* Ibid.

192 *Washburne would later write:* Ibid., 133.

192 *I no sooner got inside:* Washburne, *Recollections of a Minister to France,* Vol. II, 172.

193 *The Communards:* Hoffman, *Camp, Court, and Siege,* 283.

196 *Tuesday morning. It seems:* Elihu Washburne to Secretary of State Hamilton Fish, May 23, 1871, in Washburne, *Franco-German War and the Insurrection of the Commune,* 203.

197 *Wickham Hoffman would later write:* Hoffman, *Camp, Court, and Siege,* 282.

198 *This has been a horrible night:* Elihu Washburne to Susan Washburne, May 24, 1871, Washburne Papers, Library of Congress.

199 *On the Place de l'Opéra:* Washburne, *Recollections of a Minister to France,* Vol. II, 156.

199 *Others were shot:* Hoffman, *Camp, Court, and Siege,* 280.

199 *Young children:* Ibid., 281.

199 *When I closed my dispatch:* Elihu Washburne to Secretary of State Hamilton Fish, May 25, 1871, in Washburne, *Franco-German War and the Insurrection of the Commune,* 205.

201 *I have neither been excited:* Elihu Washburne to Secretary of State Hamilton Fish, May 25, 1871, Washburne Papers, Library of Congress.

201 *The fighting is still going on:* Elihu Washburne to Secretary of State Hamilton Fish, May 26, 1871, in Washburne, *Franco-German War and the Insurrection of the Commune,* 208.

201 *As the final savage battles:* Washburne, *Recollections of a Minister to France,* Vol. II, 146.

201 *"His activity in these moments":* Ibid., 145.

201 *Rigault was determined:* Horne, *The Fall of Paris,* 364.

203 *The insurrection is suppressed:* Elihu Washburne to Adele Washburne, May 28, 1871, Papers and Journals of Elihu Washburne, Washburn-Norlands Living History Center, Livermore, Maine.

204 *After an insurrection of seventy-one days:* Elihu Washburne to Secretary of State Hamilton Fish, May 31, 1871, in Washburne, *Franco-German War and the Insurrection of the Commune,* 209.

205 *I remained here during the whole period:* Elihu Washburne to George Bancroft, May 31, 1871, Washburne Papers, Library of Congress.

206 *Ten days earlier:* Horne, *The Fall of Paris,* 397–398.

Epilogue

PAGE

207 *On the morning of June 7, 1871:* Washburne, *Recollections of a Minister to France,* Vol. II, 185.

207 *Washburne was deeply moved:* Ibid., 185–186.

207 *You beheld around you:* Hunt, *Israel, Elihu, and Cadwallader Washburn,* 259.

208 *Although Washburne knew:* Washburne, *Recollections of a Minister to France,* Vol. II, 163.

208 *"Alas! Could such efforts":* Hunt, *Israel, Elihu, and Cadwallader Washburn,* 253.

208 *His Majesty has commanded:* Count von Bismarck to Elihu Washburne, June 13, 1871, in Washburne, *Franco-German War and the Insurrection of the Commune,* 214.

208 *Paris was deserted by the titled:* Undated news article, Scrapbooks, Washburne Papers, Library of Congress.

209 *The* New York Tribune: Quoted in undated news article, Scrapbooks, Washburne Papers, Library of Congress.

209 *Hasn't our Minister in Paris:* Diary of Frank Moore, Sept. 30, 1871, Frank Moore Papers, New-York Historical Society.

209 *"We have been through fire and blood":* Elihu Washburne to Bayard Clarke, June 16, 1871, Washburne Papers, Library of Congress.

209 *"Paris, the Paris of civilization":* Galignani's Messenger, June 3, 1871.

209 *"There has been a marvelous change":* Elihu Washburne to Secretary of State Hamilton Fish, June 2, 1871, Washburne, *Franco-German War and the Insurrection of the Commune,* 211.

210 *"It is a healthy spot":* Elihu Washburne to [unknown], June 18, 1871, Washburne Papers, Library of Congress.

210 *"I am a good deal":* Ibid.

210 *"I have not been as well":* Elihu Washburne to George Eustis, Oct. 5, 1871, Washburne Papers, Library of Congress.

210 *"All is quiet":* Elihu Washburne to Edward McPherson, Oct. 2, 1871, Washburne Papers, Library of Congress.

210 *Our great and beautiful city:* Elihu Washburne to [Kusmann?], Oct. 15, 1871, Washburne Papers, Library of Congress.

210 *He raised $30,000:* Ibid.

211 *Despite these successful efforts:* Elihu Washburne to Thomas Hoyne, Dec. 26, 1871, Washburne Papers, Library of Congress.

211 *A month later: American Register,* Nov. 14, 1871; undated article, Scrapbooks, Washburne Papers, Library of Congress.

211 *The dinner was held at:* Ibid.

211 *He was presented: American Register,* Nov. 4, 1871.

211 *By late 1872: Galignani's Messenger,* Jan. 12, 15, 1872; July 18, 1872.

211 *He hosted a number of formal dinners: New York Times,* Aug. 2, 1872; *Galignani's Messenger,* Aug. 2, 1872.

211 *He also helped promote:* McCullough, *The Greater Journey,* 334.

212 *In the fall of 1872: Galignani's Messenger,* Oct. 5, 1872.

212 *Washburne found him:* Elihu Washburne to Judge R. W. Branch, June 16, 1871, Washburne Papers, Library of Congress.

212 *"The hour has come finally":* Elihu Washburne to Adele Washburne, Sept. 2, 1876, Washburne Papers, Library of Congress.

212 *In dying he has left:* Elihu Washburne to Cadwallader Washburn, Sept. 4, 1876, Washburne Papers, Library of Congress.

212 *In accepting his resignation: American Register,* April 7, 1877.

213 *The passengers on the train: Chicago Tribune,* Oct. 4, 1877.

213 *Mr. Washburne has returned from France:* Undated news article, Scrapbooks, Washburne Papers, Library of Congress.

214 *That evening a formal welcome: Chicago Tribune,* Oct. 17, 1877.

214 *The stage in the hall:* Ibid.

214 *After thanking the people of Galena:* Ibid.

214 *I have long looked forward:* Ibid.

215 *"That little old law library":* Elihu Washburne to Thomas Hoyne, Dec. 26, 1871, Washburne Papers, Library of Congress.

215 *"I am not vain enough":* Hunt, *Israel, Elihu, and Cadwallader Washburn,* 264.

215 *The* Boston Herald: *Galena* (Illinois) *Gazette,* March 4, 1879.

215 *The* New York Sun: Quoted in *Chicago Tribune,* Jan. 6, 1879.

215 *"He is one of the few": Galena* (Illinois) *Gazette,* Jan. 31, 1879.

216 *He knew many:* Hunt, *Israel, Elihu, and Cadwallader Washburn,* 269.

216 *One Republican Party leader:* Hesseltine, *Ulysses S. Grant, Politician,* 435.

216 *As support for Grant began to dwindle:* Ibid., 435, 436.

216 *Washburne, however, dismissed all such encouragement:* Years after the election, Adam Badeau, a close friend of Grant's, was quoted on Grant's treatment of Washburne and the fractured relationship of the two old friends: "That is the darkest spot on Grant's life. Grant had a thousand good qualities of head and heart, among them gratitude for unworthy frauds and nobodies whose character he had not enough knowledge of human nature to discern." However, when it came to Washburne and the 1880 campaign, "he was a *bad friend* of his friend Washburne, of the same friend who, (foolishly enough) sacrificed himself for a man who never was able to appreciate the sacrifice." (Hunt, *Israel, Elihu, and Cadwallader Washburn,* 281.)

216 *Some in Grant's inner circle:* See Hunt, *Israel, Elihu, and Cadwallader Washburn,* 269, 279–283.

217 *In fact, the* St. Louis Globe-Democrat: Grant, *The Papers of Ulysses S. Grant,* Vol. 29, 398.

217 *After his defeat:* See *Chicago Tribune,* June 12, 1880, for Fred Grant's comment on Washburne.

217 *Grant himself:* Hunt, *Israel, Elihu, and Cadwallader Washburn,* 440.

217　*Washburne's face and form: Chicago Tribune,* Feb. 8, 1880.

218　*Since returning from Paris: American Register,* Oct. 20, 1877.

218　*He and Adele:* Hunt, *Israel, Elihu, and Cadwallader Washburn,* 290.

218　*On December 17, 1886: New York Times,* Dec. 18, 1886.

218　*"Our hearts are all broken":* Diary of Elihu Washburne, Papers and Journals of Elihu Washburne, Washburn-Norlands Living History Center, Livermore, Maine.

218　*"The world is nothing to me":* Elihu Washburne to his daughter, Feb. 23, 1887, Papers and Journals of Elihu Washburne, Washburn-Norlands Living History Center, Livermore, Maine.

218　*Just three months later: Chicago Tribune,* March 19, 1887.

219　*Washburne was "crushed into the earth":* Elihu Washburne to his daughter Marie, July 18, 1887, Papers and Journals of Elihu Washburne, Washburn-Norlands Living History Center, Livermore, Maine.

219　*Feeling alone:* Ibid.

219　*That fall: Chicago Tribune,* Sept. 22, Oct. 23, 1887.

219　*On the morning of October 23:* Ibid.

219　*The next day, the Department of State: Times* (London), Oct. 25, 1887.

219　*President Grover Cleveland:* Ibid.

219　*In Chicago an immense funeral: Chicago Tribune,* Oct. 27, 1887.

220　*On an arrangement of flowers:* Ibid.

220　*After the service:* Ibid.

221　*With nothing "to aid him": Chicago Tribune,* March 6, 1880.

221　*Washburne's casket arrived: Chicago Tribune,* Oct. 27, 28, 1887.

221　*He was buried:* Elihu Washburne to Judge R. W. Branch, June 16, 1871, Washburne Papers, Library of Congress.

BIBLIOGRAPHY

Manuscript Collections

Papers of Frank Moore—New-York Historical Society, New York, New York.

Papers of Elihu Washburne—Diary and Correspondence, Library of Congress, Washington, D.C.

Papers and Journals of Elihu Washburne—Washburn-Norlands Living History Center, Livermore, Maine.

Books and Articles

Donald, David Herbert. *Lincoln*. New York: Simon & Schuster, 1995.

Fowler, Marie Washburne. *Reminiscences: My Mother and I*. Livermore, Maine: Norlands, the Washburne Historic Site, n.d.

Grant, Ulysses S. *The Papers of Ulysses S. Grant*. Vols. 20, 21, 29. Edited by John Y. Simon. Carbondale: Southern Illinois University Press, 1995, 1998, 2008.

Hess, Stephen. "An American in Paris." *American Heritage,* February 1967, 18–73.

Hesseltine, William. *Ulysses S. Grant, Politician*. New York: Dodd, Mead & Co., 1935.

Hoffman, Wickham. *Camp, Court, and Siege: A Narrative of Personal*

Adventure and Observation During Two Wars: 1861–1865; 1870–1871. New York: Harper & Brothers, 1877.

Horne, Alistair. *The Fall of Paris: The Siege and the Commune, 1870–71.* New York: St. Martin's Press, 1966.

Howard, Michael. *The Franco-Prussian War: The German Invasion of France, 1870–1871.* New York: Macmillan Co., 1962.

Hunt, Gaillard. *Israel, Elihu, and Cadwallader Washburn: A Chapter in American Biography.* New York: Macmillan Co., 1925.

Kranzberg, Melvin. *The Siege of Paris, 1870–1871: A Political and Social History.* Ithaca: Cornell University Press, 1950.

Marsh, Diann. *Galena, Illinois: A Brief History.* Charleston, S.C.: History Press, 2010.

McCullough, David. *The Greater Journey: Americans in Paris.* New York: Simon & Schuster, 2011.

Washburne, Elihu B. *Franco-German War and the Insurrection of the Commune. Correspondence of E. B. Washburne.* Washington, D.C.: U.S. Government Printing Office, 1878.

———. *Recollections of a Minister to France, 1869–1877.* Vols. I, II. New York: Charles Scribner's Sons, 1887.

Washburne, Mark. *A Biography of Elihu Benjamin Washburne: Congressman, Secretary of State, Envoy Extraordinary.* Vols. III, IV. Philadelphia: Xlibris, 2005, 2007.

Wawro, Geoffrey. *The Franco-Prussian War: The German Conquest of France in 1870–1871.* Cambridge and New York: Cambridge University Press, 2003.

Welles, Gideon. *Diary of Gideon Welles.* Vols. I, II. Boston: Houghton Mifflin, 1911.

INDEX

Trochu, Louis Jules, 50, 61–62, 63, 64, 68*n*, 69, 70, 75, 99, 115, 121, 138–39, 140, 145, 146, 177
Turner Hall, 214, 221

Unity Church, 219

Versailles, 63, 64, 136, 149, 160–63, 166, 169, 170–71, 175, 177, 178, 179, 180–81, 185, 187, 193–206
Vicksburg, Battle of, 15, 29
Vieille Église, 198–99, 203, 209–10
Vincennes prison, 74, 116
Vinoy, Joseph, 139, 145
Virgil, 108*n*

Washburn, Cadwallader, 8, 12–13, 59, 212
Washburn, Israel, 5–6, 85, 212
Washburn, Israel, Jr., 12–13, 28–29, 35, 58–59, 71
Washburn, Lizzie, 64–65
Washburn, Martha Benjamin, 6, 220
Washburn, William, 12–13, 45
Washburne, Adele Gratiot, xiv, 9, 16, 17, 18, 19, 21–23, 25–26, 28, 37–41, 56, 64, 65–66, 71, 77, 80, 81, 96, 103, 104–5, 111, 125, 149, 150, 161–62, 203, 218–19, 221, 233*n*
Washburne, Elihu Benjamin:
as abolitionist, xiv, 13–14
appointment of, 4–5, 20–21, 51–52, 232*n*–33*n*
articles published by, 218
banking account of, 132, 143*n*
in Berlin, 29
biographies of, 8, 9, 232*n*–33*n*
birth of, 5
Bismarck's communications

with, 63, 67–69, 79, 82, 83, 100–101, 102, 103–4, 109, 112–13, 125, 130–31, 133, 139–40, 143, 184, 208
in Boston, 7, 8
in Brussels, 149, 150, 153
Burnside's meeting with, 61–64
cabinet appointments and, 14, 16, 19, 232*n*–33*n*
cables of, 37, 43
at Carlsbad, 20*n*, 25–26, 27, 77, 210, 233*n*
carriage of, 93, 163, 166
character of, 4–5, 213, 217, 249*n*
in Chicago, 218–19
Chicago Fire donations administered by, 210–11
childhood of, xiv, 4, 5–7
in Civil War, xiv, 6, 13–17, 27, 32, 33–34, 72
as congressman, xiv, 9–19
correspondence of, xviii, 3–4, 45, 47–48, 55, 58–59, 64–65, 71, 72, 90, 119, 121, 129–30, 147, 190, 198–99; *see also* Fish, Hamilton; Washburne, Adele Gratiot
death of, 219
depressions of, xvii, 59–60, 64, 71, 80, 81, 96, 104–5, 116, 122
diary of, xvii–xxi, 1, 3, 4, 30, 155, 218, 220
dispatches of, xv, xvi, 3, 42, 46, 63, 74, 82, 86–87, 99–101, 102, 103–4, 111, 112–13, 118, 119, 121, 129–30, 131, 144, 186, 190, 191, 196, 204–5
duty as important to, xiii, xiv, 3, 77, 81–82, 96, 99–100, 154–55, 186, 190, 203, 205, 212–13
education of, xiv, 7–8
European trips of, 19*n*–20*n*, 211